A Biography of Philosophy

A Biography of Philosophy

Julian Marías

Translated
by
HAROLD C. RALEY

The University of Alabama Press

Library of Congress Cataloging in Publication Data

Marías, Julian, 1914-
A biography of philosophy.

Translation of: Biografía de la filosofía.
Includes bibliographical references and index.
1. Philosophy—History. I. Title.
B92.M2813   1984   190   83-6939
ISBN 0-8173-0180-1

Contents

Contents

Contents

Contents

Translator's Preface

The present work by Julián Marías cannot be classified as a
history of philosophy in the conventional sense of a purely ex-
egetical and chronological treatment of themes, nor is it limited
to an investigation of specific problems of a given era. In some
ways the book must be viewed as pre-philosophical because Marías
begins from a point previous to any interpretation and treatment
of problems themselves. Over against a notion of philosophia
perennis, perennial or unchanging philosophy, Marías maintains
that philosophy has meant many different things to different ages.
If in its outward manifestations philosophy seems to be mainly a
history of ideas as is quite widely supposed today, this is only
because men have confronted certain problems that have remained
more or less constant throughout great spans of time. Ideas themselves are endued with a life and history of their own only insofar as they partake of human life. Marías reminds us that if men
philosophize, they do so in response to problems, circumstances,
and conditions that often may be formally and historically identified. The real problems of philosophy belong to real men. For
this reason philosophy cannot simply be interpreted as doctrine;
it must first be understood as a human activity. This means that
in order to understand a philosophy, or better, a philosopher,
insofar as possible we must first understand the problems and conditions that created both the possibility and need of that particular mode of thought. As Marías himself observes: "Philosophy
is understandable only to the degree that one can reinsert it in
the situation whence it originated. The real understanding of
any page of philosophy requires the reader to recreate at least
to a certain point the task of the philosopher who wrote it, that
is, the philosopher who 'had' both the obligation and the ability
to create that philosophy" (Obras, II, 534).

Conversely, if, as is often the case, we uproot a philosophy
from its social and intellectual habitat, we shall probably not
understand its innermost meaning; for in removing it from its
world and time, in reducing it to mere unrooted abstraction, we
deprive it of the personal and hence ultimate motives that inspired and shaped it. In every mode of thought to a greater or
lesser degree, human needs, struggles, and bias rise eventually
to the surface. The fondest dream of modern philosophy seems to
have been to speak impartially for all men and all ages. Time
and again it has attempted to gain some ultimate and utopian point
of view from where its contentions would be beyond question and
reproach. But each time its gesture has turned out to be vain
and thus petulant. Each "absolute" view has been shown to be
merely penultimate and thus provisional.

The guiding intuition behind Marías' work has long been deeply ingrained in Spanish thought. Shunning the utopian and abstract
and going counter to prevailing philosophical aims, Unamuno once
remarked (not without his usual exaggeration) that even the most
abstract work of philosophy, Kant's Critique of Pure Reason, for
instance, is really a novel. What he meant was that in every

such work we may glimpse something of the human drama and effort that went into its creation. Ortega, in turn, noted the "imperialistic" tendency of philosophy whereby in true nineteenth-century style it had attempted to extend its influence and control over all disciplines until it encompassed the whole of reality. Ortega himself had no such ambitions. Rather he was aware that his own system would necessarily be merged with subsequent views. He shared Unamuno's Iberian suspicion of so-called unchanging truths, but he never doubted that philosophy could have its moment of truth. Ortega's view was not a denial of immutable truth but rather a realization that because men change they have a need for different truths.

Going a step farther than his predecessors, Marías sets about in this work to recreate in at least a minimal way those conditions and problems that gave rise to a variety of human views and activities to which we give the uncertain name of philosophy. When viewed from this perspective, far from being the mere exercise of idle and detached curiosity, philosophy exhibits from the outset the urgency of unavoidable, irrevocable human problems. It has its full share of drama and despair. For only the irrevocable is dramatic; only the unavoidable creates despair. Yet removed from the arena where its purpose and meaning originated, philosophy often becomes a lifeless and ridiculous series of abstractions, retaining its complexities while losing its aim. This is probably one reason why in the popular mind philosophy may be esteemed for its difficulty and shunned at the same time for its meaninglessness.

At this point the preceding remarks should be tempered with a note of caution. To say that philosophy arises as a response to human problems does not imply a deterministic process whereby thought may be interpreted as a mere function of certain difficulties in which man finds himself. The mere presence of problems does not create philosophy any more than certain oils will automatically assure the creation of a painting. Marías does not attempt to explain away genius but rather tries to show that genius, far from being alien to its age, is really its embodiment and its link to other ages.

In this regard also, it should be noted that a philosophy must be considered not only for what it is, but also (and perhaps equally) for what it is not. We understand a philosopher better when we know which problems he faces and which he avoids, which possibilities he actualizes and which he shuns. We must consider what he says and what he does not say. In human terms, the remark that history does not reveal its alternatives is only partially true. Behind the realities man has selected to follow and become trail the unreal images of what he could have been. Far from being idle fancies, such images prompt us to pass judgment on ourselves and our history. It is only in view of what could have been that we can express satisfaction or regret with what we are. This is why Marías often tries to show us what options a given thinker had, and at times he will longingly watch a great possibility fade into disappointment or rejoice when a flash of insight is rescued from oblivion. Of course in any absolute sense Marías has proposed an impossible task. We can never wholly immerse ourselves in another man's world. What he sees and feels and hopes for must always retain some essential mystery, which we, like Marías, can only acknowledge and respect.

This brings us finally to the title of the work: <u>A Biography</u> <u>of Philosophy</u>. We have already seen how Marías attempts to link philosophy to human history and the problems of mankind, and in this sense the "biography" of philosophy is the setting wherein men come to think in certain ways because they have been obliged to react to specific problems of real life. But in speaking of "biography" Marías has in mind not only a setting but also a story. If we know the alternatives men faced in a given period and if we know the things to which they aspired, we have the minimal plot, the barest argument perhaps, of their life. And insofar as we can follow their progress from problem to aspiration-- or disappointment--we have told something of their story. In this way we understand the dramatic nature of all thought and thus come to see it as a human adventure rather than a mere chronological series of ideas of one kind or another. But more than this, according to Marías, in order to understand human things we must tell a human story. This is really what Marías tries to do in <u>A Biography of Philosophy</u>: tell the dramatic story of philosophy. If the attempt itself is made in obedience to Marías' own epistemological canons, the result is a clear and original account of philosophical tradition interpreted from a unique point of view. I hope that I have been able to render to the English-speaking reader something of the spirit and form of Marías' superb prose.

Houston, Texas   Harold C. Raley

Prologue

This book is considerably more extensive than the Spanish work bearing the same title. To the chapters that make up the Spanish edition I have added others written at different times (the last in 1971) in order to bring the work to its completion. A Biography of Philosophy is, therefore, made up of diverse sections written independently of each other over a period of many years, but the central idea of the book predated them all. This is not a book "composed," as it were, of scattered writings, but rather the very contrary: it is a unified book written in fragments that only now appears in its true form.

A Biography of Philosophy is not a "history of philosophy." The latter was the theme of my first book (in English, History of Philosophy, Dover Publications, New York). Rather, it is a history of what philosophy has meant, and of what has been meant by it, from Greece to our own time.

Aside from the differing content of their thought and the succession of philosophical doctrines that have appeared in the West since the seventh century B.C., the men who have philosophized have done so in quite different ways and with different purposes because the aims and situations of their lives differed from those of other men. There is a history of what philosophy has been over the centuries as a purely human activity. Thus it possesses a "life," and it is the story of that life that I call the "biography" of philosophy. It seems to me that without an understanding of this biography the meaning of the deepest level of the history of philosophy will elude us.

The present work places particular stress on the Greek, medieval, and continental European tradition in philosophy. The English-speaking reader will find that the thought with which he is probably most familiar occupies a relatively minor position and that philosophy written in other languages is treated in much greater detail. It was hard to avoid the "injustice." Since the Renaissance, when Latin was either abandoned or relegated to a secondary role and the living languages came to the fore, a schism has existed between the British Isles and the Continent. Strictly speaking, there is no single European philosophical tradition (such as existed in the Middle Ages) but rather two traditions that are in frequent contact with each other. Furthermore, in dealing with a "biography" one must keep one's own "trajectory" in mind. The philosophy of the English-speaking world is seen herein through "continental" eyes from a vantage point that bespeaks a very precise manner of living in the world and in history. The "injustice" that may thus be done to philosophy is necessary in order to do justice to its biography.

Madrid, March 1972

A Biography of Philosophy

CHAPTER I

Greek Philosophy from
Its Origin to Plato

1. On the Origin of Philosophy in Greece

It is important that we understand the meaning of the expression,
"philosophy of Plato." It does not imply an inquiry into Plato's
philosophy, except perhaps to a minimal degree. Rather it points
to something previous and more elemental, something both much
simpler and yet involving a special kind of subtle difficulty.
Leaving aside, then, at least in principle, the specific content
of Plato's thought as an intellectual system, our problem may be
stated as a question: what was the task facing Plato as he set
about philosophizing?

This leads at once to the larger problem--in a sense, an impossible problem--of understanding the ancients. All we have left
of an ancient author, at best, is his writings. Yet when someone
speaks or writes, he only says a part of what he wants to say;
the rest, indeed most, of what he means is expressed by his circumstance. In the case of a contemporary, who may even be unknown,
we are familiar with the portion of his situation that is in common with our own. When we read an ancient writer, however, we
lack this familiarity. If we are aware of this, we must realize
that this writer is, in the strictest sense, unintelligible. If
we ignore the differences and project our own situation into his
(as entire periods have done with the Greeks), then he can be
"understood." But what is "understood" is, of course, something
other than what the bygone writer meant. In other words, he is
understood, but at the same time misunderstood.[1] How, then, are
we to proceed?

In considering an ancient writing, we must begin by "restor-
ing" it, as we would do in the case of an old parchment half
erased by time. Yet this interpretative restoration is more
difficult than the purely physical task of the paleographer, for
three reasons. First, the paleographer's mutilated text of itself
points out the existence and location of its mutilations. Secondly, these mutilations refer to the written content and are there-

1

fore closely tied to the factual information offered. Finally, once the text has been theoretically restored, the more uncertain and negative task still lies ahead. In fact, in order to restore an ancient text to viable reality, we must come to know the general situation of its author, including not only the elements of his world but also its structure. In the broadest sense this is impossible. Moreover, we must exclude all elements from our own situation that did not pertain to the ancient writer: everything we believe that he did not believe, everything we know that he did not, everything we can do that he could not. Naturally, all this is even more impossible.

Philology and history are techniques that allow us to circumvent these impossibilities up to a certain point--technology is always a means for doing the impossible, and its purpose is to convert the world into possibility--but it would be idle to attempt to comprehend the world in which Plato found himself and from which he philosophized by simply relying on his writings and on the historical context in which he lived. Plato's world was a dynamic situation; it was rooted in an earlier world and led in turn to a later one; it was defined, then, by both its past and its future aim. This is why a situation cannot be "described" but rather must be told or narrated. If we wish to understand Plato's situation, we must observe how that situation came into being and how it could not endure because men longed for a different way of life. To put it more succinctly, we must try to use the method called <u>historical reason</u>.[2]

Plato is the <u>first philosopher</u> whose writings have been preserved. He and Aristotle have bequeathed to us, if not their complete works, at least the essential portions. And this is exceptional; both before and after them (the latter point must not be overlooked) Greek philosophy is obscure. Only fragments remain of the work of the great majority of philosophers from the sixth to the first century B.C. In speaking of the greater <u>importance</u> of Plato and Aristotle, this fact cannot be ignored, for it reveals the dimension that chance occupies in history. Nor would it be permissible to deny the role of chance in explaining the importance of Plato and Aristotle to the generations immediately following them. In any case, would our notion of Greek philosophy, its hierarchies, and the fate of later philosophy be the same if all or most of the writings of Parmenides, Heraclitus, Democritus, Chrysippus, or Posidonius had been preserved? It does not seem likely.

This survival of the philosophical work of Plato and Aristotle, along with scattered fragments of Greek thought, has been one of the reasons, the decisive reason if not the only one, why we are so wont to repeat what both men said and thought and to make immediate use of their ideas in our own thinking. This is especially true of Aristotle, who from this viewpoint has been the unluckier of the two. From time to time Plato creates a small intellectual scandal that keeps us on the alert. Just as we are expecting a reasoned thought, he offers us a myth and talks to us of winged chariots, cicadas, a cave, Theuth and Thamus, Atlantis. Usually these scandals have not been stressed--perhaps because the exegetes of Plato have been insensitive to their scandalous nature. For instance, Plato, at the end of Book VI of the Republic, explains conceptually--and even with a diagram--the structure of reality according to the theory of ideas. Yet immediately afterwards he tells us the myth of the cave. This would be more readily under-standable if he did it in reverse order, if he were to derive a conceptual conclusion from the figurative and mythical explanation. Once this anomaly is noticed, one realizes that he is not under-standing Plato, and this leads one to question the earlier and apparently clear idea that Plato is explaining the same thing in both passages. Aristotle offers fewer scandals of this kind, or at least they are not as apparent in his work; rarely have problems of this nature been noticed in his writings. This is why his thought has seemed nearer and more familiar to us; it has been the decisive--and perhaps pernicious--factor in his philosophical influence.

It is not my aim to resolve these problems. Furthermore, it cannot be said that reality must always be intelligible. I am interested in a more modest and, in appearance, negative conclu-sion. And this conclusion is that we have fallen far short of understanding what Plato and Aristotle really did.

First of all, the very name given to their task is question-able. The expression philosophy does not mean the same thing to both men, and of course their understanding of the term is quite different from what passes under that name in modern universities. Aristotle, in particular, uses the term uneasily and tries a series of other names along with it: sophia, first philosophy, reasoned knowledge. (Perhaps the last term is the best.)

By the fourth century B.C. in Greece the term "philosophy" had been in use for two hundred years. In the sixth century, after several attempts (which to be properly understood would re-quire a detailed history of their own), a new form of thought arose that was to bear this strange name. In an especially impor-tant passage of his Metaphysics,[3] Aristotle refers to those who formerly devoted themselves to the investigation of entities and who "philosophized about Truth" (περὶ τῆς ἀληθείας). Later, in connection with the opinion of Thales of Miletus, he adds: "There are besides some who think that the earliest theologians, far dis-tant from this generation, also held this opinion about nature. In fact, they thought Oceanus and Thetis to be the forefathers of creation and that the gods swear by the water which the poets themselves call Styx. That most deserving of honor is, in fact, what is most ancient. And the most honorable thing is such an oath."[4] As I have stated elsewhere: "Aristotle distinguishes between two very different occupations: that of the ancients who 'theologized,' and the moderns who 'philosophized' (θεολογήσαντες, φιλοσοφήσαντες).[5] He stresses the fact that the former are now

remote in time. This means that the new attitude has been predominant for a long time by the fourth century B.C. What is this
attitude? In my opinion, it is precisely what we call knowledge;
to philosophize is to philosophize 'about Truth.' This expression is often found in Aristotle,[6] and it does not of course mean
a theory of knowledge. One looks in vain for such a theory among
the pre-Socratic thinkers. Rather, what is meant is an inquiry
into things themselves; it is a manifestation or revelation of
what things really and essentially are. We find nothing of this
in those who said that Oceanus and Thetis were the forefathers
of creation. For even though in the final analysis this myth
affords us something to rely on to a certain degree and thus
allows us to approach philosophy,[7] what it really does is to
appeal to an example beyond things themselves and alien to their
nature. In reality there is no pathway leading from things as
we find them to the example to which they are appealed."

At this point one may ask what it was that men did in Greece
before the sixth century B.C. in order to discover those things
about which they could be certain, and why after that period
they were obliged to do something different in order to ascertain
those same things. Naturally, nothing called theology appears
before that time. This expression was used by Aristotle in a
very different situation to interpret certain activities of his
remote ancestors. In the strictest sense, the term is understandable only as it is used by Aristotle in the historical, mental,
and social context in which he lived.

Above all, one must keep in mind that when a few men started
to philosophize, most men continued as always. Only a very few
found the old insufficient and began to do something else that
would, in time, come to be called philosophy. This new activity
displeased their fellow citizens, who did not understand the odd
task to which these men had set themselves. Aristotle states
that men living in pre-philosophical times appealed to myths. But
in a passage in his aforementioned Metaphysics he declares that
the lover of myths, the "mythophile," is a philosopher in a certain way, since a myth is made up of prodigies.[8] And in his old
age he observed further that ". . . the more alone I am, the more
I turn to myths."[9] Aristotle means by this that a myth represents
something analogous and homologous to philosophy. But this concept of homology is a static notion; it must be made dynamic.
For this reason it is more exact to say that philosophy is a vi-
carious function of myth. For the time came when myth alone was
no longer sufficient. Something happened--later we shall have to
see what it was--that caused men to substitute vicariously philosophy for myth.

According to Aristotle's example, the "theologizers" held
that Oceanus and Thetis were the source of creation. Thales said
that "everything is water." The similarity of these notions in
content is evident; the difference lies in the real meaning of
the two ideas. Through myth, pre-philosophical Greeks could

ascertain those things that might be reliably accepted; but this same assurance is not apparent in Aristotle's example, which simply refers back to Thales and smacks of professorial learning. We can understand the situation better by reading a historian such as Herodotus or Xenophon.

The Greeks resorted to divination (μαντεία, μαντική) in order to orient themselves with respect to the future and to make decisions as to their activities. By examining the entrails (τὰ ἱερά) of sacrificial victims or, better still, by heeding the sayings of the oracle (μαντείου), for example, Delphos and Dodona, they learned what the course of events would be and could then make their decisions. In Chapter IV of Book VI of Anabasis--as a random example--Xenophon gives a minute account of the Greek military expedition in Calpe in Asiatic Thrace. Xenophon offers a sacrifice in order to discover whether they should leave their encampment (ἐπ' ἐξόδῳ ἐθύετο). The entrails reveal a favorable response (τὰ ἱερὰ καλὰ ἐγένετο), and they bury the bodies. The next day Xenophon gathers the troops and tells them that it is evident (δῆλον) that they must march overland, since they have no boats, and necessary (ἀνάγκη) that they march at once, since they have no provisions. Accordingly, he orders a sacrifice, but the signs are unfavorable, and they remain at the encampment throughout the day. Some murmur that Xenophon deliberately construed the unfavorable interpretation as a pretext to stay and found a city, and so the following day everyone is permitted to witness the sacrifice of three victims. However, the interpretation is again negative. With his soldiers becoming increasingly restive because their provisions have run out, Xenophon recommends new sacrifices. Some say the omens are justified because they have heard that boats are coming. They all think they should wait, but they must go in search of provisions. Three more victims are immolated without a favorable omen. The soldiers come to Xenophon's tent to tell him they have no food, but he tells them that he will not order them to decamp until the signs are favorable. The next day there are further sacrifices as the anxious army surrounds the altar. But they are running out of victims, and since they have no sheep, they buy oxen and sacrifice them. Even so, the signs are not favorable. Neon, the strategist, seeing the terrible condition of the soldiers and wishing to ease their plight, organizes an expedition of two thousand men to search for supplies; the enemy cavalry surprises the expedition and five hundred men perish. On the following day a boat from Heraclea arrives with provisions. Xenophon again makes sacrifices, and this time the signs are favorable from the start. At the conclusion of the ceremonies, the soothsayer Arexion spies an eagle of good omen and advises Xenophon to begin the march. And so, finally, the army leaves the encampment.

Thus we see how men in grave and urgent circumstances are guided by the results of sacrifices. Though considering it evident and necessary to act in a certain way, they do the contrary

if the omens so indicate. In other words, when it becomes a
question of knowing what to rely on, really and truly, they do not
depend on their rational assessment of the apparent facts of their
situation but rather on hidden reality that is revealed in the entrails of sacrificial victims. At other times they heed the joy-
less, unsweetened, and unadorned words uttered by the Sybil's
delirious lips.[10] Is the problem, then, the nature of the reality
they heed and interpreting the meaning of the way in which it is
manifested?

Elsewhere I have answered this question in detail by examining three modes of "thought" that are not "knowledge" in the
strictest sense: primitive ordeals, "wisdom," and the Hellenic
oracles.[11] Permit me to cite some of these earlier references:

> What presupposition lies behind the words of the Hellenic
> Oracles? That is, what latent notions are revealed in
> their utterances? An especially clear answer to this
> question is found in Herodotus: when Croesus, conquered
> and deposed by Cyrus asks Apollo whether he is not
> ashamed of having deceived him with his Delphic Oracles
> and of having sent him to war and to his doom against
> the Persians, Pythia not only scolds him for his impru-
> dence at not having properly interpreted the ambiguous
> Oracles, but also gives him a direct answer: Τὴν πεπρω-
> μένην μοῖραν ἀδύνατά ἐστι ἀποφυγεῖν καὶ θεῷ--even a god
> cannot escape his fatal destiny.[12] In other words, the
> Oracle's presupposition and at the same time the reason
> for his limitation and insufficiency is destiny itself,
> μοῖρα. Destiny outreaches the gods themselves, although
> in a secondary sense it is sometimes identified with a
> divinity, Moîra. Destiny is also the source of ancient
> tragedy. Moîra means in the first place part or lot and
> is akin to the term μέρος. It is the portion allotted
> to each person; it is what chance grants us and thus
> comes to mean luck itself. Finally, destiny, fate or
> fatality is that which must needs happen, what must be.
> This inescapable reality is oblivious to all will, even
> the will of the gods who are also under its sway. Des-
> tiny, then, is the inexorable structure of reality and
> it must be necessarily considered in all things. . . .
> Although it is an obscure question that would require
> a careful and detailed investigation, it is possible
> to see in at least one dimension of this idea of Moîra
> a pre-theoretical analogy to the idea of nature, some-
> thing resembling a mythical version of physis. . . .
> For nature is, in fact, the immutable; it is that which,
> because it admits no change, is always certain. Now
> Moîra in mythical terms implies this same certainty
> and immutability. The final reason for apparent things
> is found in their latent destiny. Yet strictly speaking,

there is no pathway leading from one to the other, and for this reason it remains inaccessible to men. They can only accept the certainty of things as stated by the gods, or in a concrete way, by the Oracle.

There is, then, an absolute discontinuity between the manifest world and the latent reality by which I must guide and decide my life. I cannot go to the latent world; it must come to me through the agency of the gods. There is no way I may assume the validity of latent things merely by the structure of things I find about me. In Greek, one would say there is no method of going from one to the other. Now then, when life becomes sufficiently complicated and man finds periods of leisure and certain resources at his disposal, when he has behind him a past stretching far into time, and when by that same process of time he has accumulated a wealth of life experiences of all kinds, then he can make long-range projections which, because of the nature of the projects, need a minimum of precision. Only in this way is the internal complexity of his projections possible. Faced with this long-term need, man must orient himself with respect to things around him in a new sense. He needs to know not so much what will "happen" but rather how things themselves act, and especially how they will continue to act. This means that now man himself needs to cross over from the manifest world to the latent and the possible. This is especially so regarding the future behavior of things. He needs, then, a method in the most rigorous meaning of the term. This need is to become the remote origin of philosophy.

In the Greek view, things appear to be multiple and changing. Their multiplicity and especially their decline mean that man cannot be certain of them. Yet it is only with these things, it is only by relying on them, that he can fashion his life. This basic fact of the inherent decline of things led the Greeks to assume three different attitudes concerning them. The first is the view expressed in lyric poetry, which is moved by the fleeting span of things and of men who appear and pass and shape a certain life view on their ephemeral world. The second is history, which would commit these passing things to memory (not all of them, to be sure, but at least the most memorable), and which appears, then, as a safeguard against oblivion; Herodotus states this idea explicitly. The third attitude leads to the idea of nature, which is the origin of science and philosophy.

Things are, in fact, first one thing and then another. Their mutability prevents one from knowing with certainty what they are. I do not know what will become of what I have before me; I cannot say how it will behave henceforth. There is no assurance that it will continue to be or that I shall be able to count on it. But there is one case where things are clearer and in which the ephemeral nature of things can be circumvented. This is the case of generation. Father and son are two people and are different from

7

one another. Yet it happens that the one springs from the other, as an oak grows from an acorn. In both cases we find different things, yet basically they are the same. In a generational line we may go from A to B and from B to A. How is this possible? We do so by way of identity, for fundamentally they are the same thing.

This idea is basic to what follows. For if I apply the same generational scheme to the mobile multiplicity of things, I have a way of going from what is patent or evident to what is merely latent or possible, and conversely, from the latent to the evident. In one of the obscure fragments of his work, Heraclitus states that the upward road and the downward road are one and the same. This road is what may properly be called method, an open avenue on which one may come and go. This is what the Greeks called physis, or "nature." Strictly speaking, nature is not a thing nor is it any given reality. It is rather the name of a solution to a problem, an interpretation of what I find about me. Nature is how I understand the way in which things arise and are born of each other. In applying the generational scheme to the multiple and moving reality about me, I interpret it as nature.[13]

Basically, then, generation coincides with identity. To say that nature exists is to say that natural things are fundamentally the same. And because of their identity it is possible to go from A to B and vice versa. Such is the overriding supposition of the interpretation.

But this alone is not enough. This identity exhibits, at least cursorily, a temporal form. The son is fundamentally the same as the father once was; he is also the same as his sons will be. This means that the fundamental identity, that which really exists today, is the same that was and will be. It is permanent; it is what remains throughout all change. The permanent underlies all passing things; it is what was already; it is ancient. Nature is essentially old, though perennially renewed and young. This is why the Greeks called it arkhé, "beginning," that which is ancient. The beginning of things is what they have been and therefore what they will be. The notion of identity allows us to go from the source to the things arising from this source and back again.

Thus, latent reality, the reality revealed in the Oracles or in the entrails of sacrificed animals through the agency of the gods, can now be unveiled by man himself because there is a way, a method of access to it. This means that man uncovers a means of reaching and dealing with this reality on his own. What formerly was darkly revealed by omens is now unveiled and made manifest by man. This process is what the Greeks termed alétheia, that which is patent, in other words, "truth."

This serves to clarify Aristotle's expression concerning those who "philosophized about truth." What he meant was that they spoke of patent or manifest things. The first men to philosophize did so in regard to those things which truly exist. This method, which is the contrary of myth, is really philosophy itself; for philosophy does not have a method but rather is itself method.

This new mode of thought, which strictly speaking and in contrast to other forms of thought is knowledge, is based on the supposition or belief that things are, that is, that they have a certain consistency and that this consistency is accessible by means of a certain intellectual operation which is precisely the phenomenon of knowing. In its most developed form this consistency of things is called nature. Nevertheless, does this alone constitute philosophy?

Undoubtedly it does not. There are forms of knowledge other than philosophy; for example, science which is dedicated to investigating the consistency of things. Therefore, something else is needed before we may talk of philosophy in Greece. To begin with, what causes man to consider the consistency of things and the need to know their structure? When a portion of my world fails, either by disappearing or by behaving in an unusual way that I had not "counted on," this fact alone puts me ipso facto in another situation. In this new situation I have no certainty of waht may be relied on. I am, so to speak, in a condition of uncertainty. In order to escape from my uncertainty I must master the new situation and discover what has happened. But this involves a previous question: how must a thing be made if this could have happened to it?

This explains man's astonishment (θαυμάζειν) at things and the subsequent decision "to do nothing" which Aristotle pointed out in the man who contemplates reality in wonderment. The failure of things to behave as expected makes it impossible to plan on them. Hence man does nothing because he does not know what to do. He then considers things from a new point of view: he searches for the innermost quality of things, for their consistency. This kind of knowledge, growing out of the unexpected behavior of things, may be called science. But it is still not philosophy.

The fact that I live within a circumstantial world of patent, evident things bounded by a horizon of latent and possible things gives my life unity and structure as well as limits. This horizon brings into question, therefore, not only certain ingredients of my life but also life itself in its entirety. My horizon of latent, unrealized things and possibilities means that I must know how to conduct myself regarding the totality of life. And this postulates some form of ultimate and integral understanding. Yet this is not to say that this understanding must be knowledge. This happens only when man finds himself in a situation where in order to know how to conduct himself he must know the consistency of things. For in such a situation man also finds himself fundamentally believing that things have a certain consistency that he may describe. When this situation coincides historically with the need for some ultimate form of knowledge, then philosophy becomes possible.[14]

This explains, at least in part, the real historical setting in which it has been possible for philosophy to exist. We must, nonetheless, bear two obscure facts in mind: first, science came

9

into being in Greece at the same time as philosophy; second, the polemic temper shown by all the earliest Greek philosophers, their thematic opposition to opinion, to dóxa or the current interpretations of reality. For the question was not so much to discover real things as it was to discover the reality of things, the portion of reality things may contain. Only when this distinction became clear did philosophy arise in Greece.

2. The First Philosophizers

The problem we are interested in here is the philosophy of Plato. We must see the vicissitudes through which philosophy passed in order to become what it was for Plato. This would necessitate a history of pre-Socratic or, if you prefer, pre-Platonic, philosophy. But we are going to attempt something different and in a certain way more basic and radical. We shall examine not so much what the pre-Socratic thinkers did as what they intended to do. In other words, we shall observe how the need that led these men to philosophize at a given moment in history is gradually transformed along with the very reality of philosophy itself. It will be necessary to examine, if only cursorily, the situation of these men whose aims altered in correlation to their changing circumstances.

Elsewhere I have shown that at the bottom of the notion of necessity in man lies the concept of purpose. Necessities arise as such in relation to the pressure, different in each case, brought to bear on things by the force of my purpose. I refer the reader to my earlier discussion of the topic.[15] It is sufficient for our purpose here to note that this is the point of view from which we must consider pre-Socratic Greek philosophy.

Above all, we must bear in mind that only a very few men began to philosophize in the sixth century B.C. Their circumstances were common to those of many other men, and yet only they felt the need to philosophize. No historical situation is sufficient of itself to explain any human reality, for in any given situation many different forms of conduct are possible, arising from all the possible human purposes at work. I am enclosed in a room because my purpose is to leave it; I am ignorant because I wish to know; I am poor because I would be rich. Those men who first philosophized had to do so because their purpose was different from what it had been formerly and different still from that of their countrymen who had no such purpose. The idea of purpose is the principal factor here.

Since the history of Greek philosophy has been written mainly from the viewpoint of "ideas" or "doctrines," the speculation by the School of Miletus and especially by Thales of Miletus is usually given as the starting point. But we must remember that to the Greek mind Thales appears as one of the Seven Wise Men and is associated with men who seem to us to be of a very different type:

Solon, Pythacus of Mitilene, Bias, occasionally also Periander
of Corinth and Cleobulus of Rhodes, and sometimes Epimenides
and Anacarsis, Chilon, etc. These men are usually not names
included in the history of philosophy. They were rich and powerful, involved in business and technical activities. Great travelers, they were men who lived in intimate contact with reality;
they had their feet on the ground rather than their heads in the
clouds. They do not strike us, in sum, as meditative men who
might choose to spend their lives contemplating in a cell. If on
the one hand the story is told of Thales that he once fell in a
hole because he was looking at the stars, it is also said, and
in greater detail, that he was an astute political adviser and
that on one occasion when a river had changed its course, Thales,
foreseeing a fine olive crop, rented several mills and became
rich. Herodotus relates that Solon traveled "in order to see"
(θεωρίης εἵνεκεν), a trait that the Orientals always found admirable in the Greeks. What was it that these men, Thales, Solon,
Herodotus himself, saw? They were interested primarily in the
cities, people, and in what the inhabitants of strange countries
did. They visited monuments and enumerated in detail the gifts
of kings and tyrants to sanctuaries and temples. They tell us of
the local customs in each country. Rather than trade with or war
against strange peoples, they consider them: they seek their
characteristics, what we might call their "consistency," in order
to understand their conduct and to have a clear idea of what they
are like. To the Greeks humans appear in the form of peoples, as
units defined by a certain behavior; Egyptians, Lydians, Persians,
and Scythians are human "varieties." As for themselves, their
own consistency or nature is that of people who observe and see
things. They are endowed with a certain superiority that lies in
questioning the consistency of things and of other men and in knowing what to look for in other men. Within the context of this
general attitude we must determine the moment that philosophy
appears. How is Thales of Miletus different from his contemporaries? What is there about him that sets him apart from the loosely
associated group of "Seven Wise Men" (of course, there were not
seven) and makes him the initiator of a new and mysterious occupa-
tion of man?

    According to extant testimonies, he was powerful, rich, in-
fluential in the politics of his city, a businessman, engineer,
traveler, and astronomer; he appears as the founder of philosophy
and at the same time--though not by chance--of mathematics. A man,
in other words, familiar with the real world in its diverse forms;
he was fully immersed in it. He was capable of technical invention,
that is, capable of that kind of novelesque fiction of which technical thought primarily consists.[16] Thales was probably a man of
much imagination, able to make projections both in his own life
and in the world about him. Thus he could foresee the movement
of celestial bodies and thereby predict an eclipse or plot the
future course of a river, the behavior of olive oil merchants, the

11

result of the war between Croesus and Cyrus. He was a futurist, and he had to be. Thales visited Egypt where he came into contact with priests who taught him certain techniques, for instance, how to reestablish the boundaries of farms after floods, how to calculate the height of a pyramid by measuring the length of its shadow, how to determine the distance of a ship at sea far from the coast. Thales learned all this, but when he returned to Greece and thought about it, he applied his knowledge in a different way that was to have unexpected consequences.

Instead of limiting himself, as the Egyptians or the Chaldeans usually did, to the manipulation of numbers and figures, to what was called logistiké, or calculus, and land survey, Thales began a new form of mental manipulation of numbers, triangles, and polyhedrons, which consisted in viewing them as something given to a permanent way of behaving. There are triangles, circles, octahedrons, pyramids; there are even and odd numbers, and each of them, because of its being what it is, is endowed with a fixed and constant reality. Each has certain "properties" belonging only and forever to it. Likewise, there are Lydians, Persians, and Massagetae, with their respective habitual manner of behavior that allows one to foresee their conduct. The same thing happens with mathematical objects. Thales does to them what analogously Solon did to the unfamiliar peoples he visited: rather than "manipulate" them in trade or war, in the case of peoples, or count and measure in the case of mathematics, Thales takes their very consistency into consideration. The passing from the one attitude to the other was not as obvious as it might appear today: a total modification of the suppositions on which man lived was necessary. We must now ask why Thales found it necessary to bring the consistency of things into question, especially mathematical objects.

I have stressed the fact that Thales of Miletus and those who appear with him in this initial step of philosophy were men who lived in intimate and varied contact with reality. They had tried to discover a sound and reliable means of dealing with the things and events of life through the habitual procedures dominant in that time and place. Probably they had experienced frequent failures that had induced in them a state of uncertainty and insecurity. The experience of leadership, technical difficulties, and the need to foresee the outcome of historical actions no doubt gave rise to a growing distrust of the usual modes of thought handed down by their more immediate tradition. On the other hand, these men had also been great travelers. The positive side of travel is usually stressed; much is said of the enrichment it lends in the form of new knowledge and facts. But we must equally be aware of its negative ramifications, for it also may lead to a perplexity caused by contact with a multitude of beliefs and ideas. Thales and others like him had known other means of dealing with situations; they had seen ways, different from those of their country, which men of other countries felt were effective. Thales felt indifferent toward Apis, but when he realized that the Egyptian did not react in the same way but rather really and truly depended on the sacred bull to guide his life, he could see that the situation was reversed in the case of the Delphic Oracle. While the Greek based his decisions on the sayings of the Oracle, these utterances meant nothing to the men of the Nile. This repeated experience, this confrontation of the system of beliefs in which man dwells with others that are different, forces one to take a different attitude toward his own. His own system of beliefs now appears as simply one of many possibilities. He may continue to adhere to it, but not simply because this is the only system he knows but for some conscious reason. This explains his uncertainty and the need to appeal directly to things themselves, to reality as such, in order to determine in truth what may or may not be relied on, and indeed so that he may decide between traditional and new or foreign beliefs. There appears, then, a higher method which may be appealed to in order to escape that uncertainty of things. And this new attitude is indeed evident in the "examination of the Oracles" which, according to Herodotus,[17] Croesus (a contemporary of Thales), a man who was by no means given to theory, insisted on before he would give credence to them or guide his policies by what they uttered. Faced with the failure of time-honored means to ascertain the certainty of things, new questions of an unexpected type now confront man: what is the nature of things if this is what happens to them? What finally is all this? The day a Greek--Thales or anyone else--did not really know what he could or could not be sure of and so began asking these questions, philosophy had been born.

3. Nature and Consistency

In a significant passage in his Metaphysics in which he associates myth with philosophy, Aristotle notes that men first philosophized in order "to flee from ignorance" (διὰ τὸ φεύγειν τὴν ἄγνοιαν).[18] By ignorance he means uncertainty or insecurity; ignorance is a threat to man lost in a multiplicity of bits of knowledge. The only solution to man's dilemma is this new attitude, which takes in the whole of reality so as to question it and thus disclose what ultimately may be relied on.

This manner of inquiry--what is all this?--which not only does not exclude but rather presupposes a multitude of partial bits of knowledge corresponds in the sixth century to the idea of nature, or phýsis. This general answer to the problem consists of thinking that things are fundamentally the same. It holds that a certain reality underlies all things and that it is out of this reality that they arise or are born. Moreover, this birth or emergence operates by way of identity; there is a road leading in both directions. Man may go from nature to things in nature (and thus understand them) because previously he had gone from things to nature itself. By proceeding in one direction man discovers natural things; if he goes in the other direction, he comes upon the nature of things.

This idea of nature implies that the process of knowledge is not mere explanation, since the latter in the final analysis consists of reducing certain things to other things. To explain something is to unfold what was implicit, that very substance which, beneath their multiple and mutable appearances, what things implicitly were to begin with. The experience of the Greek--and this should be remembered--was nevertheless the contrary. In the eyes of Hellenic man, things are not only different; they are opposed to one another. They appear in life experience in contrasting and opposing ways. Hot and cold, light and heavy, wet and dry, masculine and feminine, even and odd; reality manifests itself in antipodes. How, then, can opposites basically be the same despite their appearance? This is the problem.

The idea of <u>physis</u> involves a general structure and is a pattern of interpretation. It alludes to the fundamental supposition that things spring by generation from a primary source to which they may also be "reduced" by virtue of their fundamental identity. But something else is needed to explain how this is possible, and before we can proceed effectively with a <u>natural</u> interpretation of things. Greek philosophy appealed very early to another concept, that of arkhé, or "principle." This does not mean that <u>physis</u> and arkhé refer to the same thing, or even that they are necessarily coetaneous notions. What happened was that the Greeks, at a certain moment in their thought which cannot be easily ascertained, were to say that <u>physis</u> is <u>arkhé</u>, or principle. This means that the concept of <u>principle</u> is an interpretation of nature. We shall see later just what that interpretation was.

In his <u>Metaphysics</u>, Aristotle enumerates the different ways in which the word ($ἀρχή$) is used.[19] There is no need at this point to go into the different meanings of the term in Aristotelianism. It is enough to indicate the three primary meanings of the Greek word ($ἀρχή$) that are, moreover, closely related to one another. First of all, it has the meaning of <u>antiquity</u>, that is, that which came first, the oldest and most archaic. Secondly, it contains the idea of <u>beginning</u>, that which concerns the origin of things. Thirdly, it means <u>rule</u>, that which governs or holds sway.

There is, then, a certain authority vested in the archaic substratum from which things come that continues to exercise power over them. This view has some rather momentous consequences that culminate in Eleatic philosophy. However, there is an intermediate link: the Pythagoreans, a group of thinkers whom no one seems to know quite what to do with. They represent the first <u>social</u> manifestation of philosophy in Greece. They are the founders of Hellenic mathematics and greatly influenced Plato. They are clearly a necessary link in understanding Greek philosophy, but a link that unfortunately does not fit very well and that produces some rather troublesome notes.

Aristotle tells us that the Pythagoreans were concerned with the principles of mathematics.[20] A modern reader coming across this sentence thinks perhaps of something like the principle of contradiction or the axioms. Yet Aristotle understands the principles (ἀρχαί) of mathematics to be figures and numbers, the same things that we might call mathematical objects. But this is not all; according to Aristotle, mathematical principles to the Pythagoreans mean the principles of all things. In other words, for them certain very peculiar entities, numbers and figures, but especially numbers, are the principles of reality. Yet the Pythagoreans do not formulate a theory of mathematics; rather, they explain the relationship of things to mathematical principles by saying that things exist in imitation of numbers (οἱ μὲν γὰρ Πυθαγόρειοι μιμήσει τὰ ὄντα φασὶν εἶναι τῶν ἀριθμῶν).[21] At first glance and without other clarification, this statement cannot be understood. As a matter of fact, the very opaqueness of this assertion is its first positive result, as well as a point of departure. To attempt to understand it, we must go back to some earlier things so as to shed light on the meaning which, it must be reiterated, is incomprehensible at this point.

Thales had said that everything is water. Aristotle took this to mean that everything is wetness and that entities are engendered through moisture. This explanation is similar to the myth of Oceanus and Thetis as the forefathers of creation. Accordingly, Aristotle makes a point of the similarity of these ideas.[22] In both cases, the origin of things is to be explained through a reference to water. But whereas in the first case we are led to something inconsistent with engendered or produced reality, in the second a way is opened leading from water to things and vice versa. Things may be "reduced" to water and for this reason, water acts as a principle of explanation. In Anaximander we find the concept that all things spring from the ápeiron, or reality that is unlimited, undefined, and grandiose. Things consist of something definite; they are cold or hot, dry or wet, they are stones or animals. They are definite manifestations of something that has no definite consistency but that produces them generatively. When Anaximenes adds that all things are engendered through condensation or rarefication, the idea of physis is beginning to be articulated in a coherent intellectual pattern. Things arise in accord with the mechanism of generation. This was, in sum, the first notion of the idea of "natural law."

If now we return to the Pythagoreans, their assertion "things exist through the imitation of numbers" now takes on a certain meaning. The Pythagoreans stressed the idea that things are consistencies, as numbers are, because they consist of something. The Pythagorean statement means, finally, that things consist, and in this aspect they resemble numbers. But things, far from being fixed and immutable consistencies, such as the number seven or a triangle, exhibit change. This means that their consistency is deficient and hence a mere imitation. Other Pythagorean texts state that numbers are things themselves (αὐτὰ τὰ πράγματα),[23] which means that fundamentally things are numbers.

While the Milesians emphasized creation and therefore the fundamental reality from whence things emerge, the Pythagoreans insisted almost exclusively on the consistency of things as exemplified by the model of numbers and paid less heed to the creation of things. Although at some risk of exaggeration, we could say that for the Pythagoreans numbers are the nature or phýsis of things.

This brings us to a new problem: the matter of reconciling both dimensions of the question and combining the dual views of the natural interpretation of reality. The Milesians, with an energetic appeal to their original substratum, phýsis, are nevertheless able to explain only very crudely things as they actually appear. On the other hand, the Pythagoreans view these interpretations as overly metaphorical and instead point to the consistency of things. But if both concepts are joined, the question must be raised (as it was raised to the Pythagoreans) of how generation beginning with numbers is possible. This leads us to the very heart of the problem that in one form or another was to be debated throughout the fifth century B.C.

But before taking up this problem, a few words concerning dóxa are in order. Dóxa is opinion, fame, glory, public opinion, and belief. Now, in Greece, philosophy assumes a formal structure in view of dóxa. The assertions of the pre-Socratic thinkers have the meaning that things are in a certain way and not some other way; that is, they are not the substance of common opinion or belief.[24] This attitude is so evident in the Pythagoreans that it comes to be associated with the group itself rather than with its doctrines alone. They are a group surrounded, defined, and set apart by dóxa, and it is from this point of view that the dramatic vicissitudes of the school must be understood. As for their doctrinal theses, they consisted of the most open negation of any inherited opinion. On the other hand, their notion that reality is number ought not to be taken too seriously. To them, philosophy is rather a denial that reality is what it is believed to be; it casts aside opinion and inherited interpretations in order to discover and display reality itself. This attitude is apparent as early as Thales, but it becomes more obvious in Parmenides. "Interpretation" and "patency" are better translations of δόξα and ἀλήθεια than "opinion" and "truth" in Parmenides' work. Of course this does not make Parmenides an enemy of dóxa; such an attitude would, after all, be meaningless in his case. Yet he finds it absurd to confuse the two points of view. One may manipulate things according to the interpretations of dominant "opinion," or dóxa, or he may choose to uncover and reveal the reality of things (alétheia). What one may not do is to mistake one approach for the other, because this is precisely where the error lies.

As is well known, Parmenides is closely associated with the Pythagoreans and his work represents a mature development of the Italic philosophy. His position coincides with theirs inasmuch as it represents a repudiation of dóxa and the view that things are to be interpreted as consistency. Nevertheless, the differences between them are also important.

The Pythagoreans still exercised a primitive form of thought; although residual, we see in them what Ortega called pensamiento confundente, thought that tends to commingle things, and to see associations where mere observation is all that is justified. It is a phenomenon we see in children. Predication in this case also becomes a form of identification or association such as we might find in the statement: "Snow is that which is white." Realizing that such a sweeping association is unjustified, one may then restate it in a more restricted form: "Snow is white." Similarly, since both numbers and things consist, the Pythagoreans thought that things were numbers. Parmenides was not satisfied with this way of thinking and so began a new inquiry into the consistency of things. It was in this way, so it is generally stated, that the discovery of "being" came about.

It so happens, however, that Parmenides did not invent the verb to be (εἶναι). It is a word taken from the spoken language of his time. In Spanish, through a linguistic privilege hitherto little used philosophically, we have two verbs (ser and estar) to express being, whereas most languages, including Greek, have only one. Greek has only one verb to say that a drink "is hot" (está caliente) or that the sun "is hot" (es caliente). Hence the Greek word for is contains not only the notion of essential characteristics but also temporal state or temporary present. We must distinguish in the word is temporal state (for instance, this fruit is [Spanish está] green), quality (the leaf is [Spanish es] green), and what we may call consistency (the sun is [Spanish es] hot). Being, therefore, is not necessarily associated with consistency.²⁵ Consistency is more fundamental than quale, i.e., any given set of attributes or qualities. What later thinkers would consider qualities, the Greeks saw as modes of consistency. This explains their propensity for using the neuter expressions: the white, the wet, the cold, etc. From this notion also comes their tendency to divide the world into opposites: the cold and the hot, the wet and the dry, etc., which by no means are to be viewed as "differing" degrees of heat or moisture.

Hence things exhibit a certain consistency; but the time comes when it is also apparent that they have a certain consistency, and here "consistency" must be emphasized more than any of its several manifestations. Things consist of something, but our attention is not on that "something" but rather on the very fact of consisting, regardless of the particular form of consisting. This means that above all things appear as consisting things; and this is the real meaning of the participle ἐόν which lies at the very heart of Parmenides' philosophy.

Now we could say that things consist of this or that because first of all it is their nature to consist. In other words, they consist of that which is consistent (τὸ ἐόν). I have had to

resort to this circuitous means of stating these ideas instead
of merely saying, as simplicity might warrant, that things are
this or that or something else because previously they are, i.e.,
they are entities. But I could not do so because although this
may be true, it is an abstract truth that neither reveals how it
was discovered nor shows us the intellectual pathways by which
men came upon it. In short, the abstraction does not show what
makes a truth of it. Parmenides' discovery, therefore, might
be formulated by saying that previous to all subsequent forms,
things consist of consisting.

But here our difficulties begin. To think, as well as to
live, is inevitably to exaggerate, for it means placing something
in a certain perspective and not some other, deciding something
in one way rather than another. The exaggeration lies in rejecting
the alternatives, and it can only be surpassed when it is recognized
as such; thus thought must reject in a certain sense its own position by denying the absolute and exclusive nature of its assertions,
wreathing them instead with other possible positions. Now clearly
Parmenides exaggerates excessively, for his great presupposition,
what he tacitly says, is that things consist solely of consisting.
Their existence is spent in consisting. Yet this is by no means
evident. Perhaps there are indeed some things that could be said
to consist only of consisting: mathematical objects, numbers,
and figures. It is no coincidence that these things are precisely the point of departure in Parmenides' conception of things in
general. Now we can understand the Pythagorean thesis that things
exist in imitation of numbers. Although in a less perfect and
permanent way, things exhibit a consistency that reaches its
fullest realization in numbers. To the degree that things may be
said to have consistency, they imitate numbers and approach their
manner of consisting (κατ' ἐξοχήν). On the other hand, we would
think that whereas numbers exhibit only consistency, things have
something else as well: reality.[26]

This fundamental exaggeration on the part of Parmenides in
making his discovery leads to a series of related exaggerations.
The consistencies of things dissolve into consistency as such
and are reduced to the status of dóxa, or appearance. The fundamental fact is that things consist. When a flame is extinguished
or a man dies, their concrete consistency vanishes but they continue to consist, though perhaps in some other form. From this
view are derived the Parmenidean predications of entity that later
were to become "traditional" predications: one, immovable, present,
eternal. . . .

This was to have extraordinary repercussions, for it effectively means the elimination of physis, or nature. If reality consists
of entity, then it ceases to be physis because there is no φύειν,
or active nature. Reality is rather an inherent and imperishable
consistency. Things, therefore, are not engendered and nothing
springs up or comes into being. We should not forget that the
idea of physis grew out of an original treatment of patent or

manifest reality. Fundamentally, things are latent entities.
This latency may be comprehended from a standpoint of things,
and on the other hand, things may be explained from the vantage
point of the latent reality underlying them. This avenue leading to and from latent reality and things is known as nature.
But with Parmenides this avenue disappears, because he holds that
there is no such thing as phýsis in the sense of generation. We
have gone from the patent to the latent, but now we discover that
we cannot return. We must remain in a world of latency interpreted as being, ón. The primary reality that induced us to begin
our inquiry is relegated to mere dóxa. The situation represented
by the idea of moîra is reversed. Moîra implies that there is
no way to go from things as such to the latent reality underlying
them, but rather only a one-way avenue from latent inner reality
to things open only to the gods and revealed in their oracles.
Now men may travel along this avenue on their way to being, but
it is not possible to return to things themselves by the same
route.

In the strictest sense, philosophy does not have a method;
it is a method. Whereas other philosophers had merely made use
of method, Parmenides was the first to question the concept of
method itself. The method resorted to was that of noûs or noeîn
(mind, intellect, thinking). Whereas through aísthesis I find
myself among things, that is, among visible, surrounding things
(strictly speaking, only from the point of view of noûs does
aísthesis take on a sense of method), noûs leads me to discover
the latent, being or ón. The latent is present, says Parmenides,
but only because I seek it, because I attempt to comprehend it.
It is here that the well-known duality apparent throughout all
Greek philosophy develops. The idea of phýsis was an attempt to
articulate visible or patent reality with a latent world beyond
things. But this attempt was rendered impossible as soon as
reality was interpreted as consistency and nature as such disap-
peared.

Philosophy is shaped with Parmenides, but from this moment
thence it also begins to debate within itself. This leads us to
think that philosophy has perhaps been affected by an initial
error, always the hardest kind to discern. This does not mean
that Parmenides told something false, but that he offers only
one truth. And philosophy requires not only that the truth be
told (as do the sciences, for example) but also that the whole
truth, the basic truth, be shown in its entirety rather than in
parts. But if no single interpretation can encompass all reality,
is not philosophy itself fundamentally an error? This might be
readily admitted provided we keep in mind that the moment we admit the possibility, it ceases to be an error. For having made
this admission, we see that a partial truth would no longer be an
error, if by error we mean mistaking a part for the whole. Philosophy must take error into account and thereby absorb it, though
in a way different from Hegel. Error must be viewed not as error

so much as a condition attached to all limited perspective; in
other words, it must be seen as partial and deficient truth.
Any specific truth is verified (literally, "made true") by other
truths. And truths not visible from a given perspective exercise
a "verifying" function on the truth that foresees them and comprehends their structure.

But to ask this attitude of Parmenides would be historically
naïve. Every notion has its moment, and the attitude in question
presupposes a very long philosophical past. Parmenides was fully
entitled, perhaps even obligated, to make his mistake because it
was the price to be paid for one of the most important of truths:
that things consist of consisting. Very probably we have science
in the Western world today just because Parmenides boldly, and at
great risk, chose to follow the way of this truth.

The principal fact is that Parmenides demonstrated the consistency of reality but not the natural basis of things. He pene-
trates into latent reality but leaves closed the way whereby we
might retrace our steps back to tangible things. If this were a
matter of whim or of a theory of being we might then immediately
turn to the ón and begin our speculation from that arena. But
there is no evidence for assuming that metaphysics is first and
foremost the science of being as such. The reason for the existence of philosophy in the first place was that man did not know
what portions of the reality in which he found himself, and with
which he had to contend, could be depended on. Parmenides' idea
of being is unsuitable for explaining things; these are abandoned
to dóxa. Later we shall see how the followers of Parmenides es-
pouse the idea of being as their basic assumption. It is from
this point that they attempt to find a way between being and
things. But we must remember that they philosophize from the
notion of being, that is, from the Eleatic concept of being. In
the final analysis, their enormous efforts in trying to reconquer
reality are voided because of this fact. Pre-Socratic philosophy
after Parmenides is unable to overcome the rift between the two
worlds.

It is no wonder, then, that in the fifth century we find certain men, the Sophists, who literally pick up from the streets
the things that had been abandoned there since Parmenides. The
setting for their activities implies more than is readily apparent.
For the Sophists, who had a profound sense of reality, based their
efforts to discover what they might depend on in things on those
very things in question. And as an arbiter of reality they in-
cline rather toward dóxa than alétheia, which is to say they disregarded truth itself, which had been reduced to mere being. The
influence of the Sophists is not to be underestimated, for they
were the ferment that led Socrates, and later Plato and Aristotle,
to approach things from a different direction and to formulate a
very different type of philosophy.

The problem lies in determining just how successful Socrates
and Plato (and Aristotle in his own right) were in surpassing

both the Eleatics and Sophists at the same time. The struggle
between these two examples is well betrayed in the peculiar un-
easiness one senses in Platonic philosophy. Plato speaks of contemplation and theoría, yet he also mentions effort, gymnásia,
and the tremendous weight attached to being. This matter will
concern us again when we take up the question of why Plato wrote
dialogues. It is a question of course that may be answered in
many ways, and while they are all probably true, they are also
insufficient. But first of all we must consider certain steps
that the human activity we know as philosophy had to take before
reaching Plato.

4. Natural Things

The contemporaries and successors of Parmenides--Heraclitus,
Empedocles, Anaxagoras, Democritus--based their philosophical
thought on being, for in fact they begin with the assumption of
ón as it was discovered and formulated by the Eleatics. This
means that they base their thought on consistency, on a fixed,
immovable, immutable, and universal mode of being. For the sake
of complete accuracy, we should have to note some exceptions to
this overall view in Heraclitus, whose relationship with the
Eleatics is unclear. But at this point we shall only point out
the difficulty involved in placing him with this group.
    The problem during these decades is the dualism between
nature (physis) and natural beings (physei ónta). Several difficulties are implied by the expression physei ónta. In the first
place, we must understand what is meant by ónta, for Parmenides
had said categorically that being is one. Thus, the plural ónta
would really be meaningless. There are many things, prágmata,
but only one being. What, then, does physei ónta mean? This
expression is really the formula for the whole problem and leads
us immediately to the second difficulty. For in fact what we have
here is an attempt to explain things through nature. The dative
physei indicates that things exist in reference to nature, through
the agency of nature. The form being, or natural thing, is quite
vague, but "natural" is a reference to nature. We would be in-
clined to say that natural beings are the things of nature or
that they are in nature. The Greek, on the contrary, would say
that they exist through or by nature. Here nature as principle,
arkhé, or origin, reappears. It is nature that causes natural
things to be what they are. It is, therefore, their principle
or origin. They are not mere parts or ingredients of nature,
but rather things that are because of nature and from it they
derive their reality. Things are what has been brought into being
through this principle, or arkhé. This is most important, for it
clarifies the idea of nature held by the Greeks of this period.
    But there is more to consider. In a strict sense, things,
prágmata, appear as ónta only insofar as they are physei ónta,

21

that is, only insofar as phýsis, or nature, bestows entity on them. Now we should remember that from the Eleatic point of view entity means consistency. Things acquire entity or the quality of consistent being from phýsis or ón, and phýsis is said to be the origin of things because the latter exist only through nature.

Once we have grasped the meaning of the expression "through nature," the problem becomes one of determining the content and mechanism of being through nature. In other words, it is a question of discovering the way that things are brought into being. This problem can be seen in the uncertainty of all Eleatic thought regarding the dualism of nature or phýsis. On the one hand, nature is one (ἕν), quiescent within itself; on the other, it is seen as bringing things into being. Nature then consists of acting, of "naturalizing." But "naturalizing" what?, we might ask. The answer is the many natural things we find. Resorting to medieval terminology, we could say that the universal natura naturans is diversified in a multiple natura naturata. In the Greek view, there is a creating nature (ón) and a nature created (natural things).

In order to explain how phýsis or nature gives rise to multiple and variable things, a new concept is introduced which cannot be approached too cautiously: that of element, or στοιχεῖον. Things are relegated to dóxa and hence disparaged. But when seen as created things, that is, when viewed in reference to phýsis, they appear reduced to their "elements." Elements are diversifications of phýsis, the latent and only reality. At the heart of this idea lies Empedocles' doctrine of the four elements, which for him are the source of all things (ῥιζώματα πάντων) and indeed what things are fundamentally. It was with this notion in mind, remembering that things were interpreted as earth, water, air, and fire, that it has been said that Thales, Anaximenes, and Heraclitus considered true reality or phýsis as consisting of only one of its four elements. Still, this is not very clear and in any case perhaps reveals an anachronism. Rather, is this not an interpretation of these philosophers based on the theory of the four elements? Was Anaximenes, for example, thinking of the elemental quality of the "element" air? Probably not, but in any case this shows the danger of imposing a later theory on an earlier philosopher's thought.

Each of the four elements preserves the Eleatic properties of being: unity, invariability, and permanence. But their plurality would permit an interpretation of the genesis of things by using the elements as a starting point. Nevertheless, this leads to a serious error, that of identifying principle or origin with element, arkhé with stoikheíon. As a matter of fact, this error is evident throughout nearly all philosophy, as Zubiri has astutely pointed out. Furthermore, both concepts appear as synonyms of a third, that of cause (αἴτιον, αἰτία). They are all used without an exact distinction, though there is a general awareness that they are not strictly the same. This is shown in the opening paragraphs of Aristotle's Physics and in the first three chapters of Book V of his Metaphysics.

Arkhé is the first interpretation of physis as the substratum from whence patent or manifest reality emerges. Stoikheîon is viewed as that of which things consist and to which they may be reduced when interpreted from the standpoint of physis. It is the concrete form of application of the idea of nature to things as such. Hence, we are dealing with an "explicative" concept. The ultimate foundation of the idea of physis is to complete the cycle of things by linking them again with that from which they arose. Things may be understood, that is, we may ascertain what reliable relationships we can have with them, because they can be "re-duced" to that from which they were "e-duced." But this presupposes a previous eduction which is the initiating action of physis, a process that we might term "naturation." In this case, the reduction of things becomes also their natural explanation.

The difficulty interposed in this operation is, as we have seen, the suppression of the authentic function of physis by the Eleatic notion of consistency, or in other words, the identification of physis and ón. To overcome this difficulty, the intermediate concept of element is resorted to. Elements are what we consider in things when we attempt to determine their consistency. Now the idea of element conceals an uncertainty regarding thing and principle, consistency (ón) and the creating or "naturalizing" function (ἀρχή, φύσις). For a thing to be understandable, it is reduced to its elements. These elements, in turn, are viewed as creative principles, which arbitrarily preserve the attributes of Eleatic being that excludes all natural generation. From this fundamental inconsistency concerning elements arise all the doubts that permeate the philosophy of the physici recentiores, descendants of the Eleatic school. This basic error is also responsible for the further divisions of being, the reduction of reality to ever smaller elements. First, there is the so-called "plasticity" of fire; later, we find the four "roots" (Empedocles); then, the homoeomeriae of Anaxagoras; and finally, atoms (Leucippus and also Democritus).

Nevertheless, if we examine this process closely, we see that:

(1) It is perfectly clear that the so-called element "fire" in Heraclitus (it is only an element if we view it from the suppositions of later thought) is based on the idea of physis (this leads to the complex question of Heraclitus' possible but doubtful "Eleaticism").

(2) Empedocles, upon formulating the theory of the four elements, is also aware of its inadequacies and so appeals to the two principles of love and hate (Φιλότης καὶ Νεῖχος), which are decidedly mythical in nature, in order to explain movement and generation. In other words, his doctrine stresses the impossibility of reaching a "natural" interpretation of reality solely on the basis of the concept of element.

(3) Anaxagoras represents a step forward in the "elemental"

interpretation of reality. The homoeomeriae are, sensu stricto, elements. But Anaxagoras is aware that they alone are insufficient to explain reality. He then appeals to noûs, or mind, a concept that reveals one of the sources of Greek monotheism. We should keep in mind the importance Plato and Aristotle attached to this doctrine of noûs, despite their considerable misgivings about Anaxagoras' use of his own concept. It is apparent that they saw in this notion an improvement, albeit only postulated, over prior explanations that did not transcend the idea of elements.

(4) Finally, in Democritus atoms are elements or minimal "things" endowed with the attributes of Eleatic being. But at this point grave difficulties face Democritus. We shall point out only one: he is forced into a materialistic interpretation of reality, something hitherto alien to the Greek mind. This does not mean that the Greeks were "spiritualists," but rather that their philosophy had simply arisen outside this kind of duality. In addition, aside from the basic metaphysical inadequacy of all materialism, nature also eludes Democritus. It was no accident that the pre-Socratic form of philosophy, speculation perì phýseos, ended with him.

For at this time a grave crisis takes place in Greek philosophy. Many things are happening and among them is the fact that the Greeks are more and more concerned with sciences: mathematics, physics, astronomy, and medicine. Neo-Pythagoreanism flourishes with Archytas, Philolaus, and Ecphantus. The schools of Cyzicus and Cyrene with Theodorus are the forerunners of the Athenian school and the positive advancement of Platonic mathematics. Now Hellenic mathematics takes on structure and volume. Nor must we overlook the schools of medicine. The φυσιολόγοι, or "physiologists" in the ancient meaning of the term, who had begun to philosophize about nature (περὶ φύσεως), once again become physicists and seek a new knowledge about natural things.

5. The Return to Things

None of this resolves the philosophical problem, of course. Surrounded by knowledge, fifth-century man lacks the ultimate knowledge of how to deal with things. It is quite possible that this situation would have been prolonged if circumstances had not brought pressures. But we should not forget that in speaking of the urging or pressure of things, we reveal an underlying supposition: it is we who urge or compel things in a particular way; it is we who give them direction toward the future. Only inasmuch as we strive for something does reality become urgent or pressing. What does it mean to say that the cold compels us, while it only makes a slab of marble cold? The truth is that it compels us to some action because we wish to be warm. In a general sense, the pressure of reality on man, for certain dimensions of life, is very nearly the same in all ages, but its particular and specific stresses are determined by the here and now of each situation.

Things change drastically in Greece during the first half of the fifth century because Greek aims are substantially altered. This is the era of the Persian wars that caused profound changes in the Hellenic peoples. It is a commonplace that triumphant Athens, with its democracy, imposed on the rest of Greece a new way of life and especially a new form of education, or paideía, that would eventually culminate in the Sophists. This may be true, but it is only partially true at best, and it is not the most important thing to consider. It would be well to examine briefly the changes brought about by the Persian wars.

Before the Persian wars, the Greek cities were politically indifferent to one another and not infrequently openly hostile to one another's ambitions. On the other hand, they were also immersed in that inclusive and peculiar community known as the Hellenic world, a world defined by a series of beliefs and common customs: gods, games, language, a belief in Greek superiority, disdain for barbarians, and during this period at least, a secret admiration for Persian power. These cities were based on a simple technology and political structure.

The Persian wars, enormous in scope, differed from previous wars in that they brought about a total modification in the situation of the Greeks. For in fact they implied a very serious threat. I am not referring, of course, to the threat to personal safety that war always poses. If one takes into account the surprisingly greater number of survivors in comparison to those killed in some way, the actual danger of war is not so great as it might appear. The Persian wars represented rather a colossal threat to the survivors because they endangered all aspects of Greek life. Had the Greeks lost these wars, the foundations of their traditional life would have been changed.

But we are dealing not only with the possibility of defeat. A second and more important fact is that during these wars the Greek world faced the Persian world. Up until this time the Greek world, with its system of beliefs and customs, was for most Greeks the only world. But in confronting another world, questions were inevitably raised in the Greek mind. For the existence of two worlds with two different systems of beliefs automatically places man in a doubtful situation from which he may escape only by choosing. It is not even necessary for the Greek to doubt his own world; he may prefer it without hesitation. Nevertheless, he must choose it and he must adhere to it. Previously the world he lived in was simply the world; now it is his world, one of several possible worlds.

The very scope and magnitude of these wars required that they be waged efficiently and with all available resources. This could be done only with technical skills and precise use of the tools of war. The latter varied widely, from the efficient use of boats to the more difficult and complicated deployment of men. This

means, among other things, that a whole new skill was needed in
the use of human resources on a scale and under demands never
known before. It means that nothing less was asked of this people
than the immediate creation of a technology that could cope with
an undertaking that was to last half a century.

We may well imagine the influence the course of the war had
on the traditional reliance on omens, oracles, and mythical or
religious rituals. As an outstanding example, we have only to
recall the delay in sending Spartan troops to aid the Athenians
in the battle of Marathon (490 B.C.). Despite the goodwill of[27]
Sparta, the troops had to await the full moon before marching.
The building of a navy as Themistocles proposed occasioned, as is
generally known, a political transformation as well. The need
for a greater number of oarsmen meant that lower social classes,
hitherto without civil duties and rights, had to be taken into
the State and considered a part of society.

The Greeks won the Persian wars; they saved their Hellenic
way of life from the Persian threat. But the effort they put
forth to win cost them the very forms of traditional life they
had set out to defend. When a way of life is really at stake in
war, that way of life is lost regardless of the outcome of the
fray. The winning side is usually disillusioned, for it sees the
very way of life it thought to preserve slip through its fingers.
The experience of recent years shows once again the fulfillment
of this historical law, which is as unknown as it is demonstrable.

Following the Persian wars, Greece enters a period of prosperity brought about by the appearance of new material and human
skills. The material skills are put to use in rebuilding cities
that had been destroyed. The restored cities, especially Athens,
are quite different from what they had been before the wars. This
is the period of maturity in Greek art. The human skills are directed toward the establishment of a new political structure among
the Greek cities--leagues, confederations, the entire organization
that will later clash in the Peloponnesian War. Above all, efforts
are made to guide men in the new circumstances. The social groups
newly incorporated into public life demand different treatment and
a change of status. Athenian democracy, which had been extended
with some modifications to other Greek cities, views men as citizens (πολίται). Uncertainty arises about things and affairs of
daily life. This is the moment when the Sophists appear in Greece.

We must especially emphasize that the Sophists were tremen-
dously successful. They were the first in Greece to receive money for intellectual exercises, specifically for teaching. Their
fees were high; they lived in luxury and were much sought after
by the different cities. Their ironic insistence on the theme of
money, which is mentioned time and again by Socrates in Plato's
Hippias Major, together with their petulance, clearly reveals the
economic success of all the Sophists such as Gorgias, Prodicos,
Protagoras, and Hippias himself. Socrates contrasts their attitude with the unconcern or economic inability of ancient sages

and philosophers--Bias, Pythacus, Thales, Anaxagoras--perhaps not
without some polemic exaggeration of the real situation.

In the beginning, philosophy had consisted of individual
efforts; it appeared as something ambiguous even as to its name,
and it aroused distrust or hostility. Sophistry, in contrast, is
characterized from the earliest by the acceptance and obvious success it enjoyed. Yet, for a very long time philosophy was by no
means socially established but represented rather the inadequacy
of traditional portions of Hellenic society. On the other hand,
Sophistry was socially established from the first. It responded
to a need of the Greek society in which it was formulated. Sophistry filled a void. Not by accident, this rather trivial and
commonplace manner of describing the movement is quite justified
and is precise in the case of Sophistry. In serving a social
need, in "filling a void," as it were, Sophistry is clearly a
"professional" movement. The Sophists were professors.

What "void" are we speaking of? The voids that society needs
to fill have always been those left by individual lives (the only
form of life sensu stricto). In this case the void was that of
sophós. At this time that function was left to the sophistés.
Now it is known that the word sophistés was originally essentially
the same as sophós. The latter term then came to mean the peculiar type of sage or "wise man" associated with Sophistry. The
sophoí were those men who first indulged in theoretical activity
in Greece. These include the Seven Wise Men, Thales among them,
followed by the pre-Socratic philosophers, the φυσιολόγοι, and
especially Anaxagoras. In Democritus the concept of the sage is
linked also to a moral dimension peculiar to Socrates and even
more to the various small Socratic and Hellenistic schools.

The customary procedures of philology and history have for
a long time seemed insincere, and nowhere more so than with Greece.
It appears to be the practice simply to ignore those things that
are not understood in an ancient writer and to proceed as though
he had never written them. Thus, for example, when Aristotle at
the beginning of his Metaphysics speaks of a wise man as "theoretical" and "speculative," his ideas seem quite clear to us. Yet,
when he goes on to say: "It is not meet for the wise man to take
orders, but rather to give them; nor is it his place to obey another, but rather the duty of those less wise to obey him," we
find his words hard to understand.[28] We do not know the "orders"
he has in mind or why the wise man should give them. The general
tendency has been to ignore such passages.[29] But when we ignore
what Aristotle says, we do so at the risk of not understanding
him. We should not forget that in this very passage he makes an
explicit reference to arkhé. Arkhé, as we saw earlier, is principle, origin, and authority. In the final analysis, the wise
man is the man of principles, and in his own way he is also an
árkhon and thus enjoys a certain primacy or priority over other
men. Because he is in possession of principles, he becomes a
principal man. But what does this mean? It means simply that

the wise man knows what may be relied on for guidance in the world.
This means that he may decide what is to be done because he knows
how and what things are. Any act is done in view of something,
and this something determines what is done. Therefore, an insight
into things, a knowledge of how they will behave, is necessary in
order to decide what to do with these things. Because he knows
these things, the wise man, the sophós, may guide and order those
less wise.

The void left in Greek society by the almost mythical figure
of the seldom-appearing wise man and the decline in prestige of
later dispute-ridden philosophers explains the demand for a new
class of men that gave rise to the Sophists. Yet the Sophists
displayed attitudes contrary to those of their predecessors, although their role was somewhat analogous. It is this change of
attitude that reveals the profound change in circumstances between
the two eras. While the philosopher lived a contemplative life,
the Sophist preferred to spend his time in the midst of society.
The Pythagoreans, for instance, often revealed their secrets only
after a lengthy period of initiation, and according to Hippasos
of Metapontion, death--viewed as a divine punishment or vengeance--
might be justified for one who promulgated a mathematical discovery. On the other hand, the Sophist earned his livelihood by
revealing secrets; his knowledge was soon converted into money.

Philosophers first appeared in Greece when people generally
felt quite secure and safe within a system of mythical beliefs.
It was the philosophers who individually felt insecure and uncertain and who adopted a critical view of the traditional ways of
their society. This is why philosophers were always more or less
persecuted. The Sophists, in contrast, arise when the basic beliefs of the society are in doubt, when men feel insecure and are
seeking to find their way in a new kind of world. This helps to
explain the vagueness of sophistic teaching. It is well known
that Sophistry consisted largely of rhetoric. It is often stated
that the reason for this was the triumph of democracy in most
Greek cities and the subsequent interest in oratory as a way to
success in public life. The orator, the man who speaks well, is
the one who imposes his views and who gains in influence, position,
and authority. "The man who knows and does not explain himself
clearly is the same as if he did not think" (ὅ τε γὰρ γνοὺς καὶ
μὴ σαφῶς διδάξας ἐν ἴσῳ καὶ εἰ μὴ ἐνεθυμήθη), says Pericles blunt-
ly in a speech attributed to him by Thucydides.[30] It would be
hard to find a more vigorous and conclusive defense of the value
of rhetoric.

Yet in stating that rhetoric consists of speaking well, the
"well" is easily overemphasized while forgetting, perhaps, that to
speak is, above all, to speak about something; to speak at all
is to speak of things. A distinction must therefore be made between what is said and what it is said about. The Sophists taught
men to talk of everything. But strictly speaking, they meant
everything of concern to men in society: their affairs and the

things needed in those affairs (πράγματα, χρήματα); politics, kings, tributes, wars, gods, and of course money, which is the meaning of the word khrémata in the plural (χρήματα, χρήματα ἀνήρ--money, man is money). The topic of rhetoric changed from philosophy to Sophistry and, regardless of the views taken, men's interests also changed. Whereas once they spoke of Parmenidean ón and later of the variants of phýsei ónta, now they talked of prágmata and khrémata, of the affairs and things of life, the street or the agora.

But the point of departure in philosophy had also been things of this kind, the visible reality of life. It was only to understand these things more clearly that an appeal had to be made to the unapparent and latent side of things, to what came to be known as phýsis. The latter was first interpreted as arkhé and later, with the Eleatics, as being or ón. And now man has to abandon the notion of being in order to learn how to deal with things. Meanwhile, the ordinary things of life had been relegated to dóxa and were disregarded by those who would choose the way of truth. Now as men once again renew their interest in things, they assume the point of view of opinion or dóxa, for things behave in life in keeping with the opinions men have of them, and if they clash it is because opinions clash. Eleatic philosophy, arising in the arena of being and philosophizing from that concept, offers no real explanation for things. This is why the Sophists, in renouncing being and alétheia, begin to inquire anew into things from the viewpoint of dóxa.

Sophistry, then, responds to a social need and represents, in one of its dimensions, an inversion of philosophy. This was how it was viewed by contemporary philosophers. Whereas philosophy, which had arisen from the need to explain the nature of things, gravitated to noûs as its method of inquiry, Sophistry, quite correct in pointing out the inability of the "physiologists" to return from being to things, inverts the terms with which the problem had been posed. It scorns truth and being and before the eyes of scandalized philosophy makes dóxa its method.

Why does Sophistry choose such a procedure? The answer lies in the fact that this method offered the men of that time, those who gladly gathered to hear and to pay for hearing the teachings of the Sophists, the knowledge of how to deal with matters of common life. This was not, properly speaking, intellectual knowledge but rather a knowledge of what was to be done. It would enable them, for instance, to triumph in the assembly, to impose their views on others, to gain riches and glory, to settle political problems.

It has been said that the Sophists talked of the same things as the philosophers.[31] This is not true. The philosophers discussed being or phýsis; the Sophists talked of common matters and things. Nevertheless, there is no escaping the fact that underlying the Sophist attitude there is also an interpretation of reality, just as there is in every attempt, even in the least

intellectual and "theoretical," to determine the best way of
dealing with things. Sophistry, "apparent wisdom₂₂which it is
not," is not philosophy but an art of persuasion.[32] But it became possible only because it implicitly sheltered an interpretation of reality. It was left to philosophy to explain this implicit interpretation of the world and to account for the existence
of Sophistry. What was the meaning of this interpretation? Let
us turn to Protagoras and Gorgias.

Protagoras is the author of one of the most celebrated passages in all philosophy: Πάντων χηρμάτων μέτρον ἄνθρωπος, τῶν
ὄντων ὡς ἔστιν, τῶν δ'οὐκ ὄντων ὡς οὐκ ἔστιν, "Man is the measure
of all things; of things that are, inasmuch as they are, and of
those that are not, inasmuch as they are not." Generally this
passage has been interpreted in a relative sense, and, in fact,
it has been said that Protagoras was the father of relativism.
But without prejudging the outcome, let us simply try to see what
Protagoras meant. Plato took up his thesis from the viewpoint of
science, which was to be identified with sensation.[33] Aristotle
devoted an ill-humored commentary to it in Book X of <u>Metaphysics</u>,
alluding to the possible reference of Protagoras to science or
sensation and denying any importance to the doctrine.[34] We must
keep in mind, however, that Protagoras says that man is the measure of things (<u>khrémata</u>) and not necessarily of <u>beings</u>. Were he
speaking of the <u>latter</u>, the reference would then be to <u>epistéme</u>
and hence to the "consistency" of things in the Eleatic sense.
The <u>khrémata</u>, on the contrary, are evident and immediate things,
things as they are presented or appear to sensation. This is
precisely the point that Plato insists on in <u>Theaetetus</u>: φαντασία
ἄρα καὶ αἴσθησις ταὐτόν, "Fantasy (apparition or appearance) and
sensation are the same."[35]

But this is the most important point, for Protagoras converts
<u>aísthesis</u> into his method. If we juxtapose this to a passage from
<u>Sextus Empiricus</u>[36] in which he attributes to Protagoras the idea
that "Truth is a relation" (τῶν πρός τι εἶναι τήν ἀλήθειαν), the
celebrated passage now takes on a new meaning. Dilthey observes:

> His relativism affirmed without doubt the qualities of
> things that existed only in that relationship, but it
> says nothing of objectivity itself. That which is
> sweet is nothing if we remove the subject who enjoys
> sweetness; that which is sweet exists only in relation-
> ship to sensation. But his theory of perception then
> shows that he has not lost sight of the object itself
> in speaking of the sensation of sweetness. If an object
> affects a sensory organ, and if the former behaves ac-
> tively and the latter passively, on the one hand there
> originates in this sensory organ vision, hearing, the
> corresponding sensory impression, and on the other hand,
> an object that is colored or sonorous. In a word, the
> object appears with diverse sensory qualities. Only

this explanation of the process made it possible to have a theory of perception in the relativism of Protagoras. And it is clearly evident that the reality of movement without the subject could not be suppressed. Perception has its origin in that exterior movement, and at the same time it brings all objectivity into question. He explained the different states of the sensory subject and thus showed that the qualities of objects manifested are conditioned by these states. This leads to the paradox in his theory of perception that perceptions themselves are in contradiction to one another and are, nevertheless, all equally genuine.[37]

Sweetness exists only for me, but a sweet object does not depend on me for its existence. Sweetness appears when I enjoy honey, for instance, and so establish a relationship with that substance according to its qualities. Sweetness is a prós ti, a relationship of a subject with sweet honey. The characteristics of the latter are a function of man, who is their measure or métron. Now, one may like honey and another may not: two different opinions, each true because each involves a different relationship. On the one hand, there is the relationship of honey to me in which I find it sweet, and on the other, honey with the hepatic person to whom it tastes bitter. In other words, Protagoras vindicates the concern for things as well as their real and effective manipulation. For him truth consists in that which determines and measures things. The truth of things is revealed by their métron, the relationship of man with them. This means that he renounces all onto-logy and begins instead with the necessity of explaining things. But a comment by Gorgias reveals the final basis of this Sophist interpretation of reality.

It seems that Gorgias wrote a book entitled On Non-being or On Nature (Περὶ τοῦ μὴ ὄντος ἢ Περὶ φύσεως) in which he expounded a doctrine consisting of three principal points: that nothing is, for if it were, it would be unknowable, and if it were unknowable, it would not be communicable to others.[38] The reason for this, to summarize his ideas, is that nothing has the properties of Eleatic being. Things are multiple, mutable, and perishable, while being is supposed to be one, immovable, inherent, and permanent. Gorgias has the same idea of being as the Eleatics; but whereas the latter, adhering to the ón, disregard things, Gorgias, clinging to a view of things, rejects the concept of being and holds it to be non-existent. Given the attributes of being, the Eleatic thinker is forced to say that things in the final analysis do not exist. In other words, they are inconsistent and therefore a matter of dóxa. For the Sophist, in view of the fact that nothing possesses the predicates of being, the conclusion is that being does not exist. Since the time of Parmenides, things had been renounced in favor of the absolute consistency of ón. Gorgias takes precisely the opposing view, which implies of course that he begins with the same postulates. If things admittedly do not at all correspond to what being is supposed to be, then for the Eleatic this means that things do not exist. On the other hand, if nothing exhibits the attributes of being, then being itself does not exist, as Gorgias argued. In the latter case, not only things but also their radical inconsistency are admitted as real. This is why the traditional inquiry into peri physeos ultimately becomes a treatment of being, in Gorgias it becomes a treatise of non-being. Sophistry is an attempt to learn a sound way of dealing with things on the basis of their inconsistency. Was this a tenable situation? This was the problem that Socrates had to face.

6. The Consistency of Things

Had the Sophists done what their intellectual position presented as their duty--to give a satisfactory account of pragmata and khremata--they would not have been Sophists but truly wise men in the noblest meaning of the term. But since this did not happen, Greek intellectual life underwent a serious crisis that was not overcome until the advent of Socratism. What happened to the Greek mind after the Sophist experience, beginning with the second half of the fifth century B.C.? The answer to this question is fully meaningful only if we have also previously asked what could have happened. Since to a greater or lesser degree everything that might have happened did so, the question is not overly difficult.

In the first place, we must not forget that Sophistry endured throughout and beyond Socrates' life. Later it persisted as an attitude transformed by, and sometimes disguised as, Socratism. We see, then, the possibility of a continuation of Sophistry with a progressive watering down of its scanty ideological content. This is what actually happened with Cynicism, which is not a doctrine but a posture involving certain moral "principles." It was also possible to continue the negative side of Sophistry: the abandonment of peri physeos speculation. And in fact this is exactly what happened. This becomes apparent if we recall the enormous intellectual effort expended by Aristotle in Book I of his Physics, where he attempts to justify such speculation as a philosophical discipline. Likewise, under these circumstances we might expect science to flourish, and this is what we find represented by Theodorus and Theaetetus along with other mathematicians who formulated the synthesis expressed in the Elements of Euclid, and by the physicists, astronomers, and doctors during the last years of the fifth century and the first decades of the fourth. Finally, it was possible that philosophy would take seriously the Sophists' demand that the things and affairs of men be elucidated. This was the very task to which Socrates devoted his life.

32

Greek Philosophy from Its Origin to Plato

There is an especially important passage in Xenophon's Memorabilia of Socrates which, regardless of any reservations about its
intrinsic historical value, is one of the principal testimonies
about Socrates still in existence:

Unlike the majority of men, Socrates in fact did
not talk of all of Nature, nor of the workings of what
wise men call the Cosmos, nor yet of the necessities
through which each celestial happening occurs. On the
contrary, he pointed out that those who torment their
minds with these questions were foolish.

For he pondered, above all, whether men considered
such questions because they believed they had a sufficient knowledge of things concerning man, or whether
they believed that by ignoring human things and considering the divine they were fulfilling their duty. And in
the first case, he was astonished that such men could
not see clearly that man is incapable of ascertaining
these things. For not even the greatest minds agree
among themselves concerning these problems; instead,
they turn on each other like frenzied madmen. Some
madmen, in fact, do not fear even the fearful, while
others are frightened by the most inoffensive things.
Some think they do no wrong in talking or speaking of
whatever crosses their mind before a crowd, while others
dare not let people even see them. Some there are who
respect not even the sanctuaries, the altars, or anything sacred, while others of them adore any piece of
wood or stone or even animals. Likewise, those who are
concerned with all of Nature may believe that "that
which is" is a unified whole, or that it is an infinite
multitude of things. To some it seems that everything
is in motion; to others it even appears that there is
nothing that can be moved. Some think that everything
is born and perishes; others believe that nothing is
born and nothing passes away.

Socrates also observed that those schooled in the
affairs of human life may use their knowledge at will
for both their good and that of others. He then asked
himself analogously whether those who sought divine
things, after learning the necessities by which everything happens, thought they could produce wind, rain,
the seasons of the year, and all they might need, or
whether, on the contrary, they despaired of doing
these things and found they had nothing left but the
fact that such divine things do occur.

Such was Socrates' opinion of those who delved
into these things. As for himself, he discussed only
human matters, studying what constitutes the pious and
the sacrilegious. He pondered what we call the honest

and the shameful, the just and the unjust, the sensible
and the nonsensical. He considered courage and coward-
ice, the State and the ruler, leadership and the leader.
In general he was interested in all those things which
he was convinced made men more perfect and without which
they were degraded and enslaved.[39]

We find in this fragment a multitude of interesting things.
We note, first of all, that Socrates begins by agreeing with the
Sophists! This fact is quite important, for there were other
groups that also attracted him. The Atomists were his contemporaries, for example, and Socrates could have adopted their views.
To a certain degree, as we shall see, he began by veering toward
the "physiologists." Socrates was thus in agreement with Sophist
criticism of traditional philosophy, of perì phýseos speculation,
that may be summarized in four points:

(1) Do those who speak of divine and celestial things already
know about human things? This is a matter of primacy and urgency;
it is possible to speak of the heavens, but first we must know
about ourselves. This involves a pragmatic criticism: those who
concern themselves with divine things and lay claim to wisdom do
not know what to make of human things.

(2) Furthermore, Socrates offers a criticism based on the
Skeptic view: philosophers are people who defend the most widely
opposing opinions. The ancient argument over disagreement between
opinions, διαφωνία τῶν δοξῶν (discord over opinions), which is one
of the traditional topics of skepticism, now reappears in Socrates.
Those who speculate on nature merely indulge in a dialectical game
with concepts that have no relationship to reality.

(3) Whereas the Sophists simply draw these negative conclusions, Socrates goes further. He formally accuses such philosophers of irresponsibility. Some of them tell the crowds whatever
happens to come to mind. But is it wise to talk to people about
anything under the sun? Were philosophy simply a dialectical game
there would be no harm in doing so. But philosophy is the mission
of teaching men how to discover a sure way dealing with things.
The disagreement of opinions not only leads to error but also
causes men to lose faith in philosophy itself. We shall see the
serious theme of intellectual responsibility reappear in Socrates.

(4) Finally, do these philosophers really discover reliable
knowledge about the divine things that concern them? According
to Socrates, they will derive no real knowledge even of those
things that are the object of philosophy.

This, according to Xenophon, is the gist of Socratic criticism of Ionic or Eleatic speculation on nature. Until now Socrates
agrees with the Sophists, though his views are much deeper and
freer of the intellectual frivolity characteristic of Sophistry.
The latter point explains his forceful reference to intellectual
irresponsibility. Yet it would be frivolous of him to go no further. It is at this point that his pathway diverges from that of

the Sophists. We should compare the passage from Xenophon to a
text in Plato's Phaedo in which Socrates shortly before his
death recalls the course of his intellectual life.[40] As a youth,
recalls Socrates, he was eager to possess that knowledge called
"history," information or facts, of nature (περὶ φύσεως ἱστορία).
His first desire, therefore, was to become a "physiologist" in
the Ionic manner. His enemies tried to emphasize this dimension
of his thought even when it was long since past.[41] He recalls
his first encounter with the doctrine of Anaxagoras and his en-
thusiasm for the idea of noûs. This was followed by disappointment when he saw that Anaxagoras did not make effective use of
his own idea to explain reality. For Socrates this was the total
failure of perì physeos speculation. But then Socrates begins
his "second navigation," (δεύτερος πλοῦς) in search of the cause
of things. Sophistry was incapable of duplicating this deúteros
ploûs, and it is this feature that gives philosophical depth to
Socrates' philosophic attitude. But exactly what was his attitude?

The basic trait in Socrates' thought is that he seeks to
know what human things are: what is truth?, wisdom?, the state?
This what, this tí, i.e., tí estí (τί ἐστι), is what sets Socrates
apart from the Sophists. This means that Socrates takes seriously the Sophists' criticism of current philosophy. Nevertheless,
while accepting this reproach as valid, he does not stop with
mere criticism. We cannot, he says, concern ourselves exclusively with being to the neglect of things. Hence, we must speak of
things, not so as merely to adhere to dóxa and declare things inconsistent, but so as to ask ourselves what the things and matters
of life are that we need and use in order to live. Instead of
declaring the reality of manifest things to be inconsistent, since
they do not conform to the scheme of Eleatic being, let us attempt
to discover what that reality consists of. The Sophists called
attention to things and were concerned with them; in this they
were quite correct, in contrast to the "physiologists." But
they promptly forgot the aspect of consistency and concerned
themselves solely with the manipulation of things. This manner
of dealing with things requires only the way things appear to the
senses; in other words, it is enough to know their appearance
according to dóxa. Socrates, on the other hand, was not satisfied
with the mere manipulation of things. He aspired to a deeper understanding of things, to know what they consist of. The real contribution of Socrates lies in the question tí esti.

The term ésti again poses the philosophical question in the
dimension of being. This would seem to be a return to the Eleatic
point of view, and to a certain degree it is that--but only to a
degree. There is no denying that Socrates regards Parmenides as
his intellectual father. The entire Platonic dialogue under his
name centers around this underlying idea. But it is no less true
that differences immediately arise between them. The ésti refers
to being in the Eleatic sense of consisting. But the word tí is

not Eleatic. Tí, "what," goes beyond the idea of consisting and refers to the substance of such consistency. In other words, it means the consistency of the consisting being. Parmenides does not raise the question of what being is; for him this question would have no meaning whatsoever. Rather, he reaches the arena of being by means of noûs and then tells us "what does exist" (ὡς ἔστιν).

This is a renewal of the idea of knowing. In Parmenides it is a question of discerning between the way of truth and that of opinion, between alétheia and dóxa, between noûs and aísthesis.[42] Being and non-being do not apply to things. It is possible to distinguish between those things that are not and the being (ἐόν) that is. Yet things as such remain inconsistent and indistinguishable, lost in the senses and incapable of being discerned. Discernment is a quality of noûs and lógos--κρῖναι δὲ λόγῳ (to judge by reason), as the goddess tells Parmenides--and they in turn refer to being. Nevertheless, Socrates finds that he must distinguish between things themselves, not between what is and what is not. He has to combine the Eleatic point of view (consistency) with that of the Sophists (things). He must determine what is meant by "pious," what is impiety, what is just, and what is unjust. How may we make distinctions among things?

Unlike the case of the Eleatics, this is not a matter of separating consistency from inconsistency, or entity from non-entity, but of determining the consistency of each thing. The question, then, is not consistency but rather what things consist of. To make distinctions among things is to delimit them. This delimitation is termed horízein (ὁρίζειν), which means to define or discern things by associating each one with the what, or tí, of which it consists. The logical correlative of tí is a definition. This means that things are to be approached on the basis of the individual consistency of each one.

Here begins a whole series of logical and ontological problems that are neither solved nor even clearly stated in Socrates. We find an adequate treatment of them in Plato, but before delving into these problems, we must consider a question dealing with the very meaning of Socratic knowledge. Socrates proposes to know human things and this implies above all a knowledge of man himself. But this is possible only by knowing things, and Socrates is perhaps the first to realize this fact clearly. We must know what may be reliably accepted regarding man. But are we really correct in making this statement? Do we mean mankind in general? Evidently we do not. The Delphic precept γνῶθι σεαυτόν, "know thyself," is the Socratic theme. For what is really meant is that we must be certain of knowing what we ourselves are in contrast to other men. Know your areté, says Socrates. Areté is commonly translated as "virtue," but a better meaning would be virtus, potentiality or capacity, what one was born to do. Resorting again to our terminology, virtus or areté means that of which each man truly "consists." The knowledge of the consistency of things culminates

in the discovery of each man's innate qualities, of his areté.
This is why Socratic speculation is ethical in nature and why
with Socrates philosophical meditation turns again to the theme
of man. Yet this does not mean that it again takes up the question of man's inner being, but rather that it is concerned with
the individual qualities of each man.

Nevertheless, at this point we discover a serious problem.
The question posed by the term tí requires a definition, but a
definition is always universal and the human things I must discern are individually felt and experienced. I am unable to distinguish among such things because the distinctions are given in
the definition. Now definition deals with universalizable things
and hence transcends the aísthesis, which is the manner things
assume in manifesting themselves. In order to acquire a clear
knowledge of things, I must surmount their individuality and
sensorial reality. This leads to a dilemma pointed out by the
Sophists. If I am content with aísthesis, then I discover that
only appearance and opinion instead of science exist. If I appeal
to éstin and noûs, again I am led into universals and the viewpoint
of earlier philosophers.

How can one know of a certainty about things by stating what
they are? How can one begin to philosophize from being with his
eventual attention directed to things? Again there reappears the
need of an avenue between being and things. Earlier we saw how
the mythical way of life revealed no means of connecting the
evident with the unapparent. Parmenides had shown the way to go
from things to the ón, but he had not indicated how we might retrace our steps. Sophistry abruptly turns again to things, but
only at the price of renouncing any concern for being, declaring
it to be fundamentally inconsistent. The question, then, is to
find a way from being to things without the risk of losing our
way in the universality of definitions. This was precisely the
problem confronting Plato.

7. The Necessity of Platonic Philosophy

We are interested here in clarifying what is meant by the expression "philosophy of Plato." In other words, what task faced Plato
as he set about philosophizing? To understand his philosophy, we
must understand why he had to accept this task and why he felt
obliged to formulate his own philosophy. It seems to me that we
may best proceed by looking at the problem from a viewpoint that
few others have taken. Let us begin with one of Plato's little-
known writings: his seventh epistle.

It was some twenty-three hundred years ago, in 353 B.C., that
Plato, carrying the weight of seventy-three years of vigorous and
eventful living, composed this long letter, addressed to friends
and relatives of Dion. Plato had great hopes for this young man
who was later assassinated on orders of his cousin Dionysius the

Younger, tyrant of Syracuse. In some ways, the letter is an auto-
biography as well as a justification of his political life. It
is also a summary of certain later experiences in philosophy and,
finally, a confession that mingles melancholy with hope.

Syracuse was Plato's one great adventure, an adventure that
filled the last half of his long life. When he arrived in Syracuse during the time of Dionysius the Elder, Plato found it very
unpleasant. What kind of life was this? All he saw was sybaritic
luxury, endless parties, and violent sensuality--what the Italians
and Syracusans called the "happy life" (βίος εὐδαίμων). To Plato
it seemed impossible for one to experience all this in youth and
still retain good sense and moderation. Nor did it seem likely
that such a way of life would lend itself to political stability.
Still, it was here that Plato tried his great experiment. Through
Dion, his faithful disciple, who was amenable to everything, especially his teacher's words, and who understood Plato better than
anyone else, Plato tried to change the principles of Syracusan
life. Philosophy and that strange force which the Greeks called
areté, which we usually translate incorrectly as "virtue," would
replace the mania for sensual pleasure. Ultimately Plato devoted
some forty years to this undertaking. He made three trips to
Sicily and braved dangerous crossings of the sea during times of
war. He faced prison, slavery, the threat of death, and court
intrigue. He watched the deadly game between the two tyrants.
He was caught between fear and hope and his only support was his
great disciple. Dion reformed his personal life in response to
Plato's teaching, but he saw hatred and hostility in the Syracusan
society well up against him as he departed from the old ways and
followed Plato. It is said that all this proves that Plato, for
all his philosophical meditations, showed a keen political vocation. But one may wonder whether the explanation is all that
simple.

As a youth, Plato recalls in his letter, like many other
young men, he experienced the desire to take part in politics.
There were ample opportunities for him to do so. After several
grave alterations, the oligarchic government of the Thirty Tyrants
had been established in Athens. Among them were close friends
and relatives of Plato's family, who invited him to become involved
in public life. Plato had high hopes. As an old man justifying
the actions of his youth, he points to his tender years (ὑπὸ
νεότητος) and explains that he thought the new government would
lead the city from injustice to justice. But he was soon disen-
chanted, for their methods of dispensing justice were such that
the former period of injustice and unrest seemed a "Golden Age"
(χρυσόν) by comparison. They tried to persuade his friend and
teacher Socrates, "the most just man of his time," to take part
in politics and to participate in passing a sentence of death.
Socrates refused, preferring instead to expose himself to all
kinds of dangers. In a mood of indignation and revulsion, Plato
gave up politics. There followed a time of tumult, crime, violence,

and personal vendettas of all types, culminating in the fall of
the Thirty and the establishment of a democratic government of
great moderation. Nevertheless, during this period, powerful
influences brought about Socrates' death, although he had been
in the favor of a certain exile who had been persecuted and dis-
graced but whose party was now triumphant. Plato now irrevocably
renounced all political ambition.

We must ask why he reacted in this way. Can it be explained
solely by the pain and revulsion caused by Socrates' death? This
would not seem to be the case. In recalling the event, Plato
carefully emphasizes the political moderation prevailing at the
time and the part that chance played (κατὰ δέ τινα τύχην) in that
particular act of injustice. Nonetheless, it was this situation,
rather than past crimes and outrages, that led him to renounce
politics. How could this be? The crimes and vendettas of the
past were enough, surely, to cause Plato to feel alienated from
politics and to shun any active participation in it; that is, it
was serious enough when irresponsible men committed acts of violence. But how much worse it would have been for responsible men
like Socrates or Plato to share these political attitudes and to
associate themselves even indirectly with misconduct masquerading
as orderly government. This is why Plato waited for things to
improve and hoped that a time would come when he could take part.
Finally he realized the "incurable" (ἀνιάτως) nature of the situation underlying the melodramatic political events. What, then,
was responsible for this serious illness of the Athenian government?

Plato is clearly describing a period of crisis. The city is
no longer ruled by the traditions and customs of its ancestors.
There are no viable traditions; disorder rules the affairs of the
city. As for Plato, he experiences a feeling of "vertigo" (τελευ-
τῶντα ἰλιγγιᾶν) as he views a situation that only "an admirable
preparation and a certain amount of luck" (ἄνευ παρασχευῆς θαυμαστῆς
τινος μετὰ τύχης) could enable any leader to master. In other words,
it would take a vigorous intellectual reaction aided by circumstances
to surmount the situation. What is the meaning of all this?

When prevailing laws, traditions, and customs lose their force,
society ceases to exist. It leaves behind its image and the knowledge of its demise. But the decline of society is different from
the mere absence of a society. For the decline of a society means
that while it may have vanished, the need of a society has not.
The resultant state of being may be called dissociation.[43] The dis-
orderly state of things leaves Plato with a feeling of vertigo.
In other words, he does not know those things to which he may adhere. But the objection might be raised that this applies only to
politics and the affairs of Athens. How much does this situation
affect the lives of individuals and, in particular, Plato's own
life? This is precisely where the problem lies. For the crisis
of the pólis also becomes the crisis of Greek life in general.
Man cannot live, much less be happy, outside the community or, in

its highest expression, the city or polis. A few years later,
Aristotle said that to live in solitude, one must be more or less
than a man, either a beast or a god (ἢ θηρίον ἢ θεός).[44] This
radical uncertainty about the affairs of the pólis, after the
decline of traditional laws and customs on which the city had
been structured, led to uncertainty about the whole of life. Men
did not know what to do. Note that this was not simply a matter
of whether things were done well or not, whether politics was
good or bad, or whether there were abuses and crimes. None of
these conditions would be hopeless in the long view if they happened within a viable and working system of unassailable laws and
customs. If this were the case (and Plato at first believed that
it was), one could simply wait for conditions to improve and the
right moment to come. But the gravity of the situation lay in
the fact that such unshakable laws and customs no longer existed.
Society had given way to a state of dissociation. Hence, the
situation was really hopeless--hopeless, that is, so far as any
solution from within the present system was concerned. Society
would become possible again only when a new system of laws, customs,
and values had been formulated. But the uncertainty of such a
solution lay in the fact that not only was there no assurance
that a new system could be conceived, but that once formulated,
it would face the still more difficult and doubtful prospect of
winning acceptance and authority. Plato points out that this
crisis was not limited to Athens but affected all States (all
Greek States, that is).

How could this situation be overcome? There was only one
way: men had to know those things in which they could place confidence. They must know the just and the unjust in both private
and political life. They had to know what to do. Hence the need
to philosophize, for only through philosophy may we come to know
the nature of things and the way we must deal with them. For this
reason, says Plato, social ills will be cured only when real philosophers rule in the cities, or, to put it another way, only
when by some divine fortune those who rule truly philosophize.
Plato is repeating in a different way a well-known but poorly
understood idea that he first expressed in the Republic.[45]

Plato is clearly pointing to two ways of life in the city.
In the first, men know what they must do and how they must act,
not because they have a clear idea of what is good or bad, just
or unjust, but because conduct is regulated by the power of the
customs and conventions in which they believe. When this system
fails, the only human way to live is to find out how one must act,
or better, one must "verify" (verum facere) or mold the truth.
This is the mission of philosophy. But this alone is not enough.
For it is necessary that the truths discovered by the philosopher
exist socially and collectively; they must become prevailing truths.
This means that it is not enough to have discovered truths and to
have formulated a true philosophy; philosophy must also lead to
the reestablishment of a system of dominant beliefs. This is what

Plato means when he talks of philosophers coming to power or of
rulers becoming philosophers. This is what he hoped to achieve
in Syracuse through his disciple Dion, who had the power to convert the solitary meditations of Plato into dominant social norms.
without killing and violence, he was trying to bring about "a
happy and true life" (βίον εὐδαίμονα καὶ ἀληθινόν) by persuading
Dionysius the Younger to accept his ideas.

This is the real reason behind the Syracusan adventure. It
was not mere curiosity, as has so often been supposed, not a desire to try out the Platonic political theories in real life, but
rather the felt need to establish a new kind of society. In Plato's
view (and herein lies one of the secrets and one of the errors of
Greek thought), society means the political community. For half
a lifetime and despite many risks and failures Plato strove to
bring about a restoration of the Greek social state which he believed doomed under existing conditions. Events proved him correct
in his concern; fifteen years after writing this letter, in 338 B.C.,
Phillip defeated the Thebans and Athenians at Chaeronea and established Macedonian supremacy. But what he really conquered was
the pólis, the Greek city, that had entered a period of crisis
after the Peloponnesian Wars. It was able to emerge from that
crisis only by ceasing to exist as a way of life. Plato was already dead by this time; but years later, during the Macedonian
era when Aristotle wrote his Politics, he still considered the
same pólis, which Plato had been unable to renew in Syracuse, to
be the highest expression of collective life.

When viewed from another angle, Plato's philosophy is inseparable from his politics and consequently from his trips to Syracuse.
In the strictest sense, Plato's thought can be traced to the situation of Athens at the time. His inability to engage in politics
is directly translated into his need to philosophize. The crisis
of his time, a crisis of convention and custom, a crisis that
meant a vertiginous loss of direction, is the real motive behind
his philosophy. The uncertain state of things is what caused him
to turn to philosophy. In this context, then, philosophy appears
as an urgent task. Contrary to the customary image given us of
Plato's thought, his philosophy now may be seen as unavoidable and
necessary, arising because there were no longer any ready answers
to the questions posed by the world and the problems of everyday
life.

Nevertheless, one might ask what other Athenians, and indeed
other Greeks, were doing under similar conditions. Were they not
in the same critical situation? Of course they were, and yet seemingly their aims did not coincide with Plato's personal aspirations.
Plato speaks again and again of a happy and "true" life (ἀληθινός)
and of those who philosophize "in reality" (ὄντως) "duly and authen-
tically" (ὀρθῶς γε καὶ ἀληθῶς). Evidently the human possibility
of authenticity has become a factor in his thought. This concern
for authenticity leads Plato to an even more serious theme that
lends a dramatic tone to his seventh epistle. For it is in this

letter that he fully comes to grips with the problem of philosophy
and responsibility, topics about which we shall have more to say
later.

Regarding the supposed philosophical work written by Dionysius
the Younger and based on conversations with Plato, Plato himself
explains his own ideas about the possibility of writing for the
multitude on the ultimate questions.[46] Plato declares that he
would never write on such matters for the public. This statement
is essential to an understanding of his writings and their connection to what we may call the philosophy of Plato. The ultimate
questions may not be expressed as other forms of knowledge. Theirs
is a truth that can be grasped only as a result of long familiarity with the theme (ἐκ πολλῆς συνουσίας). Their truths arise, as
light from fire, after one has been immersed in them. If he thought,
Plato admits, that such things could be stated or written in a way
clear enough for the multitude to understand them (ἱκανῶς), then
nothing could be more pleasant than illuminating the nature of
things for all to see. But it is not good for men to argue over
these topics—except for the few (τισιν ὀγίλοις) capable of discovering the truth for themselves with only a modicum of guidance (δυνα-
τοὶ ἀνευρεῖν αὐτοὶ διὰ σμικρᾶς ἐνδείξεως). Others would only
evince scorn or foolish petulance.

Thus it is, adds Plato, that no serious man (ἀνὴρ σπουδαῖος)
writes about serious and important things (τῶν ὄντων σπουδαίων)
for the masses. Whenever we see a work of this type, we may assume
that if the author is himself a serious person, then he has not
written seriously about the theme and the most important portions
of his thought remain hidden (ἐν χώρᾳ τῇ καλλίστῃ).

In a more profound way than Socrates, then, Plato sets himself squarely against all intellectual frivolity. Only in him is
the greatest danger of Sophistry surmounted. We see now the depth
of concern in Plato for the life of the pólis, of society, which
through the decline of prevailing customs and laws and the absence
of what Auguste Comte like to call "spiritual power" had fallen
to a state of dissociation and social decay. For more than two
centuries we have been toying with the very ideas that Plato says
may not even be discussed. They have been considered from every
angle, including those professed to be the less frivolous views.
And this play of ideas has brought about a basic dissociation in
European life. It gives one a certain chill to read this letter
written by Plato twenty-three centuries ago to explain why he had
no choice but to take up philosophy.

8. The Form of Plato's Philosophy

We have seen the point of departure in Plato's thought. One must
know what may be reliably accepted concerning things, affairs, one's
fellow men, and especially oneself. One must be able to distinguish
between things according to their consistency. To do this we must

42

have definitions that give us the tí of each thing. But which things do we mean? Plato's writings for the most part have the names of people as their titles: Phaedrus, Theaetetus, Parmenides, Protagoras, Phaedo—his friends, teachers, adversaries, and disciples. Generally these works also bear a traditional subtitle with the term περί, meaning "on" this or that theme. His works deal, therefore, with matters and people (who are also "matters" of a kind), realities with which men must contend. His writings do not take up the topics of nature or being. Finally, his works are in the form of dialogues. The significance of the latter fact should be examined more carefully.

The dialogues are rooted in opinions and consist of bringing differing views together. But we should not wonder at this evident fact. Elsewhere,[47] I have compared two forms philosophy takes: the immediate form, the best examples of which are Socrates and Plato, which poses its problems from ignorance and seeks the nature of things; and the mediate, represented by the Scholastics, which begins with the contradiction between two examples or opposing opinions and attempts to decide between them in order to formulate an unassailable thesis. This is in keeping with Thomas Aquinas' distinction between a scientia dialectica, quae ordinatur ad inquisitionem inventivam and a scientia demonstrativa, quae est veritatis determinativa (dialectical science, which is meant for original inquiry . . . demonstrative science, which serves to determine the truth).[48] But how can this be if the literary form of Platonic philosophy is dialogue, that is, a dispute between several opinions which serves as a starting point?

This question might lead us to a superficial interpretation of the Platonic dialogues. Indeed, Plato does begin with dialogues and opinions, for they are all he has to begin with. If philosophy in this case begins with ignorance, this ignorance is not a pure and simple lack of knowledge, but a lack of the knowledge necessary to deal effectively with things. Men do not know how to deal with things simply because they have an inadequate knowledge of many things. A philosopher, like a lover, stands midway between the ignorant man and the sage, neither of whom philosophizes. In the Platonic dialogues differing opinions are not juxtaposed so as to decide which of them is true, but rather to show that all are false. What we are led to see is that only by rising above all these opinions can we begin to reach effective knowledge. Socrates is not a judge and he does not intend to pass judgment on the opinions of his interlocutors; rather he attempts to reveal the shortcomings of all opinions—including his own, if he has any. In this way they can surmount opinion and reach a higher knowledge. What is revealed is not the incompatibility of one opinion with another but of each one with itself. Each time one of the interlocutors tries to analyze deeply and seriously his opinions in matters of science or justice, he comes to realize that they are untenable. The Platonic dialogue consists of the destruction of opinions as such. This is an essential point. It shows the

inanity or inconsistency of common beliefs. Socrates is himself
sometimes guilty of questionable thinking, for his examination
of the opinions of others does not go far enough. Socrates is
not "in on the secret." And this is what lends a true philosophic
quality to the Platonic dialogues. We may recall the attitude of
Socrates in Phaedrus toward his own speech and that of Lysis; he
repudiates both views and launches into a new and more radical
inquiry.

Far from being a judge of opinions, Socrates is a kind of
midwife who assists in the birth of truth both in others and his
own life. He helps in the painful delivery of alétheia. Philosophical ignorance is ignorance of what must be known. This is
why opinion as such is inadequate and undependable; it is the
source of uncertainty. The fallacy of opinion is the motivation
behind Platonic philosophy. Hence the necessity of dialogue in
which opinions clash as each seeks to prove itself as an opinion.
And as each participant defends his ideas against those of the
other interlocutors he reaches a moment of personal reckoning.
This is why Plato can state that thought (διάνοια) is "the silent
inner dialogue of the soul with itself" (ὁ μὲν ἐντὸς τῆς ψυχῆς
πρὸς αὑτὴν διάλογος ἄνευ φωνῆς γιγνόμενος).[49]

Furthermore, dialogue is a way of saying something by means
of, or "via" (διά), what others say (λόγοι). It is a movement of
the mind through opinions. According to Aristotle, the Greeks
referred to that which is believed and which seems true to other
men as éndoxon.[50] The traditional translation of éndoxon as
"probable" is an error, for the probability of the éndoxa is based
on opinion and belief and not the contrary. The probable is but
the residue of opinion or belief. And while the éndoxon may be
quite probable, it assumes the appearance of belief. The under-
mining of opinion in the dialogue reveals the need for a new kind
of knowledge: the Platonic epistéme.

The way to distinguish between things is to define them. In
defining a thing we delimit it and set it apart from other things.
As I have written elsewhere:

> Now then, a definition is first of all a predication of
> the statement: A is B. This involves a problem of
> singularity and multiplicity. If I say, for example,
> that "man is a talking animal," I identify the articu-
> late animal as man. I say that two things are one,
> that A is B. But the question arises: what makes the
> truth of predication possible? We note that in stating
> A is B, A has a dual function. It acts as a subject
> when I say "A." Yet when I say that it is "B," I do
> not refer to B alone, but also to A included in the
> predicate. To put it another way, I do not refer first
> to A and then to B without any connection; rather B
> is B only in relation to A. Hence, A functions in both
> A and B. The supposition behind the predication A is B

is that A is A, or that A is identical to itself. This
identity contains two additional assumptions: (1) that
A is one; (2) that A is permanent.[51]

Predication, then, presupposes consistency. Now consistency
is precisely what is sought after in a definition, since the Sophists had denied that things were consistent. From this point
on, the problems become more involved; the idea of reality suggested by Eleatic being becomes an essential postulate, and logical thought comes to mean that which describes this consistent
being. Reality is now equated with consistency. Thought in its
fullest meaning is definition, which presupposes that same consistency. Logical thought and being are understood as functions
of each other, and both stem from identity. In a word, this is
Eleaticism.
     Apparently this would leave us foundering amidst doubts.
For Plato begins to inquire anew into things. But things, far
from consisting of identity, actually are wholly lacking in this
respect. Things are not permanent; they will not always remain
as they are now. Moreover, they exhibit a fundamental multiplicity. For example, a horse is a horse today, but he was not a
horse a century ago and he will not be one a century from now.
But even this is not the most significant fact, though it is
important. For besides being a horse, this creature is also
many other things: an animal, for instance, a mammal. With an
intellectual thrust that is typically Hellenic, Plato asserts
that in fact a horse has no being in the strictest sense. But
had not Parmenides said as much already? Have we again fallen
into Eleaticism? Were so many efforts and the implacable criticism of the Sophists all in vain?
     Plato is referring to being, of course; but it should be
pointed out that he means the being of things. This is not to
say that beyond and apart from things there may be a form of being,
or ens. What Plato means is that the being of a horse is not in
the horse. Nevertheless, there is a form of being associated
with things that in this case Plato would call the idea (εἶδος,
ἰδέα) of a horse. This view of things would be meaningless to
an Eleatic thinker, yet it is the great discovery of Platonic
thought. Plato denies that the consistency of things resides in
things themselves. This means that things are somewhat discredit-
ed (provisionally at least) in Platonic thought. They do not admit a lógos because they lack identity. Definition is possible
only in terms of the universal, the eîdos.
     If we insist on asking why this is so, logicians will usually
tell us that an individual is indefinable because he is capable
of infinite traits. Now, the truth of this statement is not immediately evident. I do not wish to take up the question, which is
one of the most difficult in all of logic. And, of course, all
logic is highly difficult. Nevertheless, I should like to pose
a few questions that may someday be answered. Is it true that

45

an individual may reveal infinite traits? As a rule, the moment
we begin to use the word "infinite" our understanding stops. Are
we justified in attributing infinity to a reality that is strictly finite? Furthermore, are these so-called infinite traits definable? Are all possible variations definable? On the other
hand, if I consider only the species, keeping in mind the supposed infinite variations of the individual, does the specific group
also exhibit infinite possibilities? If Bucephalus may display
an endless series of traits, does this mean that the species
"horse" is also infinite in its variability? If logicians are
pressed, they may also define an individual for us from time to
time, for example, the sun. And when they declare the metaphysical essence of God, are they not attempting to give a "definition"
of Him that is not a universal?[22]

The reason that it is so hard to define an individual is
that he lacks identity. If I wish to define an individual man,
I discover that the qualities I describe in him may be present
now, but the time described by the very term "is" is not the
present. Besides, the individual has these qualities because
he has acquired them, and this implies a previous state of being
when he comes and future state whither he goes. The reality of
the individual at any given moment implies a past and future
reality. Stated in another way, I have no other means of "defining" an individual than to tell what has happened to him. This
is precisely the contrary of what is generally understood by
definition.

The being of things is not within but rather without things.
It exists in ideas, and ideas are the consistency of things.
When I speak, my words refer to things—they are poured over things,
as it were. But this lógos is also reflected back to the consistency of things, to the ideas that make it possible to speak of
things and to tell what they are.

This is another source of dialogue. By means of speech we
may approach the nature of things. Dialogue is the name of a
method, of a road to reality, rather than a literary genre.
For this reason, philosophical thought is dialectic. In fact
Plato uses this term to describe logic, while Aristotle prefers
to call it analytics.[23] In Platonism logic is viewed as that
mode of thought directed toward being in the sense of identity.
Being, in turn, is identified with that form of reality which
meets the requisites of logical thought.[24]

While the Eleatic thinkers saw being, or ens, as something
totally separated from things and reduced to universal identity,
and later pre-Socratic philosophers tried to fill the vacuum left
by this separation with the ambiguous concept of element, in Plato
consistency and ideas are not completely detached from things,
but are, rather, distinguished from them. They are ideas of
things. This genitive expression contains a generic idea that
from the time of the Milesians had been associated with the latent
reality that accounts for manifest things. Parmenides counterpoised

things, prágmata, with the ón. For Plato things exist and have consistency, although the latter is external to the things themselves. In a word, things are ónta. Ideas, on the other hand, are not simply on, but rather óntos ón (ὄντως ὄν), being that is really and truly being, the "being of being," as it were. Plato is an Eleatic inasmuch as he understands being to be identity and consistency. But he ceases to be Eleatic when he heeds the Sophist injunction to speak of things and does so in the Socratic manner, which is to explain the consistency of things. Here the specific problems of Platonism begin.

Philosophical knowledge (ἐπιστήμη) is an awareness of what things are. But since their being or consistency lies without in ideas rather than within them, it becomes necessary to progress dialectically from things to ideas. Platonic philosophy begins, then, with a theory of ideas or consistencies. In other words, it starts with a concept of the form of being that fully and truly is being, with the óntos ón. Now, these ideas, I repeat, are ideas of things. Things are not inconsistent; while they have no inherent consistency or entity, they do have an acquired or, as Plato prefers to say, a "shared" consistency. But it must be clearly understood that the epistéme of Plato is not complete with the mere theory of ideas but rather depends also on an association with things. Philosophy appears as a two-way avenue (the metaphor is recurrent) leading from things, which present the problems and oblige us to philosophize, to ideas; and from ideas back to things, as we attempt to explain the "shared" being of the latter. Hence, the core of Platonic philosophy is the problem of shared being (μέθεξις).

We must now consider more closely the modus operandi of Plato in his writings as he sets out in quest of this epistéme. We must pay especial attention to the connection of definition with myth. We recall that in Phaedrus, Socrates raises a quite serious objection to both his own speech and that of Lysis on the theme of love. He says, in effect, that in neither discourse has love been defined. "Regardless of the topic," he observes, "there is only one possible principle to be followed if one wishes to deliberate clearly: one must either know the subject of his deliberations or run the risk of error in everything he says. Yet, most men fail to realize that they are unaware of the essence of things. Thus they do not agree from the start of their investigation, although they might do so if they had this knowledge. And as they proceed in their inquiry, naturally they pay for their initial error. As a matter of fact, they agree neither with each other nor with themselves. . . . Let us first define what love is and what force it has. Then let us see whether it is harmful or beneficial."[55] These procedural demands seem somewhat strange. If Platonic inquiry revolves around the tí, the what? of things, it would seem that definition should be the result of knowing. Yet it appears on the surface that this is contrary to the Platonic method of beginning with a definition. What is the significance of this?

Plato insists on a definition or delimitation (ὁρισμός), the
essential function of which is to present an object for our consideration. And this definition leads to an agreement (ὁμολογία)
that is in itself an indication of reality. Thus definition allows us (1) to bring the object of our inquiry within view and
(2) to reach an initial agreement. This agreement does not exist
in Sophist or rhetorical dialogue and it is possible to differ
widely on the supposed topic under consideration. Yet, if we
begin with a definition that might also be the aim of our inquiry,
then all our efforts would be superfluous. We must insist on
this point for it sheds light on several others.

Further on, Plato defines the soul as that which is self
moving. The soul is a self-starting entity, and "in this fact
lie both the essence and idea of the soul."[56] Plato then goes
on to tell the myth of the winged chariots. The strange thing
is that the myth follows a precise conceptual definition of the
soul. This fact demolishes the customary explanation that Plato
resorts to myth as a substitute for a concept when none is available. More importantly, Plato introduces the myth with these
words: "To describe what the soul is would require an investigation involving all the senses. It would be a long undertaking
requiring divine rather than human abilities. But it is within
the range of human capability to carry out a shorter investigation
showing what the soul is like. Let us proceed, consequently, to
undertake the latter task."[57] This proves that the initial definition in this case is not based on what the soul is, not on
the οἷον. What is the nature of the latter definition?

Plato makes a distinction between the following three categories: (1) essence or substance (οὐσία); (2) lógos or definition
(ὁ τῆς οὐσίας λόγος [the definition of substance]); and (3) the
name (ὄνομα) of things.[58] Inquiry, according to Plato, should
begin from definition and not, as is usually the case, from the
mere name. But this definition does not tell how something is
(οἷόν ἐστι). Stated in another way, the lógos or definition of
the ousía does not exhaust the reality it treats; it only delimits
or circumscribes that reality so that only that reality and not
some other is considered. Is it possible intellectually to exhaust all the ramifications of any reality? Plato states that
this would be a divine rather than human task. There is an analogy to the myth of the winged chariots in the myth of the cave
at the beginning of Book VII of the Republic, following the conceptual definitions at the end of Book VI.

The role of myth in this case is to give us a glimpse of
reality, albeit in an imperfect and partial way, so that we may
describe its similarity to other things. Myth, far from being
a mere substitute, is really superior to definition. For Plato,
true knowledge is found in myth. But the Platonic myth, rooted
as it is in definition, is unlike the prephilosophic myth. Human
knowledge cannot embrace all reality, but it can establish and
fix its limits to some degree. Any exhaustive knowledge lies

beyond the possibilities and limited time of man. In human terms, reality is inexhaustible. Life can absorb only an abbreviation of knowledge, and this is just what myth is.

But it is only by chance that myth is an allegory. If Plato had said that the soul is like a chariot, for instance, strictly speaking there would be no myth. The word μῦθος may be translated as "story" or "tale." A myth is something, then, that is told or narrated to someone else (this should be kept in mind whenever mention--excessive mention--is made of Plato's supposed immobility).

In defining the soul, Plato compares it to a wing, and in defining a wing, he thinks of its task of lifting heavy things. The unity of the two worlds, that of the cave and that of ordinary reality, hinges on man himself. For man is first in one region and then the other. Hence, the unity of reality in at least one of its dimensions depends on man.

Such, in general terms, is the method of Platonic inquiry. Beginning with a definition that fixes the object within an agreed-on frame of reference, he proceeds then to myth, through which the reality of the object is explained narratively. The culmination of Platonic philosophy, the highest form of epistéme, is the story or narrative.

At this point we may consider in greater detail what Plato understood by philosophy, never forgetting that for Plato philosophy was anything but an accumulation of information and facts. He makes a distinction between the acquisition (κτῆσις) of knowledge, its use (χρῆσις) and the habit (ἕξις) of knowledge created in the soul. It is that habit of knowledge which assures its proper use. It is because of his idea of the habit of knowledge that Plato places greater confidence in dialogue than in written works. He emphasizes this in the Seventh Epistle which we saw earlier and in the myth of Theuth in Phaedrus. When one writes, one's words are lifeless and alien--not really the words of the author. But when one speaks, one's words are personal, authentic, and alive. Philosophy is not primarily a science, but first of all a personal matter. It is not a mass of propositions but a reality experienced by man. For this reason philosophy can only be communicated in a specifically personal and erotic way. Philosophical knowledge is transmitted by a love of beauty and of ideas and through a mutual affection between the teacher and the disciple.

What is the ultimate nature of this peculiar human activity known as philosophy? In the myth of the cave, imprisoned man frees himself from his chains and the shadows of untruth in which he dwells. But it is a freedom painfully won. Plato insists on the painfulness caused by brilliant light flooding a darkened world and on the effort it requires to become accustomed to it. It is not without effort that we find the light and the world of reality; they must be attained. What does it mean for man to pass from one world to another?

According to the myth of Phaedrus, each soul is assigned to the cortège of a god. The gods feed on ideas, which are their

"nourishment." Men must subsist on opinions. Yet man was created to replenish himself with ideas, like the gods, and this is why
he is never content. If he feeds on opinion and the things of
the senses, he sinks to a bestial level and becomes less than a
man. If he does not fall, he feels a stirring in the stumps of
his wings and a longing to fly to ideas in imitation of the gods.
Man is an unstable reality ever fluctuating between being more or
less than man.

But let us not forget that leaving the cave is always a violent and temporary escape. Man must needs return to it, for he
may not live on ideas alone. He must return to his old abode
and give an account of things. Moreover, there is also a social
factor that influences his return. Man is alone as he leaves the
cave wherein he had been with his companions. He had lived there
as a member of a community, which to the Greek mind is the pólis.
The man who has escaped from the cave must return to bring the
light to his companions. He must tell them what he has seen
(pedagogy is essential to Platonic philosophy); he must give an
account of things, even describing the things of the cave as now
seen afresh under the light of true reality. If man leaves the
cave in essential solitude, he returns to communicate--to make
knowledge common--what he has seen and to explain the cave and its
shadows.

Now we come once again to the Seventh Epistle, our point of
departure. Final truths may not be written, nor can the whole
of reality be told completely. We can only show the way so that
others can find these things on their own. The mission of the
teacher is to instill in his disciples a longing for reality, so
that they themselves, with painful effort, will undertake the
conquest of reality itself.

May this also serve as an indication of the sense in which
the divine burden Plato assumed in philosophizing can be understood. Anything else will depend on the Platonic writings themselves and the effort put forth by the reader to make them live
again.

CHAPTER II

Historical Knowledge in Herodotus

There are many indications that our time has been called to regard the structure of history as a form of authentic knowledge.
One of the ways necessary to reach a somewhat precise idea of
what history is today is to have a knowledge of what it has been
in the past. But this at once presents difficulties, beginning
with the very meaning of the Greek term history and the several
more or less related interpretations it implies. A clarification
of meaning would reveal the original purpose of man in attempting
to historicize human reality, and it would shed a great deal of
light on the significance of that same task. This philological
problem is highly delicate and complex; but it is possible to
arrive at a basic interpretation of it by viewing the work of
Herodotus, the first Greek historian. We may ask what he proposes
to do and what he actually does in the nine books of his History.
Or to put it another way, what original human reality lies hidden
beneath the Ionian word ἱστορίη.

1. The Purpose of Herodotus

Herodotus of Halicarnassus lived from approximately 484 to 425 B.C.
A friend of Sophocles (though somewhat younger) and a contemporary
of Euripides, Empodocles, and Anaxagoras, he belongs to a period
when Greece can already look back on its own rather lengthy past
as well as that of other countries. And Herodotus reacts to that
past in a more active and personal way than the logographers of
the sixth century B.C. The past notwithstanding, however, the
Hellenic world still maintains a fresh and unaffected attitude
toward things; it has not yet experienced the profound change of
spirit that Socratic reflection will bring. Both features of
Herodotus' time characterize his approach to historical reality.
        The guiding purpose of his work is formally stated in the
opening lines. He would preserve the deeds of men from the ravages
of time and assure that the great works of Greeks and barbarians

shall not fade and lose their glory. Herodotus, whose principal concern is the wars between Greeks and Asiatics, goes on to say that he seeks the cause of those wars.[1] Compare Herodotus' aims with those of Thucydides, who sees his work as an everlasting achievement (κτῆμα ἐς αἰεί).[2] Historiography--history as discipline and knowledge--reacts on history sensu stricto--historical reality--and imposes a primary selection of data. In the case of Herodotus, selection is colored by his struggle with the power of time and his wish to shield deeds against oblivion. As a historian, then, he proposes to preserve certain human realities from fleeting life. But what is the real significance of all this?

The aim of history is to see to it that something remain of what has gone before, that the memory of certain things outlive their essentially transitory nature. History, then, is a discipline of the memorable. Thus we have in this concept, which will need further explanation, a basic historical category. But this presupposes a certain process of selection in history, so that the "memorable" is isolated and defined at the expense of the uneventful. From the totality of historical reality, the historian selects certain items that seem memorable to him. This means that from the very beginning, history is based on a process of abstraction.

This process arises from the nature of memory itself. The very context of memory is forgetfulness. Only through forgetfulness am I able to remember. Only because most of the past is swallowed up in a sea of oblivion, do some remaining islands appear memorable. The word "memorable" means first of all that which can be remembered, but it also implies a certain degree of preference; memorable things are those which deserve to be remembered because of certain values. Preferential selection underlies historical narration, inasmuch as what is memorable is considered important. The problem lies in determining in each case what is important and therefore worthy of being remembered.

But Herodotus proposes to go a step further. He attempts to explain "for what cause" (δι᾽ ἥν αἰτίην) peoples warred against one another. In other words, in addition to writing a chronicle of memorable happenings, Herodotus seeks an understanding of the events he records. Herodotus is very much aware that if we lose sight of the causes and motives of human reality, it becomes unintelligible. A human action cannot properly be considered as a brute fact. The age-old effort of historical thought, an effort that is just now beginning to achieve its full effectiveness, is directed towards the elimination of facts merely as facts. (One of the most lamentable errors of historiography has been its occasional ignorance of its own nature, to the point of reducing itself to a mere registry of facts.) For facts in themselves are meaningless and must be converted into something else that is not pure fact. A fact is something we come across that raises a question in our mind. Far from being an explanation, it demands explanation; and this becomes possible only when the fact is

eliminated as such and referred to its point of origin in human
life.

In human things, cause assumes the nature of motivation. If
I am walking and a stone falls on me, this is a fact; as such, however, it becomes understandable only if I trace it to its cause.
Let us assume that a man thirty feet away has hurled it at me; the
cause, then, is the physical strength of the man, who, by means
of a muscular effort, threw the stone. Is this explanation sufficient? Not at all; even with this explanation, the fact remains
incomprehensible. I must know what motivated the man to hurl the
stone; I need to know the real why? of his action. But if I recall that the man hates me, suddenly I feel a surge of understanding. I see the stoning as being motivated by hatred and its meaning is thus illuminated. It is no longer a mere "fact" but a
deed, something the man does in keeping with a certain situation.
In order to remember facts one must understand them, and this is
what Herodotus finds he needs to do.

Nevertheless, in order to reach a complete understanding of
Herodotus' aims they should be set against a contrasting background.
In fact, such a background would be what Herodotus does not propose
to do in his work. For example, he does not propose in the least
to utilize historical knowledge in current life. It does not occur to him that we need to know history in order to live our own
lives. Neither does he pursue history for the sake of erudition.
His purpose in knowing these things is not so as to be able to
construct another historical discipline from them like those dealing with man, society, and the State. Finally, his purpose is
not even to justify the state of things as they are, in the manner,
say, of Titus Livius, who wishes to demonstrate the grandeur of
the Roman Empire and to justify its entire political system.

Herodotus proposes simply to rescue certain kinds of historical events from oblivion, and to do so, he sets out, first of all,
to understand them, and then to narrate them in an artistic way
(later we shall see the importance of the artistic in his work).

From the seventh to the fifth century B.C., faced with the
realization that everything is transitory and fleeting and that
generation follows generation like leaves on a tree, the Greek
expresses his reaction in three different ways:

(1) Through lyric poetry. In poetry the Greek relives this
evanescence melancholically and derives a certain equanimity from
it.

(2) With the birth of philosophy. Before the essential im-
permanence of things, which come into being and cease to be, the
Greek appeals to something different from things themselves,
something from which they arise and to which they may be reduced:
what he called principle (ἀρχή), and ultimately nature (φύσις).

(3) Through history, which attempts to preserve and perpetuate the memorable against the threat of oblivion. In this regard,
the idea of fame or glory (δόξα) needs to be kept in mind. It is
a matter, as Herodotus puts it, of preventing great and admirable

deeds from fading into obscurity (ἀκλεᾶ γένηται), that is, from
becoming ἀκλεᾶ. But the first meaning of ἀκλεής is "without
glory," and the Ionian substantive ἀκλείη means "infamy," or lack
of fame. Glory, especially for the Classical world, was the verification of immortality and the means--hazardous, of course--of
saving oneself from nothingness. Down to the time of the Orphic
mysteries, and to a great extent after them, the Greeks have little
or no idea of immortality. In his better moments, the Greek ex-
pects life beyond the grave to be a spectral existence in a land
of shadows, but there are long periods in the Classical world when
man very nearly loses all faith, and we need look no further than
Lucretius and Lucian for examples. In contrast, Christianity
stresses personal immortality and relegates fame to a secondary
significance: the man who believes in everlasting life is likely
to be more interested in it than he is living on in the memory of
people, and even the man with personal doubts, if he is immersed
in a tradition based on this faith, will count on it and participate socially in that same belief. Concern for fame and glory
comes to the fore in periods when belief in immortality is weakened
or lost altogether. This was true of the Renaissance, for example,
whereas during the Middle Ages the desire for personal glory had
all but vanished for the most part. This goes hand in hand with
a decline in the significance of originality: the fact that we
do not know who wrote the Poema del Cid or the Chanson de Roland
is symptomatic of that medieval attitude. On the other hand, in
any provincial weekly newspaper of today even the crossword puzzle
is signed by its "creators."

2. The Concept of Importance in History

We have observed that Herodotus' desire to save certain memorable
events from oblivion involves a fundamental historical category:
importance. It is the criterion by which the historian makes
certain selections from the confused mass of information about
the past. It is a concept that conceals a degree of complexity.
Importance is not a property of things in themselves, analogous
to length, hardness, etc. (assuming that one can make this statement without reservations or restrictions); rather, things are
important to someone. Would the Ford industry have seemed very
important to Saint Bruno? We can imagine what an Indian fakir,
whose greatest ambition is to remain immobile for twenty years,
would think of building an airplane. Importance is a rigorously
circumstantial, human reality. Among the countless facts that
make up the woof of history, some are important for certain purposes, in certain situations, and from a certain point of view.
    For this reason, moreover, happenings eventually turn out
to be important historically. If someone is struck down and
killed while crossing the street, is it important? For the individual in question it is enormously important, no doubt, and yet

history will take no notice of it. Yet if the pedestrian should
happen to be Pierre Curie, the accident will, indeed, be important. A woman sits embroidering behind the windows of her bal-
cony on a provincial street. Surely this trivial fact will not
have the least historical importance. But if that woman happens
to be Mariana Piñeda,* then history will have much to say about
her embroidery. There is, then, no immediate and intrinsic way
of deciding whether or not a minor event in the course of time
is of any importance. For importance has such decisive consequences that history may consider entire periods to be more or less
important.

What seems important to Herodotus? What does he wish to
keep from fading into oblivion? Three classes of things he would
preserve: public facts, wonderful deeds, and amusing events.
These are the three categories of memorable events worthy of
being recorded.

As the first concern of historiography, public facts (τὰ
γενόμενα ἐξ ἀνθρώπων) gave rise to the chronicle which records
them. Great and wonderful deeds (ἔργα μεγάλα τε καὶ θωμαστά) are
the uncommon and unusual ones, those beyond the normal possibilities of man to perform; they are the stuff of fables, for which
Greek history always has an affinity. To Herodotus, interesting
events are those which amuse, and this attribute is what after
all seems the most important to him. This is why his work is
fragmented into many small histories amounting almost to novels,
in which he delights and displays his greatest narrative skill.

There are two things from among the diverse ingredients of
Herodotus' historiography that should be kept in mind: (1) history concerns the unusual, not the ordinary; (2) as a result of
this, it is made up of isolated and separate elements and is by
nature discontinuous. Such a view of history is approximately
the contrary of what Dilthey holds historical reality to be, i.e.,
continuity, coherence, and interdependence--in short, Zusammenhang,
to use the word on which, as Ortega has already pointed out,
Dilthey insists the most.

3. The Material of History

Herodotus wishes to tell us the truth in an attractive manner,
and he divides his attention equally between these dual responsi-
bilities. As for truthfulness, it differs according to the type
of history being compiled. Herodotus himself proposes to write
a historíe, an informative report, and to this end he seeks to be
fully informed (and on several occasions makes references to it).
A starting point for Herodotus, this type of report resembles
what we think of as news, and unlike the modern historian, Herodotus
utilizes it as historical material. In general we can say that
Herodotus bases his narration on both direct and indirect news;
in other words, he includes accounts of events by eye witnesses

or those from recent tradition. The modern historian, in contrast, prefers documents or history already written and elaborated by men of other periods. It would be interesting to investigate to what degree and in what fashion the attitude of Herodotus has persisted in subsequent historiography.

Herodotus' account amounts to reporting of a sort, but with important differences that will be pointed out later. He deals with histories, and for this reason, history in the singular slips away from him. This largely explains why he seldom uses documents, or if he does consult them, why he fails to derive their full effectiveness.

Now, documents may be used in two basic but quite different ways. The first might be termed the "testimonial": the document has an informative purpose, serving simply as the verification of a fact, which we become aware of through it. A good example would be an inscription stating that a certain king died in this or that Olympic game, nothing more. Such testimonial documents give rise to chronicles, which gather and enumerate public happenings in the most authentic way possible. Through the use of documents in this way--but we must remember that only partly in this way--history comes into being. Yet the fact must be stressed that a chronicle is not, of itself, history. The second approach to the use of documents is to see them as fragments of historical reality. In this sense, the document brings us into contact with reality, but it does so in so incomplete and fragmentary a way as to create a need for explanation and exegesis. This is modern history, which begins with the task of interpreting documents, and it is on such interpretation that historical knowledge proper is founded. History consists of the utilization of documents in order to reconstruct the vital reality that appears isolated and fragmented in these documents. In summary, the two ways in which a document can function historically are: as an exhibited document, the effectiveness of which abides entire in its presence; and as an understood account reinstated within an entire context.

Herodotus uses accounts from many different sources, and in cases of disagreement among them, he chooses the one in which to put his trust either through confidence in the source or by reason of the internal verisimilitude of the account itself. Thus, in relating the story of Cyrus' death (I, 214), he chooses the one most likely to be true (πιθανώτατος) from among the different lógoi pertaining to the event. He is guided, therefore, by two criteria: authority and verisimilitude, or coherence. Herodotus has a vast knowledge of life and the world and an intimate familiarity with things, and it is from this broad experience that he can decide on the probability of truth in differing accounts.

As for the attractiveness and artistic form of Herodotus' writings, they are primarily influenced by the materials at his disposal. The very elements with which Herodotus shapes history are themselves literary in form. On the other hand, the modern historian must deal with ingredients that either lack prior artistic expression--monuments, objects, facts, etc.--or reveal an unacceptable form that must be dispensed with before they can be utilized--books, earlier histories, etc. In contrast, Herodotus uses orally transmitted lógoi or simple accounts with a certain autonomy and development of their own that bespeak a prior artistic elaboration. In other words, these accounts amount to a literary genre in their own right, with the internal exigences that determine and define a genre. Herodotus' work is composed of these primary accounts, connected according to a cognitive and artistic purpose in order to form a secondary account. To put it another way, in a strict sense, the history of Herodotus is composed of histories, which explains its charm as well as its limitations.

4. The Suppositions of Herodotus

Herodotus' work is based on a series of suppositions originating within his historical circumstance as a Greek of the fifth century B.C. To begin with, one of the suppositions that has a lasting effect on his work concerns the role of the Oracles. History for him does not operate on a purely natural plane but also contains a divine or more exactly, mythical, element. Myth commingles in a peculiar way with human happenings. But a closer look is needed in order to determine more accurately how the divine acts on history in Herodotus.

   Let us consider three ways in which the gods intervene in the course of human events: that represented by Homer, that described in Herodotus, and that defined by the idea of Providence (πρόνοια) as it appears in the Stoics and, in a loftier form, in the Christian historians (Saint Augustine and Bossuet, for example). In the Iliad, the history of men is mingled with that of the gods, and the latter, acting almost as men, take part in battles. Aphrodite herself is wounded by Diomedes' lance in Canto V of the Iliad as she stubbornly intervenes on behalf of Aeneas. Hence the gods appear as personages who interact with men. Furthermore, they become subjects of history for this very reason. But in Herodotus the gods are no longer topics of history; that place is left solely to men. Yet the gods do intervene as a factor of immediate and detailed influence in the march of history. Through the Oracles, the gods--and especially the "numen residing at Delphos"--determine human events. Thus, a determinism of divine rather than human origin is introduced. When the Oracle speaks, it means not only that certain things are to happen, but also that men are to take measures according to this judgment. This means that in addition to natural causes, these utterances are also a determining element of history. Of course, mindful of his own health and reputation, the Oracle usually speaks in ambiguous language. On the other hand, the providentialistic historian cannot cause Providence to function as a historical element in

explaining the actual details of history. He can only begin from
the assumption that the course of history is truly in the hands
of the Divinity and that in Him a divine plan is being carried
out. Otherwise, the most that he can do is to follow a line of
thought that actually transcends history sensu stricto and attempts
to glimpse the outline of that plan within human history that,
nevertheless, continues to be understood and explained in a purely natural way. And it ought to be noted that after Herodotus,
Greek history begins to free itself more and more from that caus-
ality sui generis introduced by the Oracles.

The second supposition of Herodotus is his Hellenism. In
the first place, the mental schemes he applies to history are
Greek. He sees the world through Greek eyes, and his understanding of it is molded by a system of ideas, beliefs, and values
belonging to the Greek mind of that time. Secondly, in addition
to Greek values, he holds everything Greek in the highest esteem,
and this affects his entire interpretation of barbarian peoples.
Thirdly and most important, his Hellenism is apparent in the
very framework of understanding itself; he dwells on what seems
interesting and important for Greeks, not for Persians, Egyptians,
Lydians, or the Massagetae. This explains the predominance of
the "picturesque" in his writings. In contrast, the modern
historian tends--but only tends--to understand alien cultures from
their own point of view, not from ours, and to delve into exotic
ways of life in order to reach an internal understanding of them.
In other words, he sets out to investigate primarily that which is
"important" from the viewpoint of another culture rather than from
our own as twentieth-century Europeans. The Histoire du monde
(History of the World) under the editorship of Cavaignac is an
example of this tendency; in it, even the vast panoramas of non-
European cultures are viewed directly rather than through their
approximations to ours. If we set out, let us say, to study the
history of China, we must consider the China of the Chinese, and
not the traditional image Europe has had of China. Likewise, we
must attempt to understand and formulate that which is important
for the Chinese, that which conditions their life and therefore
makes it understandable.

The third supposition of Herodotus, and a consequence of
the first two, is that the theme of history is, above all, the
extraordinary aspects of the strange accounts he relates; it
consists of the curious and new, the unusual or entertaining.
This makes for a close relationship between journalism and historiography in Herodotus. It has been said that if a dog bites
a man, it is not "news"; but if a man bites a dog, then that is
news. Similarly, Herodotus is interested in ways of life only
when they differ from the Greek; he is attracted by the strange
and the unexpected, in a word, by the marvelous (θωμαστόν).

Finally, the articulation as units of the human subject of
history is not a matter of indifference in the kind of knowledge
sought by Herodotus. Modern universal history appears as the

history of mankind, the true subject of history. But this global subject is articulated in two ways: first, according to time, thereby obtaining the chronological groupings referred to in the broadest sense as eras or ages. This is the sense in which we speak of the Renaissance or the Enlightenment, the Napoleonic era or the Restoration. Second, according to certain historical bodies defined by a particular bond: Spain, France, England, the Roman Empire, or the Arabs. We find nothing of the sort in Herodotus; mankind is by no means the subject of his historical narrative. For him the world, in the sense of surrounding geographical regions, is divided into two parts: Greeks and barbarians. Among the latter, the Medes and Persians stand out as known peoples and what is more, as nations dynamically opposed to the Hellenes. In a remoter way, the Egyptians more or less represent the past which still survives. As for other peoples, they form a background of curious forms of humanity and are primarily interpreted by Herodotus as genealogical groupings. Thus, they remain somewhat at the periphery of history and by no means come to share fully in it. Instead, in representing certain timeless forms of conduct, they assume an almost biological appearance; for Herodotus fails to understand the social nature, much less the intrinsic historicity, of customs. As a case in point, recall the almost taxonomic filiations he attributes to diverse Libyan peoples,[3] to Scythians, and to other ethnic and geographical groups.

On these suppositions Herodotus fashions his historíe.

5. Time and History

For us history is a single unit, especially in regard to time; it is continuous and sequential. Historical things are defined by a before and after, by their appearance at a given moment of time and at a certain historical level. Is the same true in Herodotus? Evidently not. Temporal references in his work are mere accessory devices used to support the course of the narration or perhaps to resolve some doubt. Keep in mind that for a long time, until the end of the seventeenth century, the principal discipline having to do with time was chronology, which deals with "time" in a conventional rather than a historical sense, and that it was from chronology that true history based on temporality emerged.

Herodotus takes a series of stories, or lógoi, that form a certain unit. Each account is rather simple and, as we have seen, somewhat like a news item. A story is told of something that happened. No doubt it happened at a certain time, but in the final analysis the event is not intrinsically temporal. In this regard Herodotus' technique resembles modern reporting. Yet reporting differs from the "news item" in Herodotus inasmuch as it deals with recent events and the latter does not. The perfect reporter would be one capable of correctly anticipating an event, so that it would occur at the same time the public would be reading about it. In contrast, stories in Herodotus have a certain aura of age. Time in them appears as <u>distance</u>, and the things related seem <u>aged</u>.

This archaic quality is closely related to the function ascribed to time. The things told are remote, distant in time, things that have <u>resisted</u> time instead of being dragged into oblivion by it. All <u>things</u>--houses, stones, men with their words and deeds--are assaulted and corroded by time. This is the traditional image of time as the destroyer. Time <u>undoes</u> things and gradually lays waste to them. Time is a <u>silent force</u> of destruction that little by little consumes everything. With Renaissance rhetoric, time speaks metaphorically to women in the poem by Tasso:

> Ed or, mentre ch'io parlo,
> la mia tacita forza
> entra negli occhi vostri e nelle chiome,
> e le spoglia e disarma. . .
> I'fuggo, i'corro, i'volo;
> nè voi vedere (ahi cieche!)
> la fuga, il corso, il volo.[4]

This explains why in Herodotus things appear disparate and discontinuous, as islets emerging amidst a tide of oblivion, and, strictly speaking, as <u>relics</u> from the past. But another <u>viewpoint</u> stands in opposition to this interpretation. The modern historian is interested in historical continuity and connection (the <u>Zusammenhang</u> of Dilthey) and in time in its flow, precisely because <u>time for</u> him is the very substance with which life is forged. Indeed, time <u>undoes</u> things, but it does so by <u>creating</u> others. The notion of <u>time</u> as a destroyer has concealed its deeper dimension whereby life is structured and formed by temporality. Whereas modern history is based on temporality, that of Herodotus struggles against it. Stated in another way, the substance of history is atemporal in Herodotus. This is why only the strange and unusual interests him, and therefore why history as he understands it falls short of being true historical knowledge of human life.

CHAPTER III
The Meaning of
Aristotelian Philosophy

1. The Hellenic Social Situation in the Fourth Century

The Peloponnesian War ended in 404 B.C. with the complete defeat of Athens and the triumph of Sparta. Many saw in this outcome the triumph of a political ideology oriented toward discipline, military prowess, and the ability to rule, qualities which the Athenians themselves, under very different circumstances, often admired and envied. However, in reality we cannot say that one city won and another lost, but rather that all were defeated. I use the word "all" because if we look closely at events, we discover that they lead to a single result: the crisis of a form of historical life, whose socio-political unity was based on the pólis. The beginnings of this crisis may be traced back for half a century, to the end of the Persian wars, as I have previously explained ("Greek Philosophy from its Origin to Plato," 5).[*]

On the one hand, greater contact among the cities, in the form of confederations and leagues that assumed more and more importance, and on the other hand, the decline of traditional ways of life within each city, brought about a change in the framework of the pólis and a decrease in stability. We can see the reaction to the incipient situation in Aristophanes, for example, in his work The Clouds. The end of the Peloponnesian War which coincides with Plato's youth and his first contact with public life, is, as Taeger correctly says,[1] the external expression of the beginning of the decline of the pólis. Plato's Seventh Epistle is the most penetrating and intelligent description of the historical situation at the beginning of the fourth century.[2] Taeger writes that "a profound anxiety settled over Hellas and Hellenic man."[3] Plato says that he came to feel vertigo.[4] We are no longer dealing with disturbances and upheavals of external things (which in any case are never as great as those of war itself) but are concerned rather with the anxiety and disorientation of man himself and with a crisis of his socio-political world.

61

Let us consider some of the features of that world. In doing so we must bear in mind that the information about Greece is very disproportionate; compared with the great deal that we know about Athens, we know little about various other cities and next to nothing about certain regions (Aetolia, Acarnania, etc.) in which urban life had hardly developed, and where the pólis really did not exist. The conditions of Greek life thus varied greatly. Not only do we lack adequate information: the Greeks themselves were even less sure of the regions where the social structure differed from that of the pólis, and where political organization as such was lacking. What Aristotle calls éthnos--for example, Arcadia--is always a rather nebulous term. In every case, including the cities, we must think of an agricultural economy having little industry and commerce, especially if we are dealing with the cities of continental Greece.

These cities were economically dependent on other territories; the Greek ideal of autarchy was seldom realized. Even the most prosperous, industrialized, and densely populated cities were unable to produce enough food and raw materials for their generally monopolistic industries. Athens had a monopoly on ceramics; Megara, fabrics; Delos, Aegina, and Corinth, bronze; Laconia, Boeotia, and Euboea, arms and armaments. Hence, maritime communications were all-important and imposed a pressing need for naval materiel: metals, wood, tar, linen for sails, hemp for rope. Since war was a perfectly normal phenomenon among the Greek cities, a citizen had to provide himself with arms--a fact of life that was of enormous political importance. It became so important, as Aristotle insists, that the politically decisive faction in the breaking up of the cities is made up of "those who possess arms" (οἱ κεκτημένοι τὰ ὅπλα).

Greece always had both a shortage of food supplies and an excess of population, considering the mediocre natural resources of the country. This accounts for the constant and vast feats of colonization so characteristic of the Greek world. The period of greatest expansion was the second half of the fifth century, after the Persian wars. But all this changed after the Peloponnesian War. A very grave socioeconomic crisis occurred with stringent political repercussions. For one thing, a proletarianization of the masses came about, causing a decline in labor. For another, the chronic shortage of food became even more acute and there was widespread hunger in all of Greece between the years 331 and 324 B.C. This economic situation accentuated class struggle, with the social classes losing their organic and, as it were, functional character. This gave rise to the division between rich and poor, which for Aristotle (but not yet for Plato) are the principal social categories. The entire Aristotelian Politics is imbued with this concern, and his approach to government consists principally of dealing with this situation. He would make use of it as a political force, though he advocates the utmost prudence in order to avoid excessive poverty, which would make both the coexistence of the two groups and the existence of the city impossible.

Population growth has been calculated more or less accurately for Attica. Between 480 and 431 B.C. a considerable increase occurred. The population reached some 172,000 citizens and a total-- with foreigners and slaves--of 315,000 inhabitants. After a rapid decline during the Peloponnesian Wars, the population grew again but remained much lower than it had been before: some 112,000 citizens and a total of approximately 258,000 inhabitants.[6] We note that the ratio--if these data are exact--has changed. Citizens, who in the period from 480 until 431 B.C. were more than 54 percent of the total, are no more than 43 percent in the fourth century. Rostovtzeff insists that the cause of this decline in Hellenic population was not principally the losses in many battles; rather it is to be found in the atmosphere of uncertainty (which greatly inhibited the birth rate), a growing individualism, a concern for personal prosperity. In short, the decrease was due to a state of dissociation.[7] An increase in money but not in production unbalanced supply and demand and led to inflation. The inland markets were depressed because of internal struggles and a decrease in the ability of the cities to support mercenary troops; abroad, political tensions and the development of colonial industries likewise produced a restriction of the home markets. All this heightened the crisis.[8] Jaeger writes:

> By the fourth century, this way of life (the old and authentic Greek way of life) had long since been sundered by the dominance of commercial powers and interests and by the intellectual individualism which had become wide spread during the period. Probably every intelligent person saw clearly that the State could not endure unless such individualism, at least in its baser forms of wanton personal egotism, could be overcome. But it was difficult to abolish it when even the State itself was really inspired and guided in its acts by the same spirit. The predatory politics of the last years of the fifth century had gradually caused the citizens to follow these schools of thought, and now the State itself fell victim to the egoist idea, so impressively described by Thucydides and converted by him into a principle. The old State with its laws had represented the totality of "customary" norms for its citizens. To live in accord with the laws was the highest unwritten law in ancient Greece, as Plato sadly recalls for the last time in his Crito. This dialog presents the tragic conflict of the fourth century carried to absurd extremes. The State has reached a point where its laws demand that the most just and pure man of the Greek nation must drink hemlock. The death of Socrates is a reductio ad absurdum of the entire State, and not merely of the contemporary dignitaries.[9]

Writing from another point of view, Werner Jaeger also recognizes the dissociation of Greek life, the breakdown of society, and the decline of unwritten, "customary" laws. Later we shall see the implications of this. The ramifications are greater than they would appear at first glance and more pronounced even than what Jaeger notes in this context. Let us recall some instances in the historical process in question: Socrates was executed in the year 399; in 388 or thereabouts Plato made his first trip to Syracuse and on his return founded the Academy in Athens; in 371, the Thebans overthrew Sparta in Leuctra and put an end to the ephemeral Lacedomonian hegemony in Hellas (it had lasted some thirty-three years); in 338, Phillip overthrew the Thebans and Athenians in Chaeronea, thus beginning the period of Macedonian domination and the loss of independence of the Greek cities. Alexander the Great reigned from 336 until 323. During this time he carried out the conquest of Asia and brought about the political transformation of Greece and the entire Orient. It was during these same years that Aristotle, established in Athens after an eleven-year absence, founded and directed the Lyceum, composed the majority of his works, including at least most of his Politics.

Such, in broad terms, was the situation of the Greek world in which Aristotle's Politics was conceived and written. But this book deals with very specific themes and belongs to a special literary genre. What is its place and significance seen from this new standpoint? What were the implications of writing a "Politics" in Athens in the second half of the fourth century?

2. The Intellectual Tradition of the Politics

When the political works of the Greek philosophers, especially those of Plato (Politics, Republic, Laws) and Aristotle (Politics) are read without bias, a disconcerting impression is unavoidable. This impression could be expressed in a few words by stating that if, on the one hand, we recognize that decisive questions which affect the being of man and the very structure of reality are dealt with in these writings (especially in Plato), is it any the less certain, on the other hand, that in these same works we also find detailed investigations of questions concerning such things as common meals, the different possible ways of appointing magistrates, whether or not there ought to be a thousand or five thousand armed citizens in the perfect city, or the advantage of establishing 5,040 lots of land for cultivation--problems that we find it hard to take seriously if we cast aside the traditional reverence that enters into the study of things Greek.

I believe that it is very important to retain this contradictory impression. We should not silence the discontent it produces, or try to skirt the difficulty by declaring that the first things mentioned are "important" but not the others. The fact is that the seemingly trivial matters are dealt with in more detail and depth than the so-called important things. The true importance of all these matters can be ascertained only when they are placed in a certain perspective that is alien to our own. But putting them in such a perspective gives rise to many uncertainties. Can we take the totality of political writings of the Greeks as a unified and homogeneous reality? The answer is, of course, that we may not. But we must still ask ourselves: is it enough to distinguish between the philosophical works on politics by Plato and Aristotle and their other writings?

It seems to me that we must distinguish three sources of inspiration for the studies on politics, sources which are profoundly heterogeneous and which cannot be considered together if we wish to understand them. This is done not so as to separate them but rather to see how they converge in the composition of the illustrious books that we know under the titles of Republic and Politics. And we must bear in mind, reserving the possibility of viewing the theme in more detail, that the Republic of Plato and the Politics of Aristotle are not comparable as books. To put it another way, the scope of questions that the former poses greatly exceeds the latter, although not with regard to Aristotle's intellectual range. In other words, within the Aristotelian corpus the Politics is only a part of what corresponds theoretically to Plato's Republic.

Book II of the Politics (1260b, 27-36) begins with these words:

> Our purpose is to consider what form of political community is best of all for those who are most able to realize their ideal of life. We must therefore examine not only this but other constitutions, both such as actually exist in well-governed states, and theoretical forms which are held in esteem; that what is good and useful may be brought to light. And let no one suppose that in seeking for something beyond them we are anxious to make a sophistical display at any cost; we only undertake this inquiry because all the constitutions with which we are acquainted are faulty.*

After expounding and criticizing the regimes proposed by Plato in the Republic and the Laws, Aristotle says in Chapter VII of the same book: "Other constitutions have been proposed; some by private persons, others by philosophers and statesmen" (Chapter VII, 1265b, 32-33). And in Chapter VIII, which I shall treat later, he says of Hippodamus of Miletus that he ". . . was the first person not a statesman who made inquiries about the best form of government" (Chapter VIII, 1267b, 28-29).

I believe that these passages put us on the right track. The first source of political thought in Greece is, inevitably, political activity itself. According to how aware the city is of its goals and of the best way to achieve them, a corresponding amount of speculation about the affairs of the pólis is generated. Generally, as Plato notes (Laws, 63e), this activity is sporadic. But the need, which had been strongly felt since the seventh century, for a "constitution," that is, for a public preservation of the structure of the city, of rights and duties, in order that men might orient themselves in political life, resulted necessarily in a form of more general thought which questioned the primary goal of the pólis and the means of realizing it. This is what corresponds to the work of the "legislators" (Solon, Azleucus, Carondas, Draco, Pythacus, etc.) that Aristotle studies at the end of Book II. The goal of the pólis was primarily the acquisition of power, rule, supremacy over neighbors (τὸ κρατεῖν), and therefore the ability to wage war. But soon the political uncertainty of the Greek cities revealed that there was a more elemental and urgent goal, a condition of other aims: namely, the maintenance of internal peace, the avoidance of discord or civil dissension (στάσις). This turned attention towards economic matters.[10]

The first form of "technical" political thought, if one may use the expression, was soon joined to two other views. The first of these, which perhaps made its appearance slightly later than the beginnings of the second view, is represented by Hippodamus of Miletus and studied in detail by Aristotle in Chapter VIII of Book II (Politics). The introduction of this work is to the point: "Hippodamus, the son of Euryphon, a native of Miletus, the same who invented the art of planning cities, and who also laid out the Piraeus--a strange man, whose fondness for distinction led him into a general eccentricity of life, which made some think him affected (for he would wear flowing hair and expensive ornaments; but these were worn on a cheap but warm garment both in winter and summer); he, besides aspiring to be an adept in the knowledge of nature, was the first person not a statesman who made inquiries about the best form of government."[*] Who was Hippodamus? Quite obviously, he was a Milesian, a colonial man (though settled in Athens), and a collaborator of Pericles. No doubt, he was unorthodox, eccentric, and probably a snob. Architect and city planner, he built the panhellenic colony of Turios and planned Piraeus with straight streets intersected at right angles. He was a "technician." But while technicians tend to concentrate on a single discipline, he was not limited to one speciality: "For when their wealth gave them a greater inclination to leisure," writes Aristotle, "and they had loftier notions of excellence, being also elated with their success, both before and after the Persian War, with more zeal than discernment they pursued every kind of knowledge."[11] Though not a politician, though not having a direct interest in politics as such, Hippodamus did want to know the whole of nature, and in the course of pursuing this interest he tried to define the best type of government. Here we have outlined a typically rationalistic attitude: the desire to comprehend the whole of nature is joined to pure speculation which, unlike real politics,

functions in a vacuum without encountering political reality.
This speculation reaches the optimum, the unreal and extreme.
Hippodamus, who must have been an extraordinary type (except
for his lack of any congeniality), was an arch-Greek. With his
dishevelled hair and his extravagances, he was almost a carica-
ture of the Greek of the mid-fifth century. It was during this
period that the traditional ways of life began to crumble. Greece
prepared itself to live by principles, according to that strange
disturbing reality called lógos, discovered in Ionia--in Ionia,
not in Athens--a century earlier.

The ideal government of Hippodamus was a mental creation.
It was to consist of ten thousand citizens composed of three
classes: there were to be three portions of city territory,
three classes of laws, three causes of legal processes. The law-
makers would tend to legislate in accordance with the desires of
its citizens and the "plausibility" of matters. Rewards would
be forthcoming to those who made useful inventions for the city,
and food from the state was to be given the children of those
killed in war. Aristotle comments that it was "as if such an
enactment had never been heard of before." And he adds, with a
note of alarm and concern that such a proposal cannot be safely en-
acted although it ". . . has a specious sound."[12] These are plain
words, but they are among the most perspicacious that Aristotle
ever wrote. It was precisely the anxiety caused by such abstract
reasoning on the part of Hippodamus that obliged Aristotle to
pose the critical question to which we will return in time: the
possibility of changing laws, and the problem of what law and
hence the city itself really are.

The deepest and most noticeable part of Hellenic political
thought is found in the speculations of Hippodamus of Miletus,
Phaleas of Calcedonia, the theoreticians and admirers of the
Spartan constitution. Since these men did not live under Spartan
law, they could allow themselves the luxury of considering it
speculatively and extolling its virtues. Following their trend
of thought, "constitutions" are made, ideas of the perfect pólis
are formulated, social and economic orders are outlined on paper,
and legislation is regulated. Before the Greek's very eyes, in
place of the traditional prevailing reality in which he lived and
which was hardly visible, was fabricated an extensive theory of
real or fictitious politeíai that vied for prominence and that in
theory were offered as choices from which to choose. But this
means that the political community was in a state of crisis, for
society and the state are necessarily elements that may not be
"chosen." Rather, they are revealed as things that are not in
our power to choose and change; willy-nilly, we must take them
into account because of their inexorable nature. The awareness
of this situation and of its dangers is the third source of Greek
thought concerning politics. Yet only this one is, as we shall
presently see, intrinsically philosophical in two respects:
first, it stems from a philosophical consideration of political

reality; and second, it reacts on philosophy and essentially modifies its content, its method, and its repertory of problems.

The oldest form of this philosophical source of Greek political thought is Pythagorean. The aristocratic political character that Pythagoreanism assumed in Magna Graecia and especially
in Crotona is quite well known as a view that opposed both tyranny
and democracy. What is important is that the political attitude
of the Pythagoreans arises from a previous personal, religious,
and philosophical attitude, from a change in the understanding
of life. The fundamental points of agreement of that interpretation grew into a principle of conduct and caused the most adept
men of this school to band together as a league working toward
the exercise of power. The skholé functions like a hetairía, a
fraternal order which at the same time acts as a political party.
But I repeat that the principal factor is that the basis of the
latter is not, for example, family ties or economic conditions,
but a willingness to innovate; it is based on the religious and
philosophical content of its ideology. This political force,
alien to the pólis in origin and having a certain appearance of
sect about it, was at least in theory applicable to several cities.
Yet a movement whose most outstanding members were immigrants
and uprooted men was not without a certain risk. Beneath the
more or less truthful personal anecdotes--the wrath of Cilon of
Crotona for not having been admitted to the school,[13] for example,
or the violence of the anti-Pythagorean reaction which destroyed
the school and almost annihilated its power--we can surmise that
the unrest and anxiety caused by that alteration of normal politics
in the cities were quite influential. We must not forget that the
secretive nature of Pythagoreanism was incompatible with politics,
at least to the degree that the latter merges with public life.

The third form of political thought appears with features
more clearly and deeply marked in the life and works of Plato.
The document which has preserved this attitude most accurately
is his Seventh Epistle, in which he recalls his youthful reaction
to the hopelessness of the situation of Athens (and the other
Greek cities as well) after the fall of the Thirty Tyrants and
the reestablishment of democracy. The ancestral ways no longer
prevail; there are no established usages. Things occur by whim
and in the end the instability of the world produces vertigo in
men. People do not know what to do, because without usages,
without society, individual life and happiness are impossible.
There is only one solution to the problem: men must know what to
depend on; they must know what is just and unjust in political
and private life; they must know the nature of things; and they
have to know what to do with those things. But this is the function of philosophy, and this is what Plato means when he says
that a class of true philosophers must assume power in the cities;
or, to put it another way, those who rule should, by some divine
good fortune, be true philosophers.[14]

The Meaning of Aristotelian Philosophy

Normally men know what they have to do, because this is established by usages which have the force of law and exercise their automatic influence over individuals. In periods of crisis when this does not happen, man can live sanely and humanly, can be happy, only by investigating the nature of things, ascertaining what he must do with them, discovering their truth, and reestablishing this philosophy through socially accepted systems of beliefs that would make life possible in the cities. As I have observed in an earlier chapter: "In the strictest sense, Plato's thought can be traced to the situation of Athens at the time. His inability to engage in politics is directly translated into his need to philosophize. The crisis of his time, a crisis of convention and custom, a crisis that meant a vertiginous loss of direction, is the real motive behind his philosophy. The uncertain state of things is what caused him to turn to philosophy. In this context, then, philosophy appears as an urgent task. Contrary to the customary image given us of Plato's thought, his philosophy now may be seen as unavoidable and necessary, arising because there were no longer any ready answers to the questions posed by the world and problems of everyday life."[15]

This helps explain why the Republic, Plato's most important political work, is so much more than a mere treatise on politics. Rather, it is one of the most profound formulations of his philosophy and a work well-known for its metaphysical and ethical character. In effect, Plato carries out the Socratic program as Xenophon formulated it.[16] The Sophists had introduced doubt concerning fundamental questions into intellectual life; after distinguishing what is just by nature and what is just by convention, they rarely encountered the former anywhere. Hence it was but a step for them to the idea that all justice is a pact. This is the stance taken by Thrasymachus and Glaucus in the Republic.[17] The force of law, which before was a thing of nature or of the will of the gods, now disappears; the state is but a convention or the mere exercise of force. This is why Plato had to begin his dialogue with an investigation "on justice." Hence, politics demands the attention of philosophy, and the way in which philosophy poses these questions determines the subsequent development of philosophy itself.

The three sources examined so far constitute the intellectual tradition of Aristotle's Politics. The influence of actual, real-life politics is revealed by his interest in existing historical constitutions, in his examination of the circumstances in the cities, and especially in his patient work as a dedicated recorder of constitutions. On the other hand, Aristotle does not ignore the requirements of the literary genre; in complying with the demands of the genre, he must outline an ideal of politeía, and he must speculate on the "best form of government," as Hippodamus and Plato himself had done. But he speculates without the frivolous ingenuousness and petulance of the former and with more reservation and skepticism than the latter.

A Biography of Philosophy

I am not referring here to the hackneyed and platidudinized "possibilities of realization of the ideal State," but to the reservations which Aristotle had from the point of view of theory, including theory as mere intellectual construction. Finally, in Aristotelian as well as Platonic thought, the concept of political problems as a form of human problems is both explicitly stated and latently implied. Aristotelian politics is anchored in the ethics and metaphysics of that philosophy. But we must note, as I stated in passing, that these roots are almost always external to the work entitled Politics. In fact, his Nicomachean Ethics is but the first part of a total work that is continued in Politics; and the Ethics is inseparable from the "First Philosophy" or Metaphysics. Later we shall turn briefly to the setting or context in which the problem of politics appears within Aristotelian philosophy; and we shall do so in order to see it in its proper perspective and therefore in its real meaning.

3. The Metaphysical Roots of Aristotelian Politics

Aristotle's greatest intellectual undertaking was the formulation of a "sought-after science," one that would come to be identified with metaphysics. But there is a need to exercise some caution in using the term metaphysics, because many different things have been understood by it. Indeed, even as one attempts to delve into metaphysics and succeeds in doing so, he necessarily elaborates a concept of it. It would be an error to take this concept as a point of departure, when it is only a terminus or destination. If we blindly accept as a metaphysical notion what some man discovered in his consideration of metaphysics, we commit what the Greeks call "stepping into another genre," a μετάβασις εἰς ἄλλο γένος. Before finding it, Aristotle called metaphysics a "sought-after science (ζητουμένη ἐπιστήμη), "first philosophy" (πρώτη φιλοσοφία), or lastly "wisdom" (σοφία). The three definitions that Aristotle later reached, and whose unity is a problem,[18] are: "science of being qua being" (ἐπιστήμη περὶ τοῦ ὄντος ᾗ ὄν), "science of substance" (ἐπιστήμν περὶ τῆς οὐσίας), and "science of God" (ἐπιστήμη θεολογικη). Each of these definitions—each of these notions a posteriori, which Aristotle derives after having formulated his metaphysics—announces an internal thesis of metaphysics. If we say, for example, that metaphysics is ontology, this means in effect that we already possess a metaphysics and an anticipation of its central themes. In passing, there is no justification whatsoever for accepting "Metaphysica sive Ontologia" as a simple nominal designation.[19]

For Aristotle, it is a matter of knowing reality; but this poses special difficulties because natural things, either some or all, are in a state of flux, as experience proves.[20] Thus the question that arises is the mobility of things: their being and non-being; being as A first and later as B; in short, their inconsistency. Aristotle finds that he must proceed from natural things (more exactly, through nature, φύσει) to their nature. Since Anaximander, nature had been interpreted as a first cause (ἀρχή), and all the efforts of philosophy after Parmenides had consisted in eluding mutability as such, in such a way that the world was explained leaving movement aside and affirming the unity, identity, and immobility of being, and therefore, the non-existence of nature and the impossibility of physics. Plato considers consistency to be necessarily beyond things and that the latter have only a certain "shared" consistency. If the alternatives are reality and identity, Plato, good Greek that he was, would choose identity. But this leads him to the problem of the way back, of returning to the cave, that is, of the explanation of things from the view of ideas. This was the road that Plato was unable to travel.[21]

At this point Aristotle takes up the question. From the outset he was to say that ideas reside in things themselves; he converts idea into eîdos, a form which shapes or structures matter in order to form things. Nature is still a first cause or principle, but a principle of movement (ἀρχὴ κινήσεως). The key to his interpretation of reality is the idea of substance (οὐσία).

Now then, it is necessary to distinguish between the idea of substance as something by which Aristotle understands the reality of things, and the conceptual schemes that enable us ontologically to analyze this same notion of substance. This question lies beyond our present purpose and would require excessive attention for complete clarification. Nevertheless, certain references to it are necessary, even if made only in passing, for they have a bearing on attempts to explain Aristotelian politics--strange as it may seem. We shall consider only some of the more important points in order to pose the problem, the full treatment of which would imply an inquiry into all Aristotelian metaphysics.

Aristotle states in his Physics:

> Of things that exist, some exist by nature, some from other causes. "By nature" the animals and their parts exist, and the plants and the simple bodies (earth, fire, air, water)--for we say that these and the like exist "by nature." All the things mentioned present a feature in which they differ from things which are not constituted by nature. Each of them has within itself a principle of motion and of stationariness (in respect of place, or of growth and decrease, or by way of alteration). On the other hand, a bed and a coat and anything else of that sort, qua receiving these designations--i.e., in so far as they happen to be composed of stone or of earth or a mixture of the two, they do have such an impulse, and just to that extent--which seems to indicate that nature is a source or cause of being moved

71

and of being at rest in that to which it belongs primarily, in virtue of itself and not in virtue of a
concomitant attribute.[22]

Aristotle goes on to say:

Some identify the nature or substance of a natural
object with that immediate constituent of it which
taken by itself is without arrangement, e.g. the
wood is the "nature" of the bed, and the bronze the
"nature" of the statue. As an indication of this
Antiphon points out that if you planted a bed and
the rotting wood acquired the power of sending up a
shoot, it would not be a bed that would come up, but
wood--which shows that the arrangement in accordance
with the rules of the art is merely an incidental
attribute, whereas the real nature is the other,
which, further, persists continuously through the
process of making.[23]

To put it another way, substances are natural beings, but artificial things are only accidentally substances, inasmuch as they
can be made of something that is natural and therefore substance.
In the canonical exposition of the theory of substance, in Book
VII of Metaphysics, we find a provisional enumeration of substances
which are natural beings:

Substance is thought to belong most obviously to bodies;
and so we say that not only animals and plants and their
parts are substances, but also natural bodies such as
fire and water and earth and everything of the sort, and
all things that are either parts of these or composed
of these (either of parts or of the whole bodies), e.g.
the physical universe and its parts, stars and moon and
sun.[24]

This could not be clearer, but it so happens that when he
has to explain the ontological structure of substance, Aristotle
turns to two pairs of concepts, matter and form, potentiality
and act, which present many difficulties. I shall allude as
briefly as possible to some of these.
    Matter, for Aristotle, is that of which ($\dot{\epsilon}\xi$ o$\tilde{\upsilon}$) a thing is
made; form is that which shapes or structures matter in order to
constitute thus an actual individual thing ($\sigma\acute{\upsilon}\nu o\lambda o\nu$). But when
he attempts to illustrate this, he says that matter is the bronze;
the form, the figure of the idea; and the statue, the substance
formed of both.[26] Elsewhere, the example may be a table or similar object.[26] In other words, Aristotle finds the clear presence
of substance where rightly there is no substance in artificial
being ($\dot{\alpha}\pi\grave{o}$ $\tau\acute{\epsilon}\chi\nu\eta\varsigma$). It would be more difficult to specify the

matter in an olive tree or a horse, and to state what makes up
their being. In cases where this would seem easier, for example,
if we speak of water or earth, statements about their form turn
out to be uncertain. It is hard to describe the form, or eîdos,
which constitutes and shapes them. The matter-form scheme as an
explanation of substance has less application the truer the substance in question. It becomes simple and clear only when applied
to an artificial human product; for after all, the scheme is based
on such artificial things.

If we turn instead to natural beings, things are still more
complicated. In attempting to explain in depth what motion is,
Aristotle adopts the concepts of potentiality (δύναμις) and act
(ἐντελέχεια or rather ἐνέργεια). Being is divided into potential
being and being-in-fact; what is presently A can potentially be
B. To move, or change, consists in that this thing, which is
only potentially B, should pass to be fully B in fact and actuality. Let us not misunderstand: what happens, what moves or
changes, is the thing which is A and B, not A or B as such. In
this thing which provisionally is A, B is present to a certain
extent as a potentiality or possibility. When B is present, the
thing is simply B, and is no longer A, and we have a new state of
being. But when the potentiality or possibility of being B
ceases to be mere possibility and begins to be realized, when
something is being B, when the potentiality to be B--and not B
itself--is actualized, we say that the thing is in motion. This
explains why Aristotle defines motion as "The fulfilment of what
exists potentially, in so far as it exists potentially."[27]
In other words--no doubt too few for so arduous a question--
when the thing that may be B is limited to mere possibility, it
is only A; but when it is becoming B, it is a moving reality
that is neither A nor B but rather a strange state of being-in-
flux that Greek philosophy before Aristotle could not comprehend.

Under the term "potentiality" are concealed two very different categories, which Aristotle points out in Chapter V of Book
IX of his Metaphysics. Some potential qualities are inherent
and others are acquired as by habit (like playing the flute) or
by apprenticeship (like technical skills). Habitual skills require preparatory exercise, while inherent qualities of a passive
nature, like the senses, do not. Furthermore, potentialities may
be rational (μετὰ λόγου) or irrational (ἄλογοι). The former necessarily reside in a living being, but the latter may appear
either in animated beings or elsewhere. In the case of irrational abilities, when the agent and the patient approach each other,
one must act and the other suffer. Yet the same does not occur
with rational abilities. The reason for this is that each irrational ability produces only one effect, while rational abilities
produce contrary results. Should they act necessarily and automatically, they would produce opposing results simultaneously,
which is impossible. Thus the mere presence of the agent and
the patient is not enough; something else is necessary: desire

(ὄρεξις) or selection (πρ‎αίρεσις); only with these may acquired abilities be actualized.[28]

In the following chapter, Aristotle introduces another extremely important distinction. It deals with two classes of motion; in some there is a terminus (πέρας) and when it is reached, motion terminates. In others there is an end (τέλος), but no terminus, and upon achieving this end and actuality motion does not terminate, but rather continues. Aristotle refers to the first class strictly as motions; the second might more correctly be called acts (κίνησις contrasts in this sense with ἐνέργεια).[29] Ortega commented on this important passage in Aristotle with unequalled insight and depth, showing its connection to another Aristotelian text,[30] which has not been sufficiently studied,[31] but which deserves a study in depth that I cannot undertake in the present context. Still, the following paragraphs by Ortega are enlightening:

> The change from white to black begins in the thing which is white and terminates when it has become black. Every change, inasmuch as it is motion and passage, implies a terminus when it comes and another terminus whither it goes. The word "terminus" (πέρας) clearly reveals that when it is reached, change has ended. Now then, in the preceeding example the terminus is "to be black" and "to be black" is not the same reality as "to blacken." Between the change itself and its terminus exists thus a radical difference, or to put it another way, the terminus lies beyond the change; it is different from the change itself. The other examples which Aristotle gives are of the same type: it is not the same to slenderize as to have slenderized (to be slender), to learn and to have learned, to recuperate and to have recuperated.
>
> But let us consider another reality: the thinking man, the man who is meditating. To think is to bring about a change in man. From being one who does not think in A, he goes on to become one who thinks in A. This passage is precisely what we call "thinking." To enter a state of thinking A is to be already thinking A and to continue thinking the same A as long as this act of thinking persists. On the other hand, by man "not thinking A," we must understand "not presently thinking A," but always having the potentiality so to think. As all movement, to think is to free oneself from potentiality as such. But here the change is no different from its terminus, as "to blacken" is from "to be black." In the change implied by thinking, the terminus, that to which we go, is already in the change; it is inherent in the change, or, in other words, the change is not produced to enhance some being other than

74

itself, but rather for the benefit of change itself. Let us attempt to express this in another way: all movement implies the making or becoming of something; movement is movement toward a <u>terminus</u>. The act of constructing ends in a constructed work. To construct is to make, and the finished work is that which is made. And when the work is finished, the act of constructing stops, leaving the work in its place. But let us imagine that the work visualized consists necessarily of an act of doing, as when we propose not to go to a place, but to go for a walk. The act of thinking, as in all change, involves transition and movement, but it also presents the paradoxical condition that to think is not to go from thought into something else. Rather it means an increase or an advance or "progress towards itself"--εἰς αὐτὸ γὰρ ἡ ἐπίδοσις. . . . The entire paragraph from <u>De Anima</u>, to which the above cited references belong, excludes indecision. "It is not correct to call meditation change or alteration--otherwise, we should perhaps have to distinguish between two genres of change."

If Aristotle had insisted more on the disturbing question he discovered, this immediate consequence would have occurred to him: that in counterpoising the type of change or movement known as "thought," to that kind of modification that is "change into something else" (alteration or transition), that is, to what he calls <u>sensu stricto</u> movement, a new definition becomes necessary that also shows the differences between the two kinds of movement. And if it can be said that "movement" is merely potentiality as regards the present, then thinking would be the act of becoming the potentiality of itself, the present <u>qua</u> potentiality. . . . The transition from initial potentiality to the act of thinking does not imply the <u>destruction of that potentiality</u>; rather <u>it retains that which is potentially in that which exists as perfection</u> (entelechy), <u>so that potentiality and act assimilate each other.</u>[32]

In the passage from <u>On the Soul</u> cited by Ortega, Aristotle says that the human modes, such as meditating or thinking, are not rightly alterations (ἀλλοίωσις), or if they are, they must be otherwise understood. Alteration, in effect, means μεταβολή εἰς ἄλλο, a change to the other, while the thinking is literally the contrary, ἐπίδοσις εἰς αὐτό, progress towards itself.[33] This is closely related to the idea examined earlier that acquired and rational potentialities are actualized only through an orexis or proaíresis. Because of this, man, in addition to zoé--life as biological realization of his inherent potentialities--also has a bíos which he has had to select (because "the lives of men differ greatly").[34] Bíos assumes a superior and more human form as

theoría, that exceptional mode of "movement" which in the strict
sense is not movement at all but rather enérgeia, and which feeds
on potentiality.

At this point we come to the end of our long and perhaps
confusing passage through Aristotelian metaphysics, and we find
ourselves confronting the radical problem posed in his Politics.

> If, then, there is some end of the things we do, which
> we desire for its own sake (everything else being de-
> sired for the sake of this), and if we do not choose
> everything for the sake of something else (for at that
> rate the process would go on to infinity, so that our
> desire would be empty and vain), clearly this must be
> the good and the chief good. Will not the knowledge
> of it, then, have a great influence on life? Shall we
> not, like archers who have a mark to aim at, be more
> likely to hit upon what is right? If so, we must try,
> in outline at least to determine what it is, and of
> which of the sciences or capacities it is the object.
> It would seem to belong to the most authoritative art
> and that which is most truly the master of art. And
> politics appears to be of this nature. . . .[35]

And he goes on to say:

> Let us resume our inquiry and state, in view of the
> fact that all knowledge and every pursuit aims at
> some good, what it is that we say political science
> aims at and what is the highest of all goods achiev-
> able by action. Verbally there is very general agree-
> ment; for both the general run of men and people of
> superior refinement say that it is happiness, and
> identify living well and doing well with being happy;
> but with regard to what happiness is they differ,
> and the many do not give the same account as the wise.[36]

It is evident that only the laborious task undertaken previously gives full meaning to these passages and shows that they
are not plausible trivialities but a statement of the very problem
of human reality, understanding by the latter a certain way of
life which we choose in view of some good toward which we strive.
This good is not an end lying beyond life and thus alien to the
very activity in question but that state intrinsic to life itself
which is called happiness.

In formulating the program of his Politics on the last page of
Nicomachean Ethics (to which we shall soon return), and in taking up the old theme of Socratic investigation and even using
the same expression that Xenophon records for us.[37] Aristotle
states that his purpose is "to carry the philosophy of human things
to its fullest possible perfection" (ὅπως εἰς δύναμιν ἡ περὶ τα

ἀνθρώπινα φιλοσοφία τελειωθῆ).[38] In its operable and concrete
form, the latter is the third philosophical source of Greek political thought, the same source that shapes and gives impetus to
the most vital and profound dimension of Aristotelian Politics.

4. The Program of Aristotle's Politics

At the end of Nicomachean Ethics, Aristotle formulates the program of his Politics in a way closely approximating the content
of the actual work. To his way of thinking, evidently, the Ethics
and the Politics were but two parts of one and the same discipline,
two stages of a single intellectual task. It will be helpful to
cite this passage verbatim and to underline several points in
order to demonstrate that Aristotle was clearly aware of the
three sources of political thought previously considered. It
will also enable us to describe accurately the central philosophical theme of his Politics. Chapter IX of Book X of the Ethics
ends with these words:

> Must we not, then, next examine whence or how one
> can learn how to legislate? Is it, as in all other
> cases, from statesmen? Certainly it was thought to be
> a part of statesmanship. Or is a difference apparent
> between statesmanship and the other sciences and arts?
> In the others the same people are found offering to
> teach the arts and practising them, e.g. doctors or
> painters; but while the sophists profess to teach
> politics, it is practised not by any of them but by
> the politicians, who would seem to do so by dint of
> a certain skill and experience rather than of thought;
> for they are not found either writing or speaking about
> such matters (though it were a nobler occupation perhaps
> than composing speeches for the law-courts and the
> assembly), nor again are they found to have made states-
> men of their own sons or any other of their friends.
> But it was to be expected that they should if they
> could; for there is nothing better than such a skill
> that they could have left to their cities, or could
> prefer to have for themselves, or, therefore, for
> those dearest to them. Still, experience seems to
> contribute not a little; else they could not have
> become politicians by familiarity with politics; and
> so it seems that those who aim at knowing about the
> art of politics need experience as well.
> But those of the sophists who profess the art
> seem to be very far from teaching it. For, to put
> the matter generally, they do not even know what kind
> of thing it is nor what kinds of things it is about;
> otherwise they would not have classed it as identical

with rhetoric or even inferior to it, nor have
thought it easy to legislate by collecting the
laws that are thought well of; they say it is possible to select the best laws, as though even the
selection did not demand intelligence and as though
right judgment were not the greatest thing, as in
matters of music. For while people experienced in
any department judge rightly the works produced in
it, and understand by what means or how they are
achieved, and what harmonizes with what, the inexperienced must be content if they do not fail to see
whether the work has been well or ill made--as in
the case of painting. Now laws are as it were the
"works" of the political art; how then can one learn
from them to be a legislator, or judge which are
best? Even medical men do not seem to be made by
a study of text-books. Yet people try, at any rate,
to state not only the treatments, but also how particular classes of people can be cured and should be
treated--distinguishing the various habits of body;
but while this seems useful to experienced people,
to the inexperienced it is valueless. Surely,
then, while collections of laws, and of constitutions also, may be serviceable to those who can
study them and those who go through such collections without a practised faculty will not have
right judgment (unless it be as a spontaneous gift
of nature), though they may perhaps become more
intelligent in such matters.

Now our predecessors have left the subject of
legislation to us unexamined; it is perhaps best,
therefore, that we should ourselves study it, and
in general study the question of the constitution,
in order to complete to the best of our ability
our philosophy of human nature. First, then, if
anything has been said well in detail by earlier
thinkers, let us try to review it; then in the
light of the constitutions we have collected let
us study what sorts of influence preserve and
destroy states, and what sorts preserve or destroy
the particular kinds of constitution, and to what
causes it is due that some are well and others
ill administered. When these have been studied
we shall perhaps be more likely to see with a
comprehensive view, which constitution is best,
and how each must be ordered, and what laws and
customs it must use, if it is to be at its best.
Let us make a beginning of our discussion.[39]

The Meaning of Aristotelian Philosophy

Aristotle points out that politics presents a curious difference with respect to the other disciplines. Those who practice politics are not the people who teach it. As I showed earlier, Aristotle stresses the lack of true "technical" political thought proceeding from experience, from the struggle with the real problems of government. Aristotle proposes to remedy this deficiency. In this passage of the Ethics he not only states his intention of examining the existing constitutions of three different cities (an examination which he carries out in the Politics), but sets about compiling constitutions (apparently 158 in all), which he transcribed over a period of many years. Of these only the Constitution of Athens, found in an Egyptian papyrus by Sir Frederick G. Kenyon and published in 1891, has been preserved. We must bear in mind that in Aristotle, as we shall see later in detail, the trend toward the consideration of historical deeds and the real functioning of the diverse forms of government is rather pronounced; Books VI-VIII in the order adopted by Newman and used in the present work (IV-VI in the traditional order) are dedicated to these themes and constitute the most peculiar and characteristic elements of Aristotle's Politics.

With respect to the ideals of politeía, which were the principal concern of contemporary political writers (principally the Sophists), it is apparent that Aristotle had little interest in them. This does not mean that the question is not extensively dealt with in his Politics--it has been the part of it most studied, precisely because it is what was to be expected in this type of treatise. But Aristotle, who follows the norm established by this literary genre, who discusses at length various opinions on the question, and who adds another to this class of works, has a reserved and critical attitude toward the entire matter. Let us recall the beginning of Book II where Aristotle, while declaring that he proposes to ascertain the best kind of government, also adds a significant restriction: ". . . for those who are living in conditions conforming as closely as possible to their desires (κατ᾽ εὐχήν)"; in other words, it is a matter of an ideal model, and by that same measure, a model that is unreal and probably unrealizable, possible only in a favorable conjunction of nature and fortune. Somewhat later, in criticizing Plato's reasonings in the Republic and in the Laws, Aristotle notes: "In framing an ideal, we may assume what we wish, but should avoid impossibilities."[40] And in the same passage cited above, at the beginning of Book II, he feels an obligation to justify his concern with the ideal form of government, after having examined not only the theories but also the constitutions existing in various cities in order that "the search for another solution beyond them would not seem simply a sophistical display. We only undertake this inquiry because all the constitutions with which we are acquainted are faulty."[41] What happens is that Aristotle, as we shall see later, neither believed in the efficacy of this procedure, nor, therefore, in the ideal politeía.

Finally, the truly effective element in the political thought of Aristotle is, as we have seen, its philosophical basis, which leads him to emphasize the possibility of human happiness in the destiny of pólis. But more importantly, if it is true that he considers the possible forms of human life (βίοι) and discovers that one form (theoretical life) is superior to the rest, and although he believes individual life and happiness to be essentially linked to the pólis, his hopes regarding the latter are very limited. He replaces the abstract ideal of an optimal politeía with what we would term a restricted or "negative" ideal. This new ideal would require two things of the politeía: from the point of view of the individual, it should permit the development of personal life, and consequently make happiness possible (though he is far from being confident that it could positively produce or guarantee it); as regards the pólis, politeía must exist in fact and it must offer stability and security (ἀσφάλεια). This latter aspect is, in my opinion, the central concept of Aristotelian political thought. For Aristotle, beginning with a strictly philosophical problem was to make his way through the ideation of a politeía, according to the norms of contemporary authors of treatises, and end up at the question which truly mattered to him: the effective reality of the pólis and the security, or aspháleia, afforded by regimes.

5. The Reality of the Pólis

The most difficult problem posed from this point of view, not only in Aristotle but in all Greek thought, is whether, and if so to what degree, their political treatises affect social reality. In speaking of pólis, or of community or koinonía, are we dealing with society or with the State? Is this distinction even meaningful for the Greeks? In any case, whether or not the pólis is society, are there other societies? And above all, there is an even more important question: apart from whatever type of reality the pólis involves, does the pólis itself possess reality? The social atomism of the Sophists, analogous to the physics of Leucippus and Democritus, was rooted in individual reality and its attendant egoism, and it tended to interpret the city as a mere pact or agreement without any essential reality of its own.[42] What is Aristotle's position on this point?

His position is quite clear: the pólis--in general, the koinonía--does possess reality. It is "one of the natural things" (τῶν φύσει ἡ πόλις ἐστί), and "man is a social animal because of nature" (ἄνθρωπος φύσει πολιτικὸν ζῷον).[43] Why is this true? Aristotle refers to the necessity and the origin of cities: the first two chapters of Book I of Politics attempt to justify the reality of the pólis and its genesis. The genus proximum to which the "species" city belongs is the community, or koinonía; the latter is constituted with a view to some end, and, therefore, to some good. The difference between the communities is not merely quantitative, but qualitative and truly specific. In his investigation of the elements of the city Aristotle seeks to verify that both the structure of the city and the more complex organization of the pólis are natural and necessary realities. The most elemental and simple community is the household (οἰκία), that is, the "family unit" in the older sense of man and wife, children, and slaves. The incorporation of several families with the consequent formation of a "colony" of related families is the village (κώμη); the incorporation of various villages constitutes the city (πόλις), which is the perfect and sufficient community. This seems clear enough as far as it goes, but this is precisely the point where greater precision and caution are needed.

The family, in effect, is based on necessary and natural relationships: man and woman for procreation; master and slave for security and economic cooperation, the first, to lead and give orders, the second, to carry out those orders. The family is, therefore, the "natural" community, so constituted as to satisfy daily necessities. On the other hand, the village, a grouping of households, is a community structured in view of longer-range needs. The city, finally, the complete community of several villages, is sufficient: the necessities of life were its original end, but it also existed so that men might live well. Now then, the natural essence of the home and nothing more seems to be inferred from this reasoning. The formation of villages and cities would be something that might or might not occur; in any case, they would imply no intrinsic necessity, and would merely deal with secondary realities in no way arising necessarily from nature and man. In Aristotle's mind, nevertheless, this is not the case. "And therefore, if the earlier forms of society are natural, so is the state, for it is the end of them, and the nature of a thing is its end. For what each thing is when fully developed, we call its nature, whether we are speaking of a man, a horse, or a family."[44] And shortly thereafter he adds: "The city is by nature clearly prior to the family and to the individual, because the whole is of necessity prior to the part."[45] What does this mean?

We must reverse the course of our normal line of reasoning. Instead of taking the most elemental unit, the household, as a point of departure, and predicating the natural character from it (at least in a general way), we must understand that the basic element from the point of view of nature is the city, because the city is the end of the other communities--their perfection-- and they gravitate toward it. The city is already present in the family and the village as the télos, or end, which constitutes them, and is, therefore, their natural beginning. Both family and village are deficient and incomplete expressions of the community, and they reach their full natural reality only in the pólis. And this is precisely what nature is: the form that things assume once their generation is completed. The chronological

past of lower communities (on which Aristotle would not overly
insist because his purpose is not to outline historical evolution)
is not incompatible with the real and natural priority of the
city. Man is naturally destined to live in the city, and if he
does not do so it is either because he has not yet developed to
that point--but is undergoing that development--or because he is
not really a man but rather something more or less: either a
beast or a god.[46]

But then we must inquire more preemptorily of Aristotle regarding the principle of the community; in other words, why man
is destined by nature to live in cities, and why, notwithstanding,
sometimes he does not? In point of fact, man has been living
in cities for only a limited historical time; and the first man
who founded and established cities was then the cause of the
greatest good. To put it another way, how can the city be at
once "natural" and historical in origin?

Concerning this point, both the brilliant insight of Aristotle
and the limitation of his form of thought are manifested at the
same time. He begins with the fact that man is the only animal
who possesses words (λόγος); the other animals have only voices
(φωνή) with which mutually to express pleasure and pain. Words
have a higher function: to say what is good or bad, just or unjust, convenient or harmful: "the community of those things,"
he states, "is what constitutes the family and the city."[47]
What does this mean?

Pain and pleasure are private matters; a thing may be pleas-
ing or painful to me. But good or bad, just or unjust, are conditions of things: things are good or bad; with words, the logos,
man enunciates and says what things are; words make their truth
evident (ἀλήθεια). This is why be means of words men can reveal
truth that is not the private domain of the individual; it is
the truth of things, on which men can agree. This agreement or
concord (ὁμόνοια) is revealed in the ὁμολογία, or verbal agreement, which at the same time is its cause. This is why things
transcend the feelings and opinions of each man and why they
may be common or communicated. Truth and the telling of it make
the community possible.

We might ask why this is so, why men need to know what things
are, and why the mere expression of things is insufficient.
Rather man needs a meaningful logos. Aristotle's limitation is
that he does not attempt to explain this necessity; he begins
with the mere fact that man possesses words, and he joins it to
the general and abstract "principle" that nature does nothing in
vain. Withal, Aristotle really stops short of understanding.
If man possesses words, and nature does nothing in vain, then
man has to be a social animal: this is Aristotle's reasoning.[48]
A sounder approach would perhaps have been to discover and justify why man needs words, why he has no recourse other than to tell
what things are and to agree with other men, rather than simply
beginning with the faculties with which man is endowed.

The Meaning of Aristotelian Philosophy

Still, Aristotle frequently displays a perspicacity that
enables him to discover truth even when in fact he is not looking
for it. The end of the chapter reveals more than one might expect, and in part it makes up for the inadequacy of the suppositions on which it is based. Aristotle notes that the perfect
man is the best of all animals, but without law or justice he is
the worst; this is, of course, a commonplace of Greek thought.[49]
Aristotle does not stop here, however, but adds: ". . . since
armed injustice is the more dangerous, and he is equipped at
birth with arms, meant to be used by intelligence and virtue,
which he may use for the worst ends, . . ."[50] In other words,
given man's natural gifts, he still does not know how he will
use them. Both things and faculties or potentialities, as
Aristotle noted earlier, are defined by their fuction.[51] We
must consider this in relation to the distinction we saw before
in his Chapter II, that between inherent and acquired faculties.
The latter (along with rational powers) with which we are now
dealing are not automatically realized when they and the conditions necessary for their operation are given. They can be
realized in differing or even in opposing situations.

The direction they take depends on the decision made. Mere
potentiality is not enough; a desire or a choice is also necessary.
And in order to choose, in order to begin the proaíresis that is
capable of converting acquired potentialities into reality, man
needs to know what is good or bad, what is just and what is
unjust.

Social life (συζῆν) requires, then, that the meaning within
which human faculties function be commonly accepted; there must
be accord with respect to things and to justice. Only thus is
happiness (εὐδαιμονία) possible. The existence of the community,
in its concrete form as an agreement or accord, is the condition
necessary for the development of individual life, and consequently,
for their happiness. Plato's theme in his Seventh Epistle echoes
in different tones from the opening pages of Aristotle's Politics.
The meaning of human life and happiness is at stake. And since
this accord requires, as Socrates had earlier affirmed energeti-
cally, that men understand the good, the bad, the just, the unjust, the state, the ruler; and that they know what it means to
rule, to obey, etc. In short, they must know the truth about
the things of life, the science of man. Like an archer aiming
at a target,[50] he must look for his life--this need for knowledge
must culminate in an investigation of the pólis. It was for
just this reason that Aristotle felt it necessary to write a
"politics" in order to carry "the philosophy of human things to
its greatest possible perfection."

6. Pólis and politeía

Aristotle terms the agreement that makes life possible in the

city nómos, law. This fact is crucial: of all the Greek
thinkers, Aristotle is the one who comes closest to understanding social reality and yet, in the final analysis, it eludes
him, as it does all the Greeks. The Greeks viewed what we call
society as a "species" of the pólis--a word that can be translated as "state" only with a certain degree of exaggeration and
that is better rendered as "city." For to refer to it as "state"
is necessarily to have solved the problem already. In any case,
the pólis is the civil community, but at the same time, it is,
literally, the political community. In other words, the pólis
is not the "state"; the term implies, rather, a many-sided
reality that transcends the state because it is an entire society.
However, the perspective from which this society is viewed and
interpreted by Aristotle is certainly that of the state; a clearer way of expressing it would perhaps be that the pólis is the
state interpretation of society.

The fact is that Aristotle comes very close to discovering
social reality as something different from the pólis, and he
does this in the same way that leads to many great discoveries:
by analysis, the orderly separation of conglomerates. Because
Aristotle recognizes that there are other "communities" (κοινωνίαι)--
let us avoid still the term "societies"--besides the pólis: underlying it, as it were, are its building blocks, the family or home
or village, and encompassing the city is a vaster and different
unit, vaguely called éthnos. But the fact is that once Aristotle
becomes aware of these realities, he does not know what to make
of them; instead of tracing all these "communities" (including
of course the pólis) to a more basic substratum in which they
are present and possible--had he done so, he probably would have
discovered social reality in the strict and primary meaning of
the word--he sticks, more hellenico, to the pólis, and he attempts
once more to interpret social reality in strictly political ways.
Because of this, Aristotle writes a Politics and again describes
an ideal dealing with politeía, instead of advancing toward a
possible sociology. In this he repeats most of the traditional
topics appearing in writers from Hippodamus to Plato. Nevertheless, his personal experiences, enormous empirical knowledge, and
genius for remaining true to reality, will not let him stop with
the traditional; his intuition constantly overflows the mark
fixed by the "literary genre" he cultivates, and because of this
his Politics, so different from earlier works of this kind, is
more than merely another political writing.

First of all, there is always a certain hesitation evident
in Aristotle's questions about the end to which a city exists.
On the one hand, he is aware of the mutual benefits involved,
and therefore the diversity of governmental functions as well as
the obedience that go to make up a regime or constitution, e.g.,
the political aspect of the city. On the other hand, the fact
of social coexistence as such, as a form of life, "even without
any necessity for mutual aid," does not escape Aristotle. The

reason for this is that "perhaps in simply living there is a
certain degree of goodness, unless suppressed by excessive hard-
ships. It is evident that the majority of men bear many suffer-
ings because of the desire to live; and life appears to hold a
certain happiness and charm for them."[52] Now then, this bare
coexistence acquires form in the pólis. It offers "order" (τάξις),
especially with regard to power, making a systematic and perfect
structure of political life possible. In other words, in spite
of his living at the time of Alexander and--as has been repeated
so many times--in spite of his witnessing the defeat of the cities
and the establishment of great territorial monarchies, Aristotle
does not abandon the idea of the city; of all the possible social
structures, he believes, only the pólis possesses politeía. We
must delve into the significance of this view.

The only community that exhibits a precise and adequate
structure is the city, because it is a unit composed of a plurality of individuals of various classes, with a strictly qualitative
nature. It is a functional unit. If the city becomes too closely knit, says Aristotle, it will cease to be a city and will become a family or an individual. At the other extreme, the "nation"
in the old sense, the "people"--these expressions are vague because
what they describe is also unclear--lacks unity, its members do
not know each other. It is said that three days after Babylonia
had fallen many of its inhabitants had no idea what had happened.[53]
Those who maintain that Aristotle was blind to the world his
disciple Alexander was building, and that he remained stubbornly
attached to the pólis, are, so it seems to me, somewhat confused.
Aristotle was persuaded (we will soon see to what extent) that a
crisis of the city existed, but only in the city did he see the
possibility of constitution, of politeía. Alexander's conquests
and the organization of new territories, including the new order
of Hellas itself under Macedonian supremacy, were military, economic, and historical phenomena; they were not, as Aristotle
apparently saw, political phenomena in the strict sense of the
term. It must be said that Aristotle was right; the history of
Hellenism is understandable only if we recognize that the consequences of Hellenic-Macedonian expansion never attained to full
political reality, and that empire or no the cities persisted
as functioning centers of political life even after the fourth
century. For they, the cities, were the only possible communities.
This leads us to inquire about the nature of politeía.

A city, says Aristotle, is not merely a geographical unit;
it is not simply an area enclosed within walls. The entire
Peloponnesian peninsula might be encompassed so that the same
walls included Megara and Corinth, and still there would be no
city. Neither are we dealing with a law or pact of mutual assistance for the purpose of avoiding injustice; this would be an
alliance, if you will, but not a city. These are necessary conditions for a city to exist, but alone they are not enough. "And
the state is the union of families and villages in a perfect and

self-sufficient life, by which we mean a happy and honourable
life. Our conclusion, then, is that the political society exists
for the sake of noble actions, and not of mere companionship."[54]
That is, a common enterprise and not mere coexistence.

We must insist on the common character of this enterprise.
Aristotle is seeking the elements common to all cities; and he
discovers that neither geography nor race suffices; a principle
of another order is needed. The community of citizens of the
polis resembles the complement of sailors and officers on a ship.
In both are found the same division of functions, the same cooperation, the same dynamic community of the enterprise undertaken
within the same order: "For they have all of them a common object which is safety and navigation. Similarly, one citizen
differs from another, but the salvation of the community is the
common business of them all."[55]   For this reason, ". . . when the
form of the government changes and becomes different, then it may be
supposed that the state is no longer the same, just as tragic
differs from a comic chorus, although the members of both may be
identical. In this manner, we speak of every union or composition of elements as different when the form of their composition
alters."[56]

The politeía, the regime or constitution, is, therefore,
what actually gives form to the city, what constitutes it. "A
constitution is the organization of offices in a state, and determines what is to be the governing body, and what is the end
of each community."[57]   But this is to be taken more seriously
than would seem justified at first. The constitution is the
guiding principle of the city, its "life form": ἡ πολιτεία βίος
τις ἐστι πόλεως.[58]   Plato says that the politeía is "the imitation of the good life" (μίμησις τοῦ καλλίστου καὶ ἀρίστου βίου).[59]
Just as bíos determines that each individual is a certain human
type with a particular kind of life, so too is it the constitution
or politeía of the pólis. And since individual life can be realized and conditioned only within the pólis, we must return to
the beginning of Nicomachean Ethics where Aristotle expressly
says that as archers, we must finally search for our life target
in politics.

This leads us to a group of questions that serve to clarify
the meaning of Aristotelian "politics." In Chapter II of his
Politics we saw how Aristotle, in considering the ideal politeía
of Hippodamus of Miletus, at first was deeply alarmed and then
posed the fundamental question concerning the nature and modification of laws. "It has been doubted," he writes, "whether it
is or is not expedient to make any changes in the laws of the
country, even if another law be better." Then he adds: "It may
sometimes seem desirable to make change. Such changes in other
arts and sciences have certainly been beneficial; medicine, for
example, and gymnastic and every other art and craft have departed from their traditional usage, and, if politics be an art,
change must be necessary in this, as in any other art."[60]   Then

he goes on to insist upon the imperfection and rudimentary nature
of primitive laws and upon the inconvenience of following ancient
opinion. But this is only the first aspect of a problem that
conceals another more serious one. He then offers the following
observation upon which hangs the whole meaning of politics within the historical and intellectual context and experience of the
times:

> Hence we infer that sometimes and in certain cases
> laws may be changed; but when we look at the matter
> from another point of view, great caution would seem
> to be required. For the habit of lightly changing
> the laws is an evil, and when the advantage is small,
> some errors both of lawgivers and rulers had better
> be left; the citizen will not gain so much by making
> the change as he will lose by the habit of disobedience.
> The analogy of the arts is false; a change in a law is
> a very different thing from a change in an art. For
> the law has no power to command obedience except that
> of habit, which can only be given by time, so that a
> readiness to change from old to new laws enfeebles
> the power of the law.[61]

Over against the frivolity of constitutional and juridical
theoreticians, Aristotle veers in the other direction and approaches
what could have been his sociology. We cannot compare a law with
an art; law and right are not mere ideas but social realities;
they are social "norms." We are not primarily concerned at this
point with whether a law is good or bad but rather with the fact
that it exists, e.g., that the law is in force. It is impossible
to handle law as an ideology or an intellectual discipline because
it is something quite different. Aristotle says that it is a
force. And this force is social in nature, usage (ἔθος) that is
fashioned only over a long span of time (διὰ χρόνου πλῆθος). We
cannot speculate on social and political realities, on law and
constitution, because behind these ideas is the tremendous fact
of the pólis, of human social existence, in which the most mysterious and terrible powers of the world intervene: nature, fortune, and time (φύσις, τύχη, χρόνος). The city is sacred and in
the Greek mind is the handiwork of the gods; it is far too serious
a matter for a Hippodamus, with his long hair and bizarre behavior
and rationalistic frivolity, to decide how it "should" be structured.
  The most profound sphere of the constitution, the substance
of the pólis, is not even written laws (κατὰ γράμματα νόμοι),
which were conceived and legislated by someone at some particular
time, and which, after all, are merely ideas; customary laws
(κατὰ τὸ ἔθος), in short "usages," are far more important and
deal with far more important things; and if the ruler in a particular case is more trustworthy than written laws, then customary

A Biography of Philosophy

laws are far more trustworthy and powerful than even he.[62] In
the traditional usages generated over long periods of time, and
for that very reason obeyed and respected, reside all the strength
of the community, as well as the security of human life.

7. Security as a Theme of Politics

When Hippodamus, who was not a politician, began to write somewhat irresponsibly about the "best" form of government, Greek
cities still subsisted on a solid base of beliefs. It is certain,
however, that some of these beliefs had already begun to weaken; because of the above stated reasons (Chapter I), life in the Greek
cities had begun a dangerous transformation in the middle of the
fifth century. The naturalistic philosophy of the Ionians and the
Sophistic philosophy were immediate causes of it, but in the beginning they were an effect rather than a cause of the changing
situation. It is well known that in Athens new ideas, especially
philosophy, appeared quite late. The first philosopher who lived
in Athens was an Ionian (Anaxagoras); there is no Athenian philosopher before Socrates. Aristophanes' The Clouds, from the year 423,
brought to light a hostile and alarmed reaction to the appearance
of a new way of life. This hostility was accompanied by ignorance,
and consequently the two different intellectual currents (the
Ionian "physiology" and Sophistic thought) were confused, more
or less voluntarily in Aristophanes,[63] and certainly unintention-
ally by the public. In satirizing Socrates and his disciples,
Aristophanes does not even know how to classify them and their
school--σοφισταί, φροντισταί, φροντιστήριον (sages, thinkers, a
think-shop)--the very fact that such a "school" did not exist
emphasizes his lack of familiarity and exact knowledge of the
group. But the fact is quite significant and unequivocal that
in The Clouds the "just and unjust discourse" (δίκαιος καὶ ἄδικος
λόγος) enter into dialog, and that traditional education and
modern corruption are juxtaposed.

When Aristotle wrote his Politics almost a century had
passed. The process begun in times of Hippodamus, Socrates, and
Aristophanes was now complete. Aristotle, a man without a country,
as Jaeger observes,[64] had witnessed the decline of a historical
era, and in addition, his information offers an almost inexhaustible repertory of political vicissitudes. A fundamental conviction is apparent in his thinking: the life of the cities is
essentially insecure; all constitutions are affected by radical
instability; they are threatened by dissension and revolution,
and they experience first one and the other; and none of the
political forms has an easy time surviving. The fundamental insecurity of government (and therefore of cities) and the precari-
ous situation of social existence and individual life is a most
serious matter indeed. It is the primary problem of Aristotle's
Politics.

The Meaning of Aristotelian Philosophy

For this reason, the last two books, VII-VIII (V-VI in the traditional order) are devoted to investigating carefully and factually the causes of, and possible solutions to, revolution in all forms of government. At one point Aristotle clearly expresses his point of view:

> The mere establishment of a democracy is not the only or principal business of the legislator, or of those who wish to create such a state, for any state however badly constituted, may last one, two, or three days; a far greater difficulty is its preservation. The legislator should therefore endeavor to have a firm foundation according to the principles already laid down concerning the preservation and destruction of states; he should guard against the destructive elements, and should make laws, whether written or unwritten, which will contain all the preservatives of states. He must not think the truly democratical or oligarchical measure to be that which will give the greatest amount of democracy or oligarchy, but that which will make them last longer.[65]

Aristotle believes that any regime can be established and thus begin to exist. Yet the fact that a regime may last three days, for instance, does not mean that it effectively exists. Rather, its existence implies persistence. Persistence or duration is the form of existence of governments; for the latter are based on the social cohesion made possible by usages forged in the passing of time and respected because of their antiquity. Therefore, the fundamental problem of politics is not which regime is best but rather how governments may exist and endure regardless of their form. The theme of political science is not the ideal of politeía, the perfect constitution, but rather something much more modest and yet more urgent: "security" (ἀσφάλεια).

For this reason, adherence to a type of government depends not on the purity of its form but rather on its perpetuation and longevity. What carries democracy to extremes is not democratic, nor are those forces tyrannical which push tryanny to its limits. Rather, the essence of tyranny or democracy is that which assures their preservation even though it be in a diminished state that falls short of their fulfillment.

Clearly Aristotle could not have conceived of this idea without himself experiencing the instability of all governments. He had to have an utter lack of faith in an ideal of politeía. He felt himself under an obligation to outline this ideal, because doing so was "required" of any writer on politics, but it is equally certain that his heart was not in the task, not even intellectually, and he immediately divided governments into various pure forms, as distinct from their deviations or degenerations (παρεκβάσεις). And what is still more significant, he

89

gives both equal attention. With the eye of a naturalist, the commentators usually say (and with the eye of a historian, one might add), he examines the structure and internal requirements of each extant and possible regime. Of course, he does not forget the question of whether they are bad, but this consideration is not extremely important to him. He is more interested in their viability and efficiency and in the real conditions under which they exist. Shunning affectation, he studies the leaders of democracy or oligarchy who, for instance, pay the poor to attend the assembly and excuse the rich whether or not they attend.[66] He finds it perfectly reasonable that the royal guard be essentially different from the tyrannical: "Wherefore also their guards are such as a king and not such as a tyrant would employ, that is to say, they are composed of citizens, whereas the guards of tyrants are mercenaries. For kings rule according to law over voluntary subjects, but tyrants over involuntary; and the one are guarded by their fellow-citizens, the others are guarded against them."[67]

Faithful to this attitude, Aristotle poses in the broadest terms the problem of asphaleia, or security. Some constitutions are better than others, no doubt, but not all are adequate for all cities or for all circumstances. A grave political error that had deeply undermined the stability of Greek life was that leading powers, as Athens and Sparta, had tried to extend their own rule indiscriminately. He writes: "Further, both the parties which had the supremacy in Hellas looked only to the interest of their own form of government, and established in states, the one, democracies, and the other, oligarchies; they thought of their own advantage, of the public not at all."[68] And a few lines later, after discussing the best form of rule, he adds: "For that which is nearest to the best must of necessity be better, and that which is furthest from it worse, if we are judging absolutely and not relatively to given conditions: I say 'relatively to given conditions,' since a particular government may be preferable, but another form may be better for some people."[69]

The consequence of this is quite clear. In principle, the theme of politics is the reality of each form of government and, therefore, the requirements necessary for its continued existence. Men must know the nature of monarchy, oligarchy, democracy, tyranny, etc. They must be aware of what "constitutes" these forms of government, just as they must know what has to be done to keep and preserve them. Aristotle is the great theoretician of effective political conduct, and his norms are derived from the analysis of historical experience. Events that had actually occurred in Hellas and elsewhere, involving every kind of regime and government, were his source of political truth. And the melancholy and disquieting lesson he deduces from history is that all regimes are susceptible to instability and failure. This in turn implies that cities must needs change and in changing become something different as laws lose their force and individual life becomes less secure.

All this leads Aristotle to the study of an odd form of government that is not only different from all pure forms but is based on the very opposite of purity: the combination or mixture (μίξις) of several forms of government, which is superior to any single form. This is the famous "mixed government," the constitution Aristotle designates, for want of a better term, with the generic name of politeía, "republic." This hybrid regime, which earlier had so interested Plato and which was to enjoy an extremely long existence as a political idea, if not as an actual form of government in the several states, results from the skillful combination of all known constitutions. This allowed certain advantages to be derived from each of them, as it avoided the pitfalls that otherwise rendered them all unstable. Ortega has observed that this is a solution born of despair, a consequence of the absolute lack of confidence in all forms of government after they have been tried and found wanting.[70] He refers to it as the "maximum remedy" of the ancient apothecaries, that is, as a mixture of all medicines to be taken when each individual treatment has proved ineffective. By analogy, the mixed or composite form of government is the positive political expression of the failure of all regimes.

At this point Aristotle subordinates everything to two factors: first, the possibility of existence of a form of government; and second, its stability once a regime is established:

> We have now to inquire what is the best constitution for most states, and the best life for most men, neither assuming a standard or virtue which is above ordinary persons, nor an education which is exceptionally favored by nature and circumstances, nor yet an ideal state which is an aspiration only, but having regard to the life in which the majority are able to share, and to the form of government which states in general can attain.[71]

This means forsaking the traditional position of political writers: instead of hypothesizing ideal conditions in order to establish therein a regime "according to one's heart's desire," Aristotle sticks to real possibilities so as to consider what may be done in states that are real rather than hypothetical. One must deal with real conditions because the basis of good legislation is not well-intended laws that go unobeyed, but rather laws that are first obeyed and then questioned as to their fairness.[72]

The hybrid regime is the most secure and stable; herein lie its excellence and justification. The balance between differing political forces should be used to effect the equilibrium and permanence of the regime: "In a well attempered polity, there should appear to be both elements and yet neither; also the government should rely on itself, and not on foreign aid, and on

itself not through the goodwill of a majority--they might be
equally well disposed when there is a vicious form of government--
but through the general willingness of all classes in the state
to maintain the constitution."[73] To accomplish this balance,
the government in question (the politeía or republic) should be
an intermediate regime (μεταξύ) and be politically constituted
by the middle class. To his historical experience, Aristotle
now added his theory of the golden mean (μεσότης). This idea
lies at the very heart of his ethical theory of virtue and it
has deep metaphysical roots. The intermediate regime is best
"since it is the only one free of sedition" (μόνη γὰρ ἀστασίαστος).[74]

This and this alone was the question. The cycle was complete.
Since the happier times of Hippodamus all possible experiences
had befallen, all forms of government had been tried, and attempts
based on many different views had been made to improve the political order. In the waning days of the pólis, Aristotle considered
all manners of reform. But there was something even more important than the political qualities of the cities: their very
existence. Dissociation threatened all of Greek life. Public
accord had been lost for many years; men no longer knew what
was good or bad, just or unjust. Above all, they had no clear
idea as to who should rule. Aristotle retired unto himself, and
renouncing what hitherto had been dearest to the Greek mind--the
unreal--he turned instead to historical reality, to the incessant
political activity of the previous century, and to constitutions
painstakingly collected. From this material, he attempted to
draw a formula that would permit a new accord and a minimal amount
of security, so that men might have some hope that their lives
were aimed at a target of happiness. Today there remain of
Aristotle's laborious effort the eight books entitled Politics.

CHAPTER IV
Stoic Philosophy

1. The Appearance of Hellenistic Philosophies

Aristotle died in 322 B.C. on the island of Euboea. With his
death ends a period of incomparable philosophical activity in
Greece, beginning with Socrates and lasting approximately a
century. In Plato and Aristotle, philosophy reaches hitherto
unknown heights of intellectual exactitude and rigor which have
served as examples of what philosophy should be to subsequent
ages. Over the centuries whatever has appeared under the name
"philosophy" has inevitably been compared to Platonic-Aristotelian thought. These two systems have had--and continue to have--
such an undying authority that they can be said to have given
rise to almost all medieval and modern philosophy.
     Around the year 315 B.C., Zeno of Citium, a Cypriot merchant
of Phoenecian origin, found himself shipwrecked and destitute in
Athens, where he established a school of philosophy in the Portico
of Paintings, Stoa Poikíle, a kind of museum decorated with the
paintings of Polygnotus. Henceforth, Stoicism, which was already
a flourishing movement, began to supplant older doctrines, and
eventually it very nearly became the only philosophy of the time--
a very long time, lasting at least five hundred years. We must
ask what took place. What was the nature of this doctrine, which
so rapidly replaced the greatest intellectual creations of the
Greek genius?
     Two rather different though subsequently related aspects
are suggested by the foregoing: first, the fate of Aristotelianism after the death of its founder; and second, the triumph of
Stoicism, along with several lesser doctrines, in the life of the
Hellenic peoples. It is well known, of course, that Aristotle
did not find a disciple of his own philosophical stature. Thus
Theophrastus, Meno, Dycearcus, Strato of Lampsaca, even Eudemus,
all successors to Aristotle in the Lyceum, were far less than
their master. In one sense, this is due to mere chance, but
even were it nothing more than chance, we cannot lose sight of

93

the role played by fate in human life. Without the factum of
the existence of the man Plato, what would have been the fate
of Socratism in Greece? We may hazard a guess if we consider
the other results of Socratic teaching: Xenophon in one case
and the Cynic-Cyrenaic morality in another. Within the same
historical circumstance we have a comparable example: the
appearance of Aristotle, a foreigner, in the Platonic Academy.
Without Aristotle, Plato's philosophy would have had approximately the same fate it later had in the Academy itself. Now then,
Aristotle did not have Socrates' luck in finding another Plato
or anyone else who could play the same role Aristotle himself
had in the Academy.

We are dealing not with a question of mere intellectual
ability but rather primarily with a problem of attitude toward
philosophy. Any philosophy admits of many dimensions that are
generally embryonic and function in the strict sense as possibilities. More than any other single factor, the selection of one
or another of these dimensions determines the final fate of a
philosophy. Plato had the genius to retain the most promising
possibilities of Socratic thought, possibilities of which the
Cynics, for example, had not the slightest inkling. Aristotle
began his philosophy with the central problems of Platonism,
and his point of departure is precisely those points where his
master's thought becomes ultimately questionable. Thus, in
ceasing to be Platonic, in reality he remained true to that form
of thought in the only possible way. Spheusippus and his followers in the Academy confined themselves meanwhile to mere Platonic
scholarship; and in their idle cultivation of dialectic, the
academics thus foundered in an empty scepticism, totally removed
from the real Plato.

The case of Aristotle is even more serious. The extraordinary
richness of Aristotelian philosophy involved a risk. In the first
place, there was perhaps no one after his death capable of fully
grasping the totality of his knowledge. Aristotle had created a
series of disciplines that either were entirely new with him or
only germinally present in earlier philosophy. Not only were
these disciplines hard to master in the first place, but they
also tended to cause astonishment. And in fact, we can see how
in the Lyceum, especially, the most characteristic but also the
most superficial dimensions of Aristotle's encyclopedic knowledge
are cultivated: works on the history of the physical and mathematical sciences (Theophrastus, Eudemus, Meno, Dycearcus); and
botanical, zoological, and even biological works, like those of
Theophrastus, who also wrote Characters, a series of descriptive
essays whose intellectual roots are found in Aristotle's Ethics.
The natural aspect of Aristotle's thought is so emphasized that
Strato considers the Prime Mover, God, to be the province of
physis. Together with this development of natural questions and
of Aristotelian logic as a formal discipline--both of undeniable
influence on the progress of Hellenic science--there is a growing

indifference toward the deeper metaphysical questions that confer upon Aristotelianism its highest value and unlimited potentiality. The ultimate proof of this is the fact that the eleventh Scholar of the Lyceum after Aristotle, Andronicus of Rhodes, who lived in the first century B.C., though steeped in Stoic thought, could not decide what to make of the fourteen books of the so-called First Philosophy. In his edition of Aristotle he placed them after the writings on physics, thus creating accidentally--but happily--the term metaphysics.

There was, then, a change of attitude toward philosophy. Very early within the Lyceum itself, philosophy came to be understood not so much as the próte philosophía of Aristotle, the science about being as such, but rather as secondary disciplines devoid of real metaphysical substance. These disciplines included "logic," thought of especially as a dialectical art, "physics," the sum of knowledge about natural things, and "ethics," interpreted as mere studies of character or as a repertory of the norms of life. To a greater or lesser degree, this was the view of philosophy not only of the Stoics but also, in the final analysis, of all the Romano-Hellenistic moral philosophers. This is an extraordinary fact that deserves special attention. But such attention not only does not resolve the problem but rather presents it more emphatically. Why, in fact, did things happen the way they did? Aside from fortuity, which is perhaps not so accidental as it seems at first glance, that after Aristotle there were no philosophers of comparable magnitude, why did the attitude toward philosophy change after his death? This question lies beyond the scope of this writing; nevertheless, it will be necessary to treat it cursorily later.

We have witnessed the evaporation as it were of Aristotelianism beginning as early as the end of the fourth century B.C. Within Greece itself, his thought enjoyed but slight historical vitality. This fact contrasts sharply with the eminent intellectual qualities of Aristotelianism and its later marked influence on the Christian world. The other side of the coin reveals the strange exuberance of Stoicism for some five hundred years and its lasting effect on later periods. What exactly was the fate of that historical reality we call Stoicism?

The third century B.C. is replete with the history of the ancient Stoa. Zeno was a disciple of several philosophers, especially of the cynic Crates and of Stylpo, and later of Xenocrates, Polemon, and Diodorus of Megara. In other words, he was influenced by several rather obscure moralists who adhered somewhat indirectly to Socratic thought. Zeno himself was a sailor and merchant, a man of action, remote from theoretic life, a man who traveled not to see (θεωρίης εἵνεκεν) but rather to buy and sell, though later he calmly accepts shipwreck and the loss of his wealth. These facts of his life, together with his Asiatic background (a frequent occurrence in early Stoicism), are clearly significant in the total meaning of his philosophy. After many

95

years of teaching in Porticus (fifty-eight years, according to Diogenes Laertes), Zeno died at a very advanced age, leaving another Asiatic, Cleanthes of Assos (c. 330-c. 231) as the head of the school. Cleanthes was a former boxer who had arrived in Athens with four drachmas and who, as the story goes, had drawn water from the wells by night in order to pay his way in Zeno's school by day. Cleanthes had an elemental mind of little theoretical import. Stoicism prospered through a more astute disciple, Chrysippus of Soli in Cilicia (Asia Minor), who became the third master of the school. Chrysippus (c. 280-c. 204) can be considered the true founder of Stoicism, or at least of the Stoic doctrine. Of him it is said: "Had Chrysippus not lived, there would have been no Stoa" (εἰ μὴ γὰρ ἦν Χρύσιππος οὐκ ἄν ἡ Στοά). According to Diogenes Laertes, he wrote more than seven hundred books, but only a few titles and fragments are extant. In the second century, the prominence of the principal Stoic thinkers declined (among them Diogenes the Babylonian and Antipater of Tarsus), but the doctrine itself continued to attract large numbers of adherents throughtout the Hellenistic world.

In the same century and until the beginning of the first century B. C., there occurs a renascence of the Stoa under the name Middle Stoicism. Its principal leaders were Panaetius of Rhodes (c. 180-c. 110), greatly influenced by the teachings of the Academy, and the Syrian Posidonius (c. 135-35), who actively cultivated the individual sciences. It was at this time that Stoicism began to exert a profound influence on Rome. Panaetius was a friend of Scipio Africanus and of Lelius, and it is well known that the Scipio family was one of the first to begin Hellenizing Rome. Besides, Panaetius lived in Rome several years while Posidonius taught in Rhodes, a center of learning for many cultured Romans. To a certain extent, Middle Stoicism broke down the inflexible dogmatism of the school and allowed other movements to influence it. After a time it acquired a somewhat eclectic and Romanized aspect which was to be characteristic of the final stage of the Stoa.

The new Stoicism of the first two centuries of the Christian Era is firmly Roman. It matters little that of its three main representatives, two wrote in Greek and one of these was not even a Roman. The school was essentially affected by the conditions of life during the Imperial period and therefore its center had to be Rome. Seneca (c. 4 B.C.-A.D. 65) was the most important and productive of this group, and it was he who had the greatest lasting influence. After Seneca came Epictetus (c. A.D. 50-c. 120), a Phrygian, who before being ransomed had been a slave of Epaphroditus himself a former slave and later favorite of Nero. Of Epictetus' works, his Dissertations, or Diatribes, and a short Manual, or Enquiridion, of morality are preserved. The last of this group was the emperor Marcus Aurelius Antoninus (A. D. 121-180) who wrote his famous Soliloquies in Greek (Εἰς ἑαυτόν). Subsequently Stoicism declined in influence and doctrinal purity, giving way to

various neo-Platonic and Oriental doctrines, which would completely dominate the Roman Empire until the end of the Classical Age.
    It is apparent, then, that a strong current of Stoicism
dominated the Greco-Roman world for half a millenium. Whereas
Aristotelianism lost its influence after the death of the great
philosopher, the crude speculation of Zeno of Citium was endued
with lasting vitality. And beyond the sphere of strictly "classical" thought Stoicism continued to exercise a great influence
throughout the Middle Ages. Its influence became even more
pronounced during the Renaissance, and it persists even today
in much of modern literature and philosophy.[3] This brings us
to the question of the doctrinal content of this philosophy,
which has displayed such remarkable historical longevity.

2. The Stoic Doctrine

The Stoics divide philosophy into three parts: logic, physics,
and ethics. However, they insist that these three parts are
inseparable. We need not go into detail at this point regarding
their mutual relationship and hierarchy. It suffices to say that
ethics absorbs the greater amount of attention on the part of
the Stoics, and all their efforts at philosophizing are directed
toward it. Like the Epicureans, the Stoics cling more to pre-
Socratic doctrines than to Platonic-Aristotelian philosophy.
Thus it would be a mistake to believe that the speculative tradition of the "physiologists" was dead in Greece. One need only
note the attention that Aristotle himself devotes to it, especially in Book I of Metaphysics and in the first four of Physics.
After Aristotle, there was a return to ancient doctrines, with
the Epicureans looking to Democritus, the Stoics to Heraclitus.
    The thought of the Stoa is sensualist. Knowledge consists
of an "apprehension" of its object by means of an impression made
by the object on the soul. When the representation is totally
clear, it induces a concurrence or assent in the mind which is
the active element of knowledge. This is when knowledge takes
possession of its object (φαντασία καταληπτική). Zeno was fond
of expressing the process of knowledge with the following comparison: the open hand with the fingers extended is mere vision or
representation; the half-closed hand is assent; the clenched fist
is comprehension; and finally, the clenched fist in the grip of
the other hand is science.[4] In other words, to know is to take
possession of a thing in an almost physical and corporal sense.
This idea leads to a kind of nominalism; that is, Zeno denies
the reality of Platonic ideas and instead confines existence to
individual things only.
    Universal consent is determined by notiones communes, or
common notions (κοιναι εννοιαι), held by all men. The belief
grew that such notions are innate, and this has had lasting
consequences in all modern theories of "innate ideas."

97

Stoic physics admits two principles: the "active" and the "passive" (τὸ ποιοῦν καὶ τὸ πάσχον). The passive principle is undifferentiated "matter"; the active principle is the "reason" (λόγος) that dwells in matter and is called "god" (ὁ θεός). The active principle assumes a corporal nature and mingles with matter like a generating fluid (hence their reference to it as seminal reason or λόγος σπερματικός). Furthermore, the two "principles" (ἀρχαί) are distinguished from the four "elements" (στοιχεῖα): fire, water, air, and earth.

However, the active principle interpreted corporally is identified with fire, following the inspiration of Heraclitus. The subtle element of fire imparts movement to matter and is responsible for its transformations. Nature is conceived on the model of τέχνη, of "art." This is why fire is called "artifice" (πῦρ τεχνικόν). From time to time a great "conflagration" (ἐκπύρωσις) envelopes the earth; in due course it returns to the primordial fire, when it re-emerges to repeat the cycle. This doctrine is clearly an antecedent of Nietzsche's notion of eternal recurrence.

God and the world appear as one in Stoicism. According to Zeno, the world can be expressed in three ways: the first of these is God incorruptible and ingenerate; secondly, God is both the ruler and substance of the world; and finally, Zeno affirms that the whole world is the substance of God. Nature, then, as the harmonious unity of beings ruled over by a principle that is intelligence and reason and is identified with the Divinity. Therefore, God is a living being, immortal, rational, perfect, intelligent in a state of happiness and alien to all evil, who rules the world and all in it through his providence, the artifice of everything, and who, though not of an anthropomorphic structure, is yet the father of all things.

The divine principle unites the totality of things through a law identified as universal reason, and this inexorable concatenation of things is what men refer to as destiny or fate (εἱμαρμένη). This unity affects the past, present, and future and is what makes divination possible; if man possessed divine knowledge, he would know the future, for everything is determined from the principle and all things are necessarily bound together in its workings. Cicero (De divinatione, 1, 55, 125) defines fatum as the conligatio causarum omnium (link between all causes). From this doctrine derives a determinism that tends to destroy freedom and initiative, since it teaches that whatever happens happens necessarily. If I am ill and fate decrees that I recover, I shall get well even though I do not call the doctor. This objection is what is called "inert" or "slothful reason" (λόγος ἀεργός). Zeno responded that all is determined necessarily and that, therefore, I may call the doctor and recover or not call him and die. This is the theory of the confatalia (common fate) of Cicero (De fato, 12, 28) which Leibniz, from different postulates, had to consider (Discourse on Metaphysics, 4).

The concatenation of things means that they exist in harmony with one another. The universe is like a work of art conceived in unity and order. In such a scheme of things destiny appears as "providence" (πρόνοια). The world--or God--is intelligent, as the beauty and regularity of its functions demonstrate. Moreover, the very existence of God is apparent in the contemplation of this order and harmony, for they point to the work of an intelligence. We must not forget, however, that in Stoicism this means the divine nature of the world and not the existence of a God who transcends it. This notion of providence leads to the problem of evil. In Stoic thought the necessity of a theodicy appears (though the term must be taken cum grano salis). If divine order rules everything, why is there evil? The Stoics responded to this question in two ways. They contend, first, that opposites are mutually necessary and dependent, so that without evil there is no good, nor evil without good. Secondly, they deny the ultimate reality of evil and advance the idea that things are evil in appearance only and serve to perfect the sum total of things. Complete truth could be known only if men comprehended the whole universe. Hence the only criterion on which judgment can rest is the divine, universal law we call nature, which binds all things together in an orderly and harmonious whole. This is the culmination of Stoic physics and the foundation of the school's moral concepts.

Stoic ethics is summed up in the famous expression: "Live according to nature." But this formula leads to serious complications. In the first place, nature, or physis, is not open to equivocal definition. Rather, it is understood, on the one hand, as the sum total of things and the permanent source from which they emerge, and, on the other hand, as the individual nature of each thing. In the cited passage, Diogenes notes that Zeno states in his book On the Nature of Man (Περὶ ἀνθρώπου φύσεως) that the aim is to live according to nature. But which nature is meant? Should man live according to his nature or to universal nature? Above all, man, as all beings, should be in harmony with himself. For that harmony is the good that is his. Yet it so happens that man's nature consists of reason. Man is a rational, living creature. But reason is not exclusively the property of man; rather, human reason is but a portion of universal reason, the same universal reason that rules and orders the entire universe (let us not forget pre-Socratic speculation on the noûs and lógos, "common" realities--the koinón of Heraclitus--in which men only participate). Reason, which is our very nature, puts us in accord with the entire universe, that is, with universal nature. This idea is the focal point of all Stoic morality, and Stoics from Zeno to Marcus Aurelius repeat and expound the same idea in a thousand ways. There is a passage in Marcus Aurelius' writings that expresses this profound conviction with all the noble emphasis of the Stoic Emperor: "Everything befits me that is in harmony with thee, o world! Nothing is too soon or late if it is to thee opportune. All that thy hours bring me is fruitful, o Nature! All comes from thee, all is in thee, and all returns to thee."[10]

Virtue (ἀρετή) consists of man's rational conformity to the order of things. The wise man is in harmony with nature and accepts destiny. The irrational man, the man who does not live according to his own nature, is at odds with himself and with the world, and destiny compels rather than guides him. As Seneca translates the verse of Cleanthes: Ducunt volentem fata, nolentem trahunt (The fates lead the willing man, the unwilling they compel).

Herein lies the meaning of the Stoic moral norm, as well as the criterion for all judgment. Virtue is right reason (ὀρθὸς λόγος). Man does the right thing when he behaves according to reason. The concept of duty does not, properly speaking, exist in Stoic ethics (or, in general, in the moral thought of the ancients). "Duty" (καθῆκον), officium in Latin, is instead that which is adequate or "decent" (in other words, that which is suitable, quod decet). Duty acquires a meaning that is almost aesthetic and it implies particularly the harmony of man with nature. Therefore, rightful conduct is primarily a matter of propriety. Yet true moral worth appears when this officium is not partially but rather completely involved in an act, when an act is carried out not only in accord with reason but also because of it. Then it is the act of a wise man and is called κατόρθωμα (according to the right). Furthermore, the only worthwhile things to the Stoic are those that depend on man and his rational conduct. The Stoic is indifferent to all the rest--although after he assumes this fundamental attitude, he does recognize the existence of preferable things. For this reason the wise man is self-sufficient; he finds the essential things within himself and he is therefore above all contingencies. The only thing that matters is reason and so long as he is a man he does not lose this attribute. All the rest has no effect on him and hence is, in the strictest sense, neither good nor bad. This line of thought leads the Stoics to an extreme form of autarchy--the old Hellenic ideal--expressed in the famous formula sustine et abstine, "endure and renounce," and then to a glorification of ataraxía, or serenity, above all else. Stated in the simplest way, this is the moral doctrine of the Stoics and a summary of the meaning of all Stoic philosophy.

It is quite evident that the intellectual insight of Stoic thought is quite moderate, and from the "scientific" point of view, it does not compare with Platonic-Aristotelian philosophy. It is a somewhat shortsighted form of speculation with evident conceptual shortcomings and clear lack of precision. It does not delve into the deeper implications of problems as does, for instance, the metaphysics of Aristotle. In the entire philosophical production of the Portico, nothing could be found that would compare to his analysis of substance, or to his modes of analogical being, or to his theory of categories. Nevertheless, the clear and astounding historical fact is that after Aristotle's death Stoicism supplanted his splendid philosophy and held undisputed

100

sway for five centuries. How could this be? One can hardly say that it was a matter of an inferior kind of thought being replaced by a deeper philosophy offering superior qualities. Rather, we must seek an explanation in a different direction. Is it possible that the men who accepted Stoicism were looking for something quite different from what other, radically curious men had sought in the Lyceum? Can it be that the word "philosophy" uttered by Zeno means something quite different from the same word on the lips of Aristotle?[11]

3. What Is Stoic "Philosophy"?

We must leave aside the meaning of philosophy in pre-Socratic thought; to include it would take us beyond our present scope. It is sufficient for our purposes to keep it in mind in a general way that pre-Socratic thought deals with natural things (περὶ φύσεως). In Parmenides, this mode of thought assumes the explicit form of knowledge about that which is--about being. In his successors down to Democritus, this took the form of an investigation of the elements and movement that affect nature. The real beginnings of Stoicism are to be found in Socrates, despite its connection (especially in its physics) to the thought of Heraclitus. Clearly, without the Socratic attitude the men of the Stoa could not have been what they were. But let us not forget that Plato and Aristotle also betray a fundamental debt to Socrates in their thought. It would appear, therefore, that Socratic thought first gave rise to one form of philosophy, the Platonic-Aristotelian, and then engendered another quite different mode of thought, that of the Stoa and related schools. But as we shall see, this order of appearance is somewhat problematic, and this fact leads us away from a consideration of a mere "succession" of historically documented modes of thought and instead obliges us to examine the different latent possibilities within Socratic thought itself.[12]

As Zubiri observes:[13]

> Wisdom, which since its earliest beginnings had been thought of as a knowledge of the ultimate things of life--and for that reason as something closely akin to religion--, came to be thought of along the shores of Asia Minor as the discovery or possession of truth about Nature. And this truth about Nature became a a vision of the nature of things with Parmenides and Heraclitus. On the one hand, this view of being led to rational science, and on the other, to rhetoric and culture in the civil life of Athens. This was the situation of the world as Socrates found it. The dynamic components of that situation were essential to Socrates and serve as the point of departure for his intellectual activity.

He goes on to say that Socrates was able, first of all, to withdraw from the public life of his time in order to return to the point of view of the mind (noûs) and thus to the truth. Secondly and more importantly,

> Socrates adopts a new way of life: the meditation about what the things of life really are. This means that in the view of Socrates, ethics does not primarily dwell in the things about which one meditates, but rather in the fact that one lives a life of meditation. . . Socratic wisdom does not, as it were, appeal to some ethical plane, because it is an ethics in itself. . . Wisdom as Ethics is the central idea of Socratic thought and it really constitutes a new kind of intellectual life.

Plato and Aristotle are able, as disciples of Socrates, to develop their philosophies by adopting the Socratic attitude of meditating on the reality of the things of life.   At this point three questions arise: (1) What do Plato and Aristotle understand by "philosophy"? (2) How does another mode of philosophy arise from the Socratic attitude? (3) Of what does Stoic philosophy consist?

"None of the gods philosophizes," says Plato (Symposium, or Banquet, 203 e), "and none wishes to become wise because wisdom belongs to the gods already. Neither do the ignorant philosophize or aspire to wisdom. . .Who, then, are those who philosophize, if they be neither the wise nor the ignorant? The answer is, of course, that men who philosophize stand somewhere between these two extremes (μεταξύ)." Elsewhere he identifies the philosopher as one who wishes to learn,[14] while in still other passages he defines philosophers as those who are "friends to the sight of truth."[15] He points out[16] as does Aristotle later, that philosophy is born of astonishment.   This does not mean, however, that it can be a matter of idle curiosity; rather, it means that the chronic illness of the soul is deprivation (that is, deprivation of "mind," or noûs) and that the two forms of this "demented" state are madness and ignorance.[17]   Ignorance must be overcome by means of philosophy so that the soul is then "cured" of its illness and becomes in reality what hitherto it has been in name only. Hence philosophy is not by any means a mere game, not simply an eloquent manner of speaking as the Sophists would have it but is, rather, the full possession of the knowledge of true being (ὄντως ὄν).[18]

This explains why philosophy is related to éros, or love, which is a longing, a search for something that is lacking, something needed but not present. Love based on the want of things moves the lover to seek the possession of beauty. The philosopher, likewise, must seek truth, the knowledge he lacks, because of the radical situation in which he finds himself. According to Plato, therefore, philosophy is the search for

"effective knowledge," and man seeks this knowledge because of
the human need "to live in truth."

In Aristotle's words: "It was due to their astonishment
that men, lately as in the beginning, began to philosophize."[19]
Aristotle goes on to say that ". . . if men philosophized in
order to escape ignorance, it is also certain they pursued knowledge for its own sake and not for purely utilitarian ends."[20]
This supreme knowledge, which he would later call "first philosophy," is the knowledge of causes and principles. In more precise
terms, it is ". . . a knowledge that considers being qua being
and its essential attributes," a knowledge that ". . . makes
a universal inquiry of being as such."[21] It is, therefore, a
knowledge of universal scope regarding things to the degree that
they exist as things, and it is a divine knowledge in two ways:
first, because it treats things divine, and second, because it
is first and fully a knowledge possessed by God.[22]

As we have seen, for both Plato and Aristotle (leaving aside
their many differences) philosophy is knowledge about what things
are. This knowledge is not something that is merely added to
man's being; rather, man is man only insofar as he knows. To
state it another way, to be human is to live in the truth (ἐν
ἀληθείᾳ) by revealing the patent and evident aspects of things
as they exist in the here and now. This view gives rise to the
concept of "theoretic life" (βίος θεωρητικός), which culminates
in happiness (εὐδαιμονία).[23] Therefore, philosophy is both a
form of knowledge and a way of life; or more precisely, it is a
life of theory that consists of knowing what things are.

According to Aristotelian testimony, two things may rightly
be attributed to Socrates: inductive reasoning and universal
definition, both of which concern the beginning of knowledge.[24]
Within this context Platonism is born, for it is a mode of thought
that is elevated to ideas, or essences, dialectically. In other
words, it discovers universal realities whose correlative is
definition. Socratic thought quite naturally gives rise to
Platonism and then to Aristotelianism (though Aristotle refuses
to separate ideas from individual things). At the same time,
however, Aristotle notes that Socrates devoted himself to the
study of "moral" virtues (περὶ τὰς ἠθικὰς ἀρετάς), although he
is careful to undersocre the fact that what Socrates sought in
virtue was "essence" (ἐζήτει τὸ τί ἐστιν). Hence it is in any
case a question of knowledge in the fullest sense, even though
it is knowledge directed toward moral aspects. The validity of
Socratic discipleship is apparent in Plato and indirectly so in
Aristotle. Xenophon, on the other hand, insists that Socrates
always sought after essence, the "what?," in the question posed by
human things (περὶ τῶν ἀνθρωπείων).[25]

The Socratic influence was not limited to Plato and Xenophon.
Also attributable to him are the so-called Socratici minores, the
small Socratic schools, especially the Cyrenaics of Aristippus
and the Cynic disciples of Antisthenes. These schools ignored

logic and physics and busied themselves only with the moral part
(τὸ ἠθικὸν μέρος) of philosophy, for it is the only dimension
that matters for happiness, according to the Cyrenaic Sextus
Empiricus.[26] The same could be said of the Cynics. Both groups
sought only the "good," and both tried to answer the question
of what constituted the good life. The Cyrenaics believed the
answer lay in pleasure (ἡδονή), while the Cynics, who despised
voluptuousness, thought it consisted of effort (πόνος). Neither
group was interested in knowledge as such or, in the final analysis, in truth. This is the important point: for the second time
since Parmenides (the first time was with the Sophists) Greek
philosophy abandons the way of truth. The first time it did so
was in the name of "culture" and rhetoric and the refined language
of fifth-century Athenian democracy. Now it does so again because
of self-sufficiency, of autarchy, and of the need of a people to
simplify the magnificent complexity of a way of life it had
achieved but could not sustain. The structure of the Greek
cities first began to change after the Peloponnesian Wars, and
the change became more pronounced as the Macedonian domination
grew. The Hellenic world experienced a change of posture and
came to be something quite different, what we call the "Greco-
Roman world." This transformation was fully realized after the
death of Alexander and Aristotle. The rather equivocal and misleading term "post-Aristotelian philosophy" harks back to this
period, but the tendency--and this is what I wished to point out--
was already apparent in the immediate disciples of Socrates. The
most authentic continuation of his work was the philosophy of
the Academy and the Lyceum; the superficial continuation, after
truth had been given up as an aim, was the work of the schools
of Aristippus and Antisthenes, which paved the way for Epicureanism and Stoicism.

This brings us to the third question. What does the term
"philosophy" mean to these schools? "Epicurus," writes Sextus
Empiricus, "said that philosophy is an activity that seeks the
happy life through discourse and reasoning."[27] We have, therefore,
an essential alteration of Aristotelian thought disguised in
language that sounds like Aristotle's. For Aristotle philosophy
and happiness are closely related but that relationship lies in
the fact that happiness arises from contemplation. This means
that the happy life is a life of theory. For Epicurus, on the
other hand, philosophy may lead to happiness, but the latter
differs from the former in both essence and possession. Epicureanism would dispel man's religious fears and teach him that pleasure
is the supreme good. It was only to allay such religious concerns
that Epicureanism dealt with physics. Its hostility to religion,
so visible in Lucretius, clearly reveals the religious significance of Epicureanism.[28] To state it another way, it shows the
quasi-religious nature of Epicureanism, for basically it aspired
to be a substitute for religion. We must remember that it is
during this period that the Oriental religions invade the Hellenic

world and attempt to replace the old and decadent polytheism with new beliefs.

The Stoics said that wisdom is the knowledge of things human and divine. But they added that philosophy is the exercise (ἄσκησις) of an art (τέχνη) the supreme aim of which is that very wisdom.[29] Wisdom is considered to be the highest perfection, or virtue, and is divided into three parts: that dealing with discourse (logic), the dimension that corresponds to the world (physics), and wisdom directed to human life (ethics). This explains the well-known division of the philosophic disciplines. Wisdom is directed primarily toward action; at least this is the way Cicero and Seneca understood it, and in so doing they revived the point of view of the ancient Stoics. Chrysippus strongly assailed the doctrine of Theophrastus (c. 371-287 B.C.) who, in the Aristotelian manner, had extolled the life of contemplation and theory.[30] There was, then, a complete reversal of viewpoint in the Academy and the Lyceum: philosophy was no longer thought of as knowledge or science, which has as its aim the contemplation of things in the light of truth; rather, it was looked on as an art by which life is to be guided. Even the tripartite division previously mentioned aroused opposition within the school. Aristo considered the division to be a concession contrary to the spirit of the doctrine. According to him, physics transcends our possibilities, and logic is like mud in a road, fit only to bother the traveler, or it is like a plate of crabs: many shells and little meat.[31] Ethics alone remained and was their only real interest. The other disciplines were maintained either out of respect for the Hellenic philosophical tradition and the influence the name philosophy had for centuries enjoyed in Greece, or simply as auxiliaries (inasmuch as a minimal knowledge of the world was needed in order to set the course of moral life), or finally as tools in their dialectical arsenal for use in that most ancient and abiding of Greek arts: argument and persuasion. Similarly, Epicureanism found it necessary to give some natural explanation of thunder and lightning--not to be sure to know what they were but so that man could live in peace, secure in the "knowledge" that they were not an expression of the anger of Zeus. The Epicureans offered several explanations, for they were not interested in the truth of the matter; it was enough for their purposes to point out that the phenomena could be explained and that they were natural occurrences and need not be feared.

We see, then, not only that Stoicism was a new philosophy but also that it involved a fundamental change in the meaning of the term philosophy itself. If it may be called philosophy at all, then it is philosophy in another sense. Consequently, it is obvious that the doctrine of the Stoa did not replace Aristotelian thought. If such were the case it would be incomprehensible. Rather we find that toward the end of the fourth century and early in the third man simply abandoned philosophy in the Platonic-Aristotelian sense and sought the foundations of his

life in another kind of activity and under a different sign.
Yet this activity also went under the name "philosophy" and was
intimately connected with the problems and ideas that had been
predominant in the earlier Greek world, and herein lies the
ambiguity suggested by the term philosophy. Finally, we may
ask what the expression "Stoic philosophy" meant in the life of
Greco-Roman man.

4. Stoicism in the Ancient World

One should be unable to understand the prodigious success of
Epicureanism and especially of the Stoa were it forgotten that
the entire period of that success--from Alexander to Marcus Aurelius--
was a time of crisis. At first glance this statement seems to be
blatantly frivolous. How can the greater part of the life span
of the Roman Republic and the first two centuries of the Empire,
the historical age during which was created the fabulous reality
we know as Rome, be referred to as a time of crisis? Moreover,
can half a millennium rightly be called a single period? And
above all, can a historical crisis really last that long?
        Let us attempt to clarify several points. In the first
place, a historical period not only has a temporal value measurable
by the unfeeling revolutions of the stars; it is also bound to
a circumstance that is geographically determined. As historical
realities, the European Middle Ages and the "same" centuries in
America are absolutely independent of, and irreducible to, each
other. Without going to such extreme examples, the thirteenth
century in France is not the same period, historically speaking,
as the identical years in the Moscovite realm. From the fourth
century B.C. until the second century A.D., if not later, it was
a period of crisis, though not always in the same places. In
other words, the crisis lasted throughout that period, but the
subject was not the same throughout. First of all, the Hellenic
peoples proper entered a critical period (as early as the fourth
century B.C.); they were followed by the Hellenized countries,
that is, those countries resulting from the breakup of Alexander
the Great's Empire, the Greco-Oriental kingdoms of the Diadocos:
Macedonia, Thrace, Seleucid Syria, and the Egypt of the Ptolemys.
Rome, at the time she conquered Greece, still stood apart from
Hellas and was a flourishing and thriving historical community
untouched by crisis. But participation in Greek life was to
bring about an internal transformation. Graecia capta ferum
victorem cepit (captive Greece the rude victor masters), Horace
had sung in the name of Hellenic culture, without even suspecting
the tremendous truth of his words. The Hellenization of Rome
began with the Scipios and the Greek ways of life and thought
soon began to encroach. By about the first century A.D., the
process of fusion was complete and the Hellenistic crisis was
common to both the Greeks and the Romans, though the latter were

106

affected only by its intellectual dimension. Roman ideas on
religion, on philosophy--in part this was a "contagion" spread
by the Hellenes--on the state, were affected by the crisis. But,
to use an expression of my teacher Ortega, the beliefs of the
Roman people remained intact and were still not seriously affected.
A short time later, at the beginning of our era, the specifically
Roman crisis occurred, the crisis of the Roman state itself, which
led to the critical and problematic solution of the Empire as
principatus. This was the period beginning with Caesar and end-
ing with Diocletian. Thus we can see that the crisis shifted
from one place to another as its historical subject changed.
This is why it could last for five hundred years and why also,
in ways that are often misunderstood, it could include periods
of plenitude and perfect stability.

But at this point a new problem arises. If the "subject"
of the crisis changes, if it is not the same in all cases, how
can one speak of a single crisis? We must understand the following: the subject is different in each case, true, but it is not
totally different. Human reality has dimensions, and there was
a certain dimension common to Greeks, Romans, and Hellenized
peoples, that underwent a crisis lasting more than five centuries.
This is what we may call the crisis of "Classical man." To define fully what is understood by Classical man is a task beyond
the limits of the present study and hence cannot be considered
at length. It is sufficient for our purposes to point out some
of the salient features in order to have an idea of what the
expression means. Classical man was the Mediterranean man whose
life was structured on several fundamental beliefs, including:
(1) the world is, i.e., it exists forever; (2) in this world
there are things that have a consistency and that move, or change;
(3) this world is understandable, and men may talk of it and tell
what it is; (4) things have properties that man may use to make
other things; and finally, (5) the world can be governed and
guided by virtue of the fact that it involves order and is subject
to a a law that springs from a divine principle, just as men may
live singly and collectively according to a law. In terms of
these few features we can trace a vague and blurred profile of a
kind of man who is quite different from the Asian (except "Greek
Asia"), the Egyptian, the Semite, and of course the Christian,
though the last type ranges far beyond any single historical context. In fact, the Classical world was not Christian, and to the
degree that it became so, it ceased to be Classical. Had it
been Christian, it would have exhibited quite different characteristics, and we should have to distinguish two phases of its history: that of the "pre-Christian" Classical man and that of the
Christian "Classical" man.

The historical crisis being alluded to is that of Classical
man and therefore of the Classical world. The different Mediterranean communities underwent a critical period at the same rate
at which they reached their maturity and exhausted the assumptions

107

on which their life was based. For instance, Rome was late in
becoming a Classical people in the strict sense of the term, and
she was even more tardy in becoming aware of what she had become.
Both conditions, especially the latter, came about as a result
of contact with Hellenic culture. This explains why we can say
with complete accuracy that we are dealing with a single, albeit
multisecular, crisis that unfolded throughout the far-flung
Mediterranean geography.

We must consider a highly significant fact. The phases of
the historical crisis alluded to above coincided exactly with
the stages of moral philosophy we studied earlier. The beginning
of the Hellenic crisis corresponded to the Socratic schools: the
Hellenistic crisis involved Epicureanism and the earlier Stoa;
as the crisis moved to the Greco-Roman period, the equivalent
philosophy was the middle Stoicism of Panaetius and Posidonius:
the Roman crisis corresponded to later Stoicism from Seneca to
Marcus Aurelius. This later Stoicism was Roman in spirit as was
the crisis with which it coincided. It represented a new and less
rationalistic aspect, and it was less concerned with philosophy
as knowledge and more with the outright predominance of ethics
as a quasi-juridical discipline and even as biography (for instance,
the Soliloquies of the emperor philosopher). The last stage of
Stoicism was the intellectual reflection of a crisis peculiar to
the Roman world.[32]

Now we can begin to see the role of Stoicism in the Classical
world. As Hellenic man came to question the assumptions on which
his life was structured, and as sprawling Hellenistic territorial
monarchies arose to alter the political horizon of the Pólis that
hitherto had been the scenario of his activities, he found it
necessary to formulate a new repertory of convictions in which to
root his life. The law (nómos) in which he had placed his faith
had become problematic. This is why he came to reject it and to
replace it with a "natural" legality, the legality of physis.
Henceforth, nature and law (or convention) would be opposing concepts. The task of uniting them again in the form of "natural
law" would fall to the Christian world. From this duality arose,
along with the Hellenistic moral philosophies, the concept of
cosmopolitan man, the "citizen of the world," that was to exert
a decisive influence in both Stoic thought and the actual history
of the Roman Empire.[33]

The supreme authority for the Greek was philosophy, the culmination of Hellenic culture. For this reason he turned again to
philosophy when conditions became critical. But this appeal is
quite misleading. For in this instance man did not seek what he
had earlier understood philosophy to be. Now he was looking for
a substitute for religious and socio-political convictions--in
short, "ethical" convictions in the Greek meaning of the term--
that had weakened. Thus the name "philosophy" was retained, but
it referred to a quite different reality, for now it meant a life
norm, a kind of religiosity of circumstances.

Moreover, the function of this new philosophy was to be
quite different not only in a personal, but also in a social,
sense. Individually, the primary concern for truth gave way to
the ideal of a sufficient and imperturbable life. In its social
dimensions, philosophy, which had always been the private concern
of a few, became a need of the many. Common men hardly concern
themselves with philosophy as an intellectual discipline, not
even in those historical communities with an intellectual tradition. At best they look on philosophy as something given them,
as popular and anonymous language shows quite clearly. The life
of common men is based primarily on other things. It is when
those "other" things fail him and man must turn again to philosophy to replace them--as he was obliged to do in Greece--that he
discovers he must modify philosophy in two radical ways. First
and foremost, he has to change the very content of philosophy,
for now it must serve other needs. Secondly, he must alter the
formal qualities of philosophy, since what had been the intellectual patrimony of a few now concerns the masses. This social
condition predetermines the necessary doctrinal and intellectual
inferiority of such philosophies. Far from triumphing over
Aristotelianism despite their inferiority, they are successful,
among other reasons, because they are inferior. The fundamental
difficulty of Platonic-Aristotelian thought, aside from its
content as such, rendered it incapable of serving the social
function that the Hellenistic world demanded. As an analogy
from another era, let us imagine how difficult it would be for
the average Christian to live a religious life based on theology
alone, rather than nourishing his faith by prayer, liturgy, and
the sacraments.

At this point, finally, the reasons for the predominance of
Stoicism over the remaining Hellenistic philosophies become quite
clear. Stoicism is a doctrine for difficult times; it is a morality
of endurance. Endure and renounce: it would be hard to find a
better formula of a minimal morality for turbulent times such as
the reign of the Diadocos or Nero's Rome. Classical man could
only resist as a rock in a swirling storm. Of course, there is
another possibility for such times. Man may seek a maximal morality
through which he overcomes the situation by trusting in a saving
God. And this alone is enough to reveal the absolute abyss between
the Stoic and the Christian. Despite certain superficial similarities,
the Stoic is strictly Classical man, whereas the Christian in a radical
sense is the new man.

CHAPTER V

Scholasticism in Its Own World and in Ours

A. Scholasticism in Its Own World

1. Philosophy and Situation

In attempting to understand the great historical fact we call scholasticism, it is necessary to consider two viewpoints. On the one hand, we must try to comprehend scholasticism as a reality of its own time; on the other, we must consider its historical legacy to the present, that is, scholasticism as it appears today. In other words, we must study scholasticism not only as we see it today but also, insofar as possible, as it saw itself in its own time.

The reason for this is that philosophy is inseparable from the circumstances from which it arises. Like any human activity, philosophy is created in the light of some situation, and it is only in that light that it becomes meaningful. Philosophy is linked to the man who conceives it, and each man is defined by his circumstance, which is what leads him to articulate a certain philosophy and not some other. Yet one might think that the pressure of circumstance, the necessary condition for the genesis of any philosophy, would hold no interest once a philosophy has been conceived, for then the task would simply be to understand it. Such is not the case. Philosophy is understandable only to the degree that one can reinsert it in the situation whence it originated. Real understanding of any page of philosophy requires the reader to recreate, at least up to a certain point, the task of the philosopher who wrote it, that is, the philosopher who "had" both the obligation and the ability to create that philosophy.

This explains the essential disagreement about definitions of philosophy. If we take any one of the defintions offered, it seems that all other philosophies are then excluded. Yet the other philosophies in turn appear justified by the very fact of their existence. The reason for this diversity of definitions is that <u>each philosopher believes philosophy to be what he has</u>

himself created. It is somewhat like asking for a definition of
swimming. If we were to ask a swimmer to define swimming, he
might respond by indicating the movements he makes in a certain
position with his arms and legs. Another swimmer might disagree,
insisting instead that swimming is another kind of movement, for
instance, of the shoulders. Both would be right, for swimming
can be both these movements, just as it may be any imaginable
swimming technique. Yet swimming is essentially something much
more simple and profound: it is something done to stay afloat.
Philosophy is very similar to swimming, in a sense, for it is
something man does in order to stay abreast of certainty. It is
a personal effort to reach a radical certainty. As a human activity philosophy is the same among all philosophers, notwithstanding the differences of content in what each one creates. There
is, then, a certain sameness that underlies even the most diver-
gent philosophies.

When a man discovers that he must turn to philosophy it
because his circumstance presents some problem that renders his
entire situation problematic. He realizes that in order to live
in that circumstance he must philosophize. Unless we consider
the reasons why men philosophize, then philosophy itself is incomprehensible. To omit consideration of the reasons is like
draining the water away from a swimmer: in a dry stream, his
movements are incoherent and comic.

This means that any attempt to reach a true understanding
of a human activity--in this case philosophy and a specific philosophy at that--must necessarily include not only what has been
done but also the reasons for its being done, which is to say
we must delve into the "situation" out of which that activity
arose. Specifically, we must inquire into the "situation" of
scholasticism.

2. The Problem of the Medieval "World"

To speak of scholasticism is to confront a certain ambiguity that
arises from the long span of time involved. As a historical
phenomenon scholasticism lasted for a number of centuries, but
just how many is problematical. If we set maximum limits we
have to deal with no less than eight hundred years; if we use
more restrictive criteria then the time-span can be reduced to
five hundred. Any exact limitation implies a prior interpretation,
and at the outset, at least, it is only with the greatest caution
that we can speak of a certain historical time-span characterized
by scholasticism. For it is a matter of dealing with many situations and a single philosophy. However, this very singularity
becomes questionable, in turn, for the reasons previously given.
How may this be explained?

Certain assumptions of the Schoolmen remained valid throughout the entire period when scholasticism was Western man's basic

intellectual response to the problems presented by his situation
in the world. Thus it is possible for us to speak of a single
scholasticism. Yet meanwhile other assumptions changed and it
was these changes that determined the internal evolution, the
stages and steps, as it were, of scholasticism. These changes
were correlatives of modifications in an overall scheme of things
that enjoyed a much longer life. I am concerned at this point
only with the larger "world" of scholasticism, not with its
doctrinal content, and I need refer to the latter only insofar
as it becomes necessary for an understanding of the scholastic
"situation." And in order to examine the articulation of the
different phases of scholasticism, it will be necessary to consider three focal points represented by three men: Saint Anselm,
Saint Thomas, and Suárez.

To begin with, it will be necessary to investigate the
general assumptions of the Schoolmen; or, to put it another way,
we shall have to examine the "situation" of the medieval world
as a repertory of beliefs and basic problems. This situation is
understandable only if we use a comparative method of clarifying
the peculiarities of one situation by juxtaposing it to others.
Hence we must compare the scholastic world to: (a) the Classical
world (which brings up the problem of "Christian philosophy" as
a radical innovation), (b) patristic philosophy (in order to
show the nature of scholasticism as a particular kind of "Christian" philosophy), and (c) the modern world (which will clarify
the transition to other forms of philosophy and bring us finally
to our own situation).

3. The Classical World

For the sake of brevity let us enumerate schematically some of
the concepts that constitute the basic beliefs of Classical man.
Around these fundamental beliefs is articulated the very special
and original human undertaking that we call "Greek philosophy."

(1) The world is. This is the fundamental assumption, the
original preexisting reality, that responds to particular problems
of one kind or another. The world as such is never a problem for
the Greek. Hence when the Neoplatonic thinkers--Plotinus, for
instance--encounter the idea of creation, they do not see in it
simply a new "idea," for ideas are always a delight to Hellenic
man, but rather a threat to their beliefs. This explains why
Plotinus has to muster all his metaphysics in order to be able
to comprehend with a Greek mentality the new situation of a
"created" world, and why, too, he develops the concept of emana-
tion, which is creation that avoids the question of nothingness,
a concept into which the Greek mind does not venture.

(2) The world is experienced by Classical man as a source
of reality and hence manifests itself as "nature" (φύσις) whence
spring "things," and as "principle" (ἀρχή), which gives being

to things and to which they may ultimately be reduced.

(3) This unity of principle in the world has as a correlative the plurality of things. This dichotomy presents one of the permanent problems of Classical thought; and the incompatibility of the two opposing beliefs necessitates the search for a new area of certainty that can transcend and reconcile them. This is one of the sources of Greek ontology.

(4) Plurality is thought of by Classical man as a multitude of "things," that is, real entities endowed with permanent properties. These properties assure the undeviating behavior of things and thus permit their utilization. Greek technology (τέχνη) is the art of manipulating things understood in this way. But the identity of these very things is threatened because they are mutable. Motion, another reality discovered by Classical man, presents a new problem and poses the need to investigate the inner structure of those things that are real and mutable. Finally, the properties of things are not experienced by the Greeks as quantitative gradations—for instance, as greater or lesser degrees of heat or of hardness—but as opposites: hot and cold, hard and soft.

(5) Things are interpreted by the Greeks as substance, as something that contains within it certain properties from which is derived its sufficiency. This idea of οὐσία is behind the Greek concept of freedom as independence, or "autarchy," which is quite different from the modern view.

(6) The world has an intelligible structure and thus permits both a noetic vision and a verbal account (lógos) of what it is.

(7) The intelligible structure of the world means that it is a cosmos, an order, and that it is ruled by a law. The application of this cosmic legality to the world of men establishes the possibility of a political order, a pólis, founded on law.

(8) From a very early date Classical man begins to think of a division into two worlds. This duality assumes many intellectual forms and interpretations, but they are all grouped around the fundamental belief in a dual world. Parmenides describes a world of truth as against a world of opinion. Platonic thought dwells on the world of ideas and the physical world. This duality culminates in an urge to flee from the world—a tendency latent throughout all of Greek history but seen in its extreme form in Neoplatonic philosophy. While the tendency is Greek, we should recognize its reappearance at certain moments of Christianity.

(9) Finally, to Classical man reality appears to be ahistorical. Its basic tendency is to exist forever in an essential immutability.

An interesting problem, but beyond the scope of this work, would be an investigation of the vestiges of these basic Classical concepts in later situations. The present task, however, is to see how these concepts were altered by a new belief.

4. The Basic Postulates of "Christian Philosophy"

The philosophy of the Patristic period signals an utterly new
phase of thought. The differences are not so much in "conceptual"
divergencies--for men will perpetuate the mental habits of the
Greeks for centuries--as in a change of basic assumptions that
are previous to philosophy. The internal dialectic of Classical
thought would never have led to "Christian philosophy," for the
radical innovation of Christian thought springs not from philosophy itself but from the alien concept of creation. What, then,
is the significance of the latter concept from the point of view
we have taken? In other words, what is its importance not as
a "doctrine" but as an element of a certain situation?
    In the first place, we find that the world itself has become
uncertain and problematic; what previously functioned as a support,
as solid ground and example to which the problems of Classical
man could be appealed, now becomes the radical and primary problem
for the Christian. What had been the basic belief of the Greek
now becomes the basic question for the Christian. There could
be no greater shift of emphasis in the vital function of what
we refer to as the "world." As the Christian is confronted with
the world, the first thing he must do is to ask why and how it
can be. And since any problem arises against a backdrop of beliefs
and forms of certainty, the problematic nature of the world is
appealed to, and interpreted according to, a higher and surer
reality.
    This reality is God. But the reality of God is quite peculiar
and the first observation to be made is that it is not simply apparent and evident. This means that reality is manifested through
revelation. But revelation is not to be considered so much as
something supernatural as it is as a means of revealing and discovering a latent reality. Saint Augustine in his Soliloquies,
for example, discovers God as the plenary reality that supersedes
the reality of the world. The world is no longer the source of
reality it was for the Greek; that role is now reserved primarily
for God. The alterations in the system of philosophical ideas
caused by this new belief appear during the first centuries of
the Middle Ages in the use of the somewhat ambiguous concepts of
natura naturans (creating nature) and natura naturata (nature
created).
    This divine reality is manifested in a personal and intimate
way. For this reason, although interest centered on God must also
include the soul--Deum et animam scire cupio (I desire to know God
and the soul)--the world matters only in a secondary way as the
handiwork of God and as an element in the life of the soul. The
question of the existence of the world is accompanied by an indifference toward its internal problems. Wilhelm Dilthey observes:
"For this kind of man, submerged in religious beliefs, the problems
of the cosmos are a matter of complete indifference."[1] Dilthey
goes on to say: "A powerful reality is manifested to the individual

consciousness, and this knowledge absorbs any interest in the study of the cosmos. . . . In this autognosis man perceives the essence of himself; in it he at least has an indication of the attitude he is to assume concerning a conviction of the reality of the world; and above all, in it he is able not only to apprehend the essence of God, but also to grasp, if only in part, the mystery of the Trinity." This explains the predilection for "meditations" as a literary form in the thought of that time.

"Christian" thought also introduces an element of historicity that is apparent in two ways. In the first place, Christianity establishes a historical sequence of decisive human stages: Creation, Fall of Adam, Redemption, Last Judgment. Moreover, for history to exist at all, the past must be preserved and linked dynamically with a foreshadowing future. Only then does history become meaningful and not a mere parade of dates. In the Christian God history acquires meaning, for historical reality is present in Him. And insofar as a divine plan exists to unify historical happenings, the historian can then trace and plot it to a certain extent. He thus comes to understand the flow of events. But at the same time, he still views these events as history, which involves the related categories of historiography and historical reality.

But we must remember that the form of thought we call "Christian philosophy," which is keyed to the Christian circumstances of the philosopher, does not originally spring from a Christian "world" (taking world to mean a system of prevailing beliefs). On the contrary, even in the halcyon days of Christian thought, Saint Augustine, himself converted to Christianity after maturity-- sero te amavi, pulchritudo tam antiqua et tam nova (Late I loved thee, beauty so old and yet so new)--faced a non-Christian world. Strictly speaking, his problem consisted for the most part of seeing the world in which he had lived as a pagan, as "Classical" man, from a new perspective and through Christian eyes, that is, through his belief in God. This is precisely the task he set out to accomplish in The City of God.

This first phase of Christian philosophy is not scholasticism. Between Saint Augustine and the Scholastics lie at least four centuries, or perhaps six, if we insist on greater accuracy. At this point, then, we must consider the historical situation that made possible and necessary that peculiar form of thought we know under the name of scholasticism.

5. Scholasticism in Its Own Situation

The primary fact of scholasticism is that it arises in a time when Christianity has prevailed. Contrary to Patristic speculation, scholasticism springs from a Christian "world," a world created by the fact that social beliefs--regardless of individual acceptance or rejection of those same beliefs--are Christian in nature.

It is this "world" as a system of prevailing beliefs that serves
as a starting point for scholasticism. It is the kind of world
that is implied in the term "Christendom."

But at this point one might object to what has been stated
by pointing out that there is not one but three forms of scholasticism: Christian, Arabic, and Jewish. How can we assert that
the basic foundation was Christian when many of the greatest
scholastic thinkers were rooted in Judaism or Islam? Would that
all difficulties were as easily resolved. For one thing, even
in a religious sense the three religions are inseparable; this
is obvious in the case of the first two, and as for the third,
it can be understood only as a heresy within the Judeo-Christian
tradition. Moreover, despite points of friction, the three religions exist side by side during the Middle Ages, and of the
three Christianity looms largest by far. Secondly, the three
religions agree as to what is philosophically essential: theism,
monotheism, creation, and the place of man. They also share common philosophical antecedents and assumptions in the Greek tradition, equally important to Jews, Christians, and Arabs. Above
all, during the period of greatest contact they shared the influence
of Aristotelianism. This means that the prevailing beliefs that
shaped them are approximately the same in all three religions.
Indeed, their common heritage explains the seriousness of the
situation created by the Averrhoist movement, not only for Christians but also for Orthodox Islam. Averrhoist doctrines about
the eternity of the world, the unity of understanding, and personal immortality--including the "dual truth" of Latin Averrhoism--
disrupted the continuity of prevailing beliefs and caused a serious rift in scholasticism that had not occurred, for example, in
the case of Avicenna. The fact that Christian scholastic thinkers
often cite Arabs or Jews without being aware that they are such
and the existence of works as the Summa contra gentiles are quite
clear indications of a situation common to all three peoples. Of
course, within that situation are lodged all manner of theological
differences of a more or less serious nature.

This condition of scholasticism has an essential influence
on its content and forms. What precisely does the term "scholasticism" mean? Is it a philosophy? In response to this question,
we find that, strictly speaking, there was never an independent
scholastic philosophy during the Middle Ages. Nor can scholasticism be defined as theology, for neither was theological speculation a separate activity during those centuries. In my judgment,
scholasticism is at once philosophy and theology in a very peculiar relationship that affects the meaning of both and is much
more complex and subtle than the presumed ancillary subordination
of philosophy to theology.

The relationship between these two disciplines is causal:
theological questions give rise to philosophical problems that
must automatically be postulated and resolved by philosophy in
keeping with its own exigencies, and that may lead philosophy

116

into unforeseen areas. Stated in another way, theology is inseparable from philosophy in the Middle Ages because it is a principal
component of the situation within which philosophy arises. If we
ignore theology, then "Christian philosophy"--something that has
never existed in the strictest sense--is isolated from its active
context, separated from its source of being, and hence reduced
to a mere abstraction of itself. In principle and grosso modo
at least, theology outlines the arena of medieval philosophical
problems and reveals the spectrum of problems that arise from
the situation of man in the Middle Ages and oblige him to philosophize. But I reiterate that once philosophy has begun to consider these problems, its course and its destiny depend entirely
on the requisites of philosophy itself and nothing else. These
internal criteria may even lead--as indeed happened in fact--to
an essential alteration of the situation just described.

Yet we can no longer speak of scholasticism as if it were
a single unit. Instead, we must turn our attention to the different ways in which philosophy responds to its situation as certain
elements within that situation undergo changes. In order to do
this, we must observe several stages within scholasticism, the
focal points represented by Saint Anselm, Saint Thomas Aquinas,
and Francisco Suárez.

6. Saint Anselm

Aside from the beginnings of scholasticism in the ninth century
with Johannes Scotus Erigena and his circle, whose teachings
were almost totally forgotten in the tenth century, the real
creator of scholasticism in its mature form was Saint Anselm
(1033-1109). This fact makes his position a rather peculiar one,
for by its very nature scholasticism was thought of not as an
innovation but as a tradition. Saint Anselm is aware of this
and while he realizes the innovative features of his doctrine,
he also attempts to justify and moderate them by stating that his
writings contain nothing in disagreement with the teachings of
the Church Fathers, especially Saint Augustine. This is why in
cases where doubts arise as to his affirmations he recommends
they be carefully collated to the De Trinitate of Saint Augustine.
In fact, he considers this to be so important that he vehemently
requests whoever might transcribe the Monologion to include the
prologue in which these things are explained in order to assure
that the work will be correctly interpreted.[2]

It must be noted, however, that Saint Anselm's point of departure is not previous philosophical and theological doctrines.
Rather, as we shall soon see, he begins with another kind of data.
Hence, his entire intellectual activity is really original; the
only restriction on his work is that its originality must not be
excessive (nimis novum) or contain discrepancies with the philosophical and theological tradition of the Patristic thinkers.

These guidelines give Saint Anselm's thought a peculiar and
somewhat borderline position with scholasticism. This will become more apparent in comparison with later forms.

Elsewhere I have discussed at length the point of departure
in the thought of Saint Anselm.[3] His is, of course, a religious
starting point; specifically, he begins with the situation of
man deprived of God. Man was created to see God but has never
beheld Him because He is not present. Man is thus in a kind of
exile, reduced to himself and lost from God. Yet he clings to
God in a deficient way be believing in, and missing, Him, and by
feeling a need somehow to see God and to understand His truth.
This situation is summed up in the famous expression, fides
quaerens intellectum (Faith seeks understanding). However, the
full meaning of the expression can be seen only after further
elucidation.

For Saint Anselm revelation uncovers or reveals a certain
reality that is then converted into a given portion of knowledge.
Hence revelation functions like a primary datum. The world
appears as a vestige of God and is experienced as creation, that
is, as "creature," as ab alio (from another).[4] Faith functions
in its primary meaning of belief, in which man dwells. For this
reason it is an immediate avenue to reality. In earlier thought
faith functions rather as authority, as an idea which must be
taken into account. This is still true, but it should not con-
ceal the other, more radical view of faith. Dogmas are presented
as statements of fact and as avenues by which reality may be
approached. But whereas reality as such is undeniable and undoubted, it is also incomprehensible.[5] Hence dogmas lead to forms
of inquiry, much as physical reality about us necessitates a science
in order for us to understand it. This is why faith has a function
somewhat analogous to that of experience as a means of coming into
contact with reality, the conditio sine qua non of intellection.
Experience transcends the mere sensation of a thing, as the science
of the expert surpasses the knowledge of the simple observer.[6]
This distinction is closely tied to another, which Saint Anselm
makes elsewhere, between living and dead faith.[7] The substance
of living faith is love, dilectio; living faith is operosa fides
as opposed to otiosa fides that is inert. The first consists of
credere in id in quod credi debet (to believe in that which ought
to be believed in), the second, of credere id quod credi debet (to believe that which ought to be believed). Whereas in the second
case, that which ought to be believed is simply the inert content
of belief--that which is believed--living faith is believing in
something within which man is rooted and on which he shapes his
life. Saint Anselm points out a distinction between two totally
different functions of belief, even though the content of that
belief remains the same: in almost his own words we might call
these operative belief and inoperative belief.

The situation of Saint Anselm is thus determined by the fact
of Chrisitianity in its concrete form as living faith. This faith

gives man a reality, but this reality appears as a datum and therefore as something incomprehensible and insufficient. The love that moves his faith obliges him to seek understanding and intelligence. Such is the meaning of the expression credo ut intelligam (I believe in order that I may understand) and fides quaerens intellectum (faith seeks understanding). But then Saint Anselm goes on to point out that the success of man's effort is neither certain nor necessary.[8] The latent nature of the reality revealed through faith posits another kind of presence, described by Saint Anselm as "illumination."[9] Therefore, his speculation does not deal with things so much as with the content of faith, with what is believed, though he sees in that content a means of revealing reality.

If we allow for certain modifications, this is the general situation of scholasticism in its first phase, from its beginnings to the twelfth century. During the following century that situation is radically changed. The thirteenth century is generally thought of as the plenitude of scholasticism, and this is true, especially if this assumption shuns mere critical judgments concerning the merits of individual thinkers and if scholasticism is not identified willy-nilly with all medieval philosophy. For, indeed, the culmination and plenitude of scholasticism, which Saint Anselm had only initiated, does occur in the thirteenth century. Saint Bonaventure, on the other hand, perhaps represents a period of transition to a new situation that finds its most outstanding expression in Thomism. We must now consider the most salient features of that transition.

7. Saint Thomas Aquinas

In the thirteenth century Aristotelian philosophy makes its appearance in the West and leads to a decisive change in the situation of Christian scholasticism. A similar change occurred among the Jewish and Arabic thinkers, though perhaps not at the same dates. Medieval philosophers, who until now had lived within the Platonic-- or Neoplatonic--and Augustinian tradition, with some Stoic and Aristotelian influences of a purely formal nature, now discover a perfect, complete, and polished philosophy with a scope and conceptual vitality hitherto unknown to them. Their impression of Aristotelian philosophy is simply that it is the truth. For the first time in the Middle Ages there is a dominant philosophy. This is the basic significance of the Aristotelianism imported by the Arabs to Spain and thence to all the countries of Western Europe. (In passing, let us note the historical fact, as important as it is ignored, that Aristotelian philosophy, which was replaced by Stoicism and related doctrines after the death of Aristotle, regains its dominance in thirteenth-century Europe in a world totally different from the one in which it originated. This fact alone brings up the crucial question of the grandeur and essential limitations of Aristotle.)

To reiterate, then, there is a predominant philosophy beginning with the thirteenth century. This is an absolutely new phenomenon, and for that reason it profoundly changes the entire situation. Aristotelianism had arisen quite independently of Christianity and revelation in response to other problems and assumptions. This meant that it could not immediately be juxtaposed or mingled with the other prevailing belief of man in the thirteenth century: Christianity, or in intellectual terms, scholastic theology including its philosophical dimension. Thirteenth-century man thus finds himself confronted with two beliefs, two certainties, and it is this very duality that constitutes the real problem. For he must decide between them, bring them into accord, and discover a transcendent certainty that will explain the duality and clarify man's way. This encounter with an Arabized Aristotle appearing like a meteor in the European universities was no laughing matter. We need only recall the terror Saint Bonaventure felt when he first encountered Aristotelianism in the University of Paris and heard discussions about the eternity of the world to be reminded[10] that the advent of Aristotelianism was taken most seriously.

The need arises, then, to make a decision. It was unlikely that Christian thought could create intellectual forms of sufficient maturity to permit an autonomous solution of the Aristotelian problem. Were it capable of such philosophical expansion, then Aristotelianism could be absorbed and utilized as an element of Christian thought. But attempts in this direction were of little consequence. The other solution was the formulation of an Aristotelian-scholastic philosophy. To this task the two great Dominicans of the century devoted their lives: Albertus Magnus and, in a more brilliant and fertile way, Saint Thomas Aquinas

This fact has several consequences. The intellectual problem of Saint Thomas, lest we forget, is primarily the relationship of Aristotelianism to scholastic theology. The terms of the problem are two beliefs in apparent discord. Since Aristotelian philosophy seems essentially sound and true to Saint Thomas, he does not propose to create another. On the contrary, his aspiration is to present Aristotelian thought as the authentic philosophy, and only when it seems erroneous or inadequate will he offer his own. Moreover, Saint Thomas' interest is first of all theological. This is what Etienne Gilson means when he correctly refers to the "Thomist order," which he reestablishes in his study of Thomism, pointing out the difference between the undertaking of Saint Thomas and the construction of a philosophy "from the elements taken from Thomism."[11] Furthermore, the philosophy of Saint Thomas easily establishes a body of philosophical truths that are manifested through faith.[12] Yet, because those truths are philosophical and must therefore be rational, Saint Thomas is faced with the problem of the "independence," respectively, of philosophy and theology, in other words, he must deal with the requisites of a true philosophy and theology. This is why in Saint Thomas the exigencies of rationality are the deciding factors, and why he vigorously opposes the attitude of thinkers past, present, and future, who are too ready to demonstrate the truths of faith with any pious argument. To believe is one thing, says Saint Thomas; to know and to demonstrate are quite different things. If the intention is to demonstrate, then it must be done in the most effective way possible. Otherwise, it is possible to have the illusion of believing in a thesis for the reasons put forth, and if the latter are invalid, then the belief leads to absurdity. For example, regarding the Trinity and the eternity of the world--the two problems over which Saint Bonaventure had stumbled in his encounter with Aristotelianism--the attitude of Saint Thomas is exceedingly clear: the only valid demonstration is that effectively permitted by the demonstrable. As for the rest, faith has its own justification.[13] And when attempts are made to demonstrate something directly by basing an argument on the consequences that the inadmission of the thing in question would imply, Saint Thomas demands that the impossibility of those consequences also be demonstrated directly. Thus when it is argued, in order to prove the rational impossibility of the world existing ab eterno, that this would mean the existence of an infinite number of souls, Saint Thomas first notes that God could have created a world without men or souls, and then he goes on to say: ". . . and moreover it still has not been demonstrated that God could not cause an infinite number of things at once."[14] This attitude, purely as an attitude, coincides with the view of Kant when he says that in regard to certain questions he was obliged to forego knowledge in order to give priority to belief.[15] Probably Kant was too restrictive in his determination of the possibilities of knowledge, just as Saint Thomas may have been overly inclusive. But in any case, both agree as to the criterion by which knowledge is to be determined.

From the philosophical point of view, the most important fact to consider is that the older forms of thought that had prevailed in Classical times retain only a part of their former authority in the thirteenth century, and even that vestige appears from a quite different vantage point. The problem for Aristotle was the knowledge of reality, especially of nature, and of God as a necessary extension of the problem. For Saint Thomas, on the other hand, the problem is one of coordinating two authorities when both seem true: theology and Aristotelianism. The quaestiones he treats arise from the friction between the two views.

There is one consequence of this situation that must be strongly emphasized if confusion is to be avoided. Philosophy has customarily presented its problems on an assumption of a lack of knowledge. For Socrates and Plato, the beginning of philosophy was the question of what things are. This is the idea contained in the τί of Socrates and is closely connected to the idea of astonishment (θαυμάζειν), which, according to Plato and Aristotle, was the origin of philosophy and the first formulation of the philosophical problem. Even in Aristotle, the central problem of his metaphysics is stated in the question, "What is being?" (τί τὸ ὄν). But Saint Thomas--and indeed all the Scholastics sensu stricto--present problems not from any lack of knowledge but from a contradiction. Even in its external form this situation is apparent: Videtur . . . Sed contra . . . (It is understood . . . but opposed to . . .). The Scholastics begin with two opposing authorities whose contradiction necessitates a thesis that will lead to some certainty regarding them. This means that Saint Thomas is concerned immediately more with opinions than with things and with reality. Of course, the opinions that concern him are statements, "sentences," about reality. This lends an essentially "mediate" nature to his philosophy and is quite in keeping with the actual situation that gave rise to his thought.

The conditions under which scholasticism arose explain the methodic character of Thomism and related forms of thought. In the middle of the nineteenth century in works that reveal an uncommon understanding of Saint Thomas, Father Gratry writes: "We can understand that Saint Thomas was above all obliged to deduce and proceed by means of syllogisms, since the outstanding conclusions were already formulated and available. What Plato, Aristotle, and Saint Augustine had found in philosophy, Saint Thomas did not have to seek. Of course, without exception he confirmed their findings with greater care, depth, and accuracy than anyone else. Yet, above all, his task was one of deduction . . ."[16] For this reason, Saint Thomas prefers the method which he accurately calls scientia demonstrativa (demonstrative science). This is the science or art of determining the truth, and it differs from the scientia dialectica (dialectical science), which is the method of creative or original inquiry.[17] In the case of Saint Thomas it is a matter, then, of determining or "demonstrating" the truth within several given opinions, rather than of discovering a truth that is simply unknown. This process is what I call the mediate aspect of philosophy.

Yet this stable situation is suddenly changed in the last phases of medieval scholasticism. This is the period from Duns Scotus to Ockham and his disciples, and its philosophical importance is matched only by a general lack of knowledge about it. The Thomist norm of rationality had led to a reduction in scope of philosophy and theology, although a consecutive synthesis of the two was still believed possible.[18] The interest shown by Franciscanism in nature would lead eventually to modern-day physics, but underneath that interest lies an evident theological substratum. It is apparent in the notion of the world as vestigium Trinitatis (vestige of the Trinity) and in conjunction with other elements can be found as late as Kepler. We need only recall, for instance, the latter's writings on De adumbratione Trinitatis in sphaerico (On the Adumbration of the Trinity in the Spheres).

Even Saint Thomas warned against the tendency of skipping too easily from things created to the Trinity. The fourteenth century was deeply skeptical of any possibility of the kind of synthesis sought after by the previous century.[19] Now philosophy and theology tended to draw apart. According to Ockham's definition, scientia es cognitio vera sed dubitabilis nata fieri evidens per descursum (Science begins as true but doubtful knowledge that becomes evident in the course of things). In the Tractatus de principiis theologiae (Treatise on the Principles of Theology), written by a member of Ockham's circle and sometimes attributed to Ockham himself, the difference between the "sciences" are pointed out time and again.[20]

Moreover, in Ockham there is a clear appeal to the immediate. Intuitive knowledge is the only way of comprehending existences and facts and the only one that permits us to know what a thing is or is not. This explains Ockham's predilection for experientia (experience) or experimentalis notitia (experimental knowledge) rather than for abstract or discursive knowledge. Concerning freedom of the will, Ockham declares in his writing that it cannot be proved by any ratiocinative method, but that it is knowable evidentially through experience.[21] Reason as a new trend is becoming predominant in philosophy. The subsequent fate of philosophy is generally known as far as its broad outlines are concerned. Yet one of the critical problems of philosophy is the question of Ockham. The fact that few works on Ockham exist other than incunabula or manuscript copies, and that save for rare exceptions Ockham's writings have not been reprinted since 1500, would suffice to show the existence of a historical problem of the first order. However, it is a problem we cannot even begin to consider in the present work.

8. Francisco Suárez

As the importance of reason (in the double meaning of human reason and the reason of things) continued to rise during the fifteenth century, scholastic writings proliferated. Although there were no great figures--which does not mean there were no interesting ones--the writers of scholastic treatises flourished as never before. Toward the end of the century and during the first decades of the following, scholasticism was beset not only by an internal crisis but also by the weight of its own excessive production. The entire medieval tradition centered on it, and this was precisely its principal problem. For this meant that things as they really were lay hidden under all the accumulated opinions and notions of them. Even the literary forms reflected this situation. The lack of immediacy alluded to earlier was coupled to a kind of immediacy to the second power: the writings of the period were usually in the form of commentaries on the works of earlier Scholastics, especially in the case of the

Summa Theologica of Saint Thomas. There are two positions that may be taken regarding the situation of scholasticism, and, as a matter of fact, both were taken in the sixteenth century.

The first attitude is that of the humanists and it amounts simply to a total rejection of scholasticism. They have no desire to know anything about it, and in fact their knowledge is limited. They aspire to return to Classical thought, but they fail to take into account two things: first, that the Scholastics themselves were deeply imbued with Greco-Roman thought, especially Neoplatonism, Aristotelianism, and Stoicism; and second and more important, that history precludes returning to anything past.

The second view is that of the Schoolmen. They have no wish to turn their back on scholasticism. Yet the better minds among them realize that something new must be done, something that is relevant to their real and present situation. They cannot go on emptily adding treatises and commentaries to the hundreds written during the preceding century. Furthermore, they are, at least in part, men of the Renaissance with somewhat modern problems such as law, the beginnings of nationalism in Europe, matters dealing with discovery and the treatment of Indians, and the theological and political difficulties brought on by the Reformation. The Scholastics of the sixteenth century consequently discover that they must consider and justify the entire scholastic tradition. The best example of this is found in the Disputationes metaphysicae of Suárez. Another aspect, along with the overall inquiry into tradition, is that for the first time in the history of scholasticism philosophy is separated from theology. This is the period when courses of philosophy became prevalent, such as those offered by the Carmelites, by the Universities of Coimbra and Salamanca, or by Arriaga and John of Saint Thomas. Yet the profoundest and most original response to the new situation is that of Suárez. What, then, is the nature of his work?

In the first place, Suárez is a theologian and his primary task is to write an exposition of theology. But he finds that one cannot be a competent theologian without first having established the firm groundwork of metaphysics.[22] He sees "as clear as day" that divine and supernatural theology requires the human and natural foundation of metaphysics. He observes further that he does not hesitate to interrupt his theological work in order to give, or better, to restore, importance to the doctrine of metaphysics.[23] Suárez is obliged to write his metaphysical work for this reason, though his final interest is theological. But his theology is influenced by the fact that metaphysics acts as the background of his work and indeed constitutes the very situation from which it arises.

In the Disputationes Suárez proceeds like a philosopher, but he never loses sight of the fact that his philosophy must be Christian and subservient to theology. For this reason, just as he had had to interrupt his theological work in order to substantiate its philosophical foundation, so now he must occasionally stop in the course of his philosophy and turn to certain theological questions. What is the reason for his method? It is certainly not to examine them in depth, for that would be extemporaneous, but rather to indicate to the reader how the principles of meta- [24] physics apply and relate to the confirmation of theological truths. This means that the causal relationship between philosophy and theology, a peculiarity of all scholasticism, still exists. Yet there are essential differences between the position of Saint Thomas, for example, and that of Suárez.

In Saint Thomas' view, theology can benefit somewhat from philosophic disciplines, not because the latter are necessary to the former, but because they serve to substantiate theological thought. Theology receives its principles not from other sciences but directly from God through revelation. For this reason, he goes on to say, theology cannot consider other sciences as superior to it; on the contrary, they are to be used in subservient and inferior capacity.[25] It has been stated that Suárez considers a prior metaphysical foundation essential for theology, and he goes on to insist even more forcefully on the universal validity of this procedural necessity. He continues to use the verb "to minister" (ministrare); however, the function it implies is a necessary one if theology is to be a true science. Primary philosophy or metaphysics explains and confirms those principles which comprehend all things and which support and sustain all doctrine.[26] From a procedural point of view, then, metaphysics enjoys an essential priority over all doctrines, including theology itself.

In the second place, there is a difference of method in treating disciplines. According to Suárez, the scholastic theologians indiscriminately used natural and supernatural theology in speaking of God.[27] Suárez, on the other hand, found it necessary to elaborate natural theology separately.[28] This is why Suárez had to write a treatise on metaphysics, the first such work in all scholasticism if one leaves out the somewhat problematic Sapientiale or Metaphysica of Thomas of York in the thirteenth century. And the metaphysics of Suárez, the culmination of several centuries of scholastic tradition could only take the form of the Disputationes: a discussion with the past in order to determine the structure of an independent doctrine of a purely philosophical nature.

If we summarize at this point the features found in the philosophy of Suárez insofar as it is a response to particular situation, we find the following: (1) the procedural separation of philosophy from supernatural or revealed theology; (2) the priority of metaphysics as foundation; (3) the ordering of philosophy and theology whereby the latter stands as the aim of the former; (4) the causal relationship between philosophy and theology which determines the nature of philosophical problems and which directs interest in various problems according to a theological perspective;

and (5) the mediacy of philosophy, postulated on the opinions
derived from the entire Aristotelian-scholastic tradition with
a view to determining the "true sentence" from among the many.

Nevertheless, despite his efforts to posit problems in the
light of new circumstances, despite the undeniable genius of
Suárez, and, finally, despite the official and academic prestige
enjoyed by scholasticism until well into the eighteenth century,
it is a commonly known fact that it declined rapidly after the
death of Suárez in 1617 and certainly after the passing of
John of Saint Thomas in 1644. This leaves us with the question
of the existence of scholasticism in the Modern Age and of its
place in the world today.

B. Scholasticism in the World Today

9. The Generations Following Suárez

If we group into generations philosophers and thinkers in related
fields after Suárez, using Descartes as a provisional point of
reference, we discover an order that alone sheds much light on
the thought of the seventeenth century. Following this procedure
we would have seven generations:*

1. Francisco Suárez (1548-1617); Giordano Bruno (1548-1630).
2. Francis Bacon (1561-1626); Galileo Galilei (1564-1642);
   Johann Kepler (1571-1630).
3. Herbert of Cherbury (1581-1648); Groot (1583-1645);
   Thomas Hobbes (1588-1679).
4. Juan de Santo Tomás (1589-1644); Pierre Gassendi (1592-
   1645); René Descartes (1596-1650).
5. Antoine Arnauld (1612-1694).
6. Blaise Pascal (1623-1662); Pierre Nicole (1625-1695);
   Arnold Geulincx (1624-1669); Robert Boyle (1626-1691);
   Jacques Bénigne Bossuet (1627-1704); Christian Huyghens
   (1629-1695); Samuel von Pufendorf (1632-1694); Baruch
   Spinoza (1632-1677); John Locke (1632-1704).
7. Philipp Jakob Spener (1634-1704); Nicolas Malebranche
   (1638-1715); Isaac Newton (1641-1727); Gottfried Wilhelm
   von Leibniz (1646-1716); Pierre Bayle (1647-1706).

The men belonging to these seven modern generations found
that scholasticism was still the official philosophy; it was the
philosophy taught in the universities, the one that was everywhere
studied and learned, and it was the source of philosophic terminology. It was the dominant philosophy with which Galileo contended
in Italy. Groot was imbued with it. Descartes studied it at the
Collège de La Fleche, Locke at Oxford, Malebranche at La Marche,
and Leibniz in Germany. Even Christian von Wolff (1679-1754)
found scholasticism entrenched in the German universities, though

his own scholasticism based on Leibniz was later to displace it. In Latin countries the official status of scholasticism lasted even longer. However, by the eighteenth century it had to contend with the encroaching influence of Descartes, Bacon, and Locke.

Notwithstanding the persistence of scholasticism, we vainly seek a development of scholastic doctrines in the accounts of that time. Despite considerable efforts made the books of that time offer no new doctrine. The eulogies that replace serious theoretical content are purely formal or personal: erudition, knowledge, faithfulness to thomism, etc. In fact, during this time another philosophy was coming into being as creative thinkers abandoned the inertia of scholasticism to begin their own work under the influence of Descartes, Bacon, or the modern physicists. This polemic attitude, which began with the humanists, is apparent in different ways and for different reasons throughout the seventeenth century. On the other hand, as the past is freed from its "traditional" or "immemorial" subjection to scholasticism, it is automatically rediscovered as history, and this fact accounts for the more frequent and direct appeals to ancient philosophers: Saint Augustine, Plato, and even Aristotle himself considered on his own merits without medieval interpretations. Malebranche, who had only a slight interest in history, thought that theology should regard the past in a way contrary to what was proper in philosophy. He held that the things concerning faith are known through tradition; hence one must consider the past and ask what the early fathers and evangelists of the Church believed. But ancient opinions are of no interest in matters that depend on reason, for in such cases only the truth is of importance. Therefore, whereas in theology the love of truth leads to antiquity, so in philosophy that same love would direct men to the present, since modern philosophers are capable not only of knowing the truths of the ancients but also of discovering others.[29]

But the clearest understanding of this position concerning scholasticism is found in Leibniz. According to him, two points of view should be kept in mind: that of scholastic philosophy as such (as a form of philosophizing) and that of the doctrines contained in it. As for the first view, Leibniz diverges from it completely. He finds it to be mere verbalism, a farrago of useless formulas that cause him to waste the most precious of all things, time. Leibniz, a genius at conciseness, who wrote only what was necessary and who was able to sum up his entire metaphysics in twenty pages (a feat worthy of one of his own verses: particula in minima micat integer orbis (The entire universe throbs in the smallest particle),[30] rejected the scholastic folios. Yet the doctrines themselves are another matter entirely. For scholastic writings are ". . . a treasure of the most important and absolutely demonstrative truths."[31] He did not regret his study of scholasticism in his youth, for amidst

the refuse of scholasticism there is also gold. The attitude of
Leibniz is aptly summed up in the well-known phrase: aurum latere
in stercore illo scholastico barbariei (Gold lies in the manure
of those scholastic barbarians).[32]

Therefore, scholasticism is useful, not within itself but
without, as a means of creating something else. For the first
time with Leibniz scholasticism has a philosophical role to play
in modern philosophy. Leibniz gathers all philosophic tradition
known to him, from the orientals and the Greeks to his contemporaries without leaving out the Scholastics, and he sees the truths
included in this tradition articulated in such a way as to reveal
". . . some progress in knowledge" and to constitute a kind of
perennial philosophy, perennis quaedam philosophia (a certain
perennial philosophy), the historical accumulation of philosophy
throughout the ages. He gives scholasticism its rightful place
within this perennial philosophy. But after Leibniz and until
the nineteenth century scholastic philosophy languishes and little
attention is given it from without. For example, in his Histoire
comparée des systemes de philosophie (Comparative History of
Systems of Philosophy, 1804) Degérando disposes of Christian and
Arabic scholasticism in a scant fifty of the fifteen hundred pages
of his work.

10. The Nineteenth Century

Not until Hegel do we again find even so much as a deficient understanding of scholasticism. We must remember that Hegel wrote the
first History of Philosophy as philosophy in the strict sense as
well as history. In the Hegelian structure of reality the past
in its entirety is indispensable and irreplaceable. His method
of tying the past together may seem inadequate to us today, but
there is no doubt that our own demands for greater historical
accuracy can be traced to him. The whole of the nineteenth century
in its philosophy as in all other disciplines, and even in its opposition to him, is rooted in Hegel. It would not be overly difficult to show the presence of Hegelianism in the tendencies of
the nineteenth century to turn again to scholasticism, albeit the
motives involved were quite different from those that led Hegel
to interpret it.[33]

It is a well-known fact that around the middle of the nineteenth century scholasticism came to be reconsidered broadly and
systematically. This occurred in two more or less simultaneous
ways. First, scholasticism was looked on as a way of thought that
was currently valid and thus, in a sense, of timeless value. In
this view scholasticism was of interest as a "repertory of doctrines"
independent of any historical context or circumstance. Thus for
the first time in this neoscholasticism (it was noted that Suárez
had other aims) an attempt was made to segregate philosophy from
theology in order to create a "scholastic philosophy" that hitherto

had not existed independently. This consideration of scholasticism as a body of docrines naturally directed attention to the work of Saint Thomas Aquinas, the philosopher who had symbolized the apogee of scholastic thought insofar as formal perfection and systematic construction were concerned. For this reason neoscholasticism has been principally and at times almost exclusively neothomism.

We find, then, a consideration and utilization of scholasticism based on the formal rejection of what I have referred to throughout this work as the scholastic "situation." Indeed, this rejection is carried to extremes, for it leads to each thesis, principle, and ratiocination of Saint Thomas being removed from its context. Now the immediate situation of any human utterance is its context, and yet neothomism has customarily isolated the pronouncements of Saint Thomas from whatever real context they have in his work. This is what Gilson refers to as the elimination of the "Thomist order." Naturally, references to the multisecular speculation of other Scholastics are minimal and marginal in neothomism.

The second view of scholasticism during the past century involves less unity and breadth than the first. In fact, it consists of several isolated and independent views dealing with diverse aims and interests. Their only common denominator is a tendency to situate scholasticism within history and consequently to view it in its entirety. It is these two features that set this view of scholasticism apart from the one discussed above. Among the thinkers who exemplify this second tendency--begun at the same time as the first, i.e., around mid-century--are Gratry, Brentano, and Dilthey. Auguste Gratry (1805-1872) makes a constant thematic appeal to scholastic thought, including Saint Anselm and especially Saint Thomas, and even to the forerunner of scholasticism, Saint Augustine. Yet Gratry understands scholasticism as a historic form of thought originating with the Greeks and the Church Fathers and continued in modern philosophy where it reaches a splendid culmination in the seventeenth century. To put it another way, scholasticism seems to him to be an indispensable phase of that philosophy which is so coherent and true in its overall unity, but which is still developing toward final maturity, and which in its historic entirety could be called philosophia perennis.[34] Franz Brentano (1838-1917) who was steeped in scholastic thought and who links it to Aristotelianism on the one hand and, like Gratry, sees it effectively continuing in the thought of Descartes and Leibniz on the other, is also aware in a philosophical way of the entire medieval tradition. As a matter of fact, his use of this tradition is so effective that certain scholastic notions are clearly elucidated for the first time in his philosophy. In other cases his reconsideration of some medieval doctrines is unusually penetrating.[35] Finally Wilhelm Dilthey (1833-1911), in the masterful history of philosophy that he undertakes in his Einleitung in die Geisteswissenschaften (Introduction to the

Sciences of the Spirit, 1883),[36] displays a more cogent understanding of all scholastic thought than his predecessors by including for consideration not only secondary figures but also
Arabic and Jewish thinkers. Moreover, he attempts to reach an
understanding of scholasticism by means of what he calls "historical reason."[37]

11. The Present Position

The philosophy of the present century takes a position somewhat
similar to that of the three thinkers discussed briefly above.
Those men are important forerunners of present views and to them
may be traced our insistence on a philosophic understanding that
transcends the mere manipulation of texts extirpated from temporality. For such texts are the disjecta membra of what were once
living realities and which can be brought back to life only insofar
as the circumstances under which they arose are brought into present focus. As Gratry wrote in 1853 regarding Saint Thomas: "But
Saint Thomas of Aquinas is yet to be understood! In him there
are heights, depths, and insights that contemporary intelligence
is far from being able to understand. Perhaps they will be understood a few generations hence, if philosophy comes again to prominence and if wisdom reappears amongst us. . . . Philosophy has
been discovered and rediscovered by Plato and Aristotle, by
Saint Augustine, by Saint Thomas of Aquinas, by the seventeenth
century; but it has been lost in the intervals between. Today
it is evidently lost from amongst us. We read the ancient monuments without understanding them; we do not know their language,
and we cannot understand their meaning. . . . Such is the state
of contemporary thought regarding the noble philosophy of the
past and the wisdom of the great centuries. For modern man has
before him all their monuments but not their understanding and
still less their faith."[38]
    Nevertheless, our position differs from all those taken by
the nineteenth century because our idea of philosophy is more
complex. This can be seen in apparently trivial details, for
example, in the very meaning we give to the word "problem."
Usually it is thought that a problem exists when I am unaware
of something, or perhaps when I believe two things that appear
in contradiction to each other. In other words, a problem seems
to appear whenever there is uncertainty or discord among certainties.
Yet this alone is not enough; in order for a problem to exist something else is needed, something so elementary and simple that it
appears too obvious to mention. The missing element is my need
either to know something I do not yet know or to resolve some
discord between the things I do know. Now countless things exist
which I do not know or of which the coherence and relationships
are a mystery to me. Can these things, strictly speaking, be
considered problems? Of course not, for I have no need to consider

them as far as my situation in the world goes. Problems are not theoretical statements that may or may not appear in my life. Failure to understand this is the reason why we speak so lightly of "problems" today, forgetting that a problem is always something that must be resolved.

For this reason, philosophical problems are always imposed by some real circumstance, and this is also why they are not always the same. On the contrary, problems have a history; they come and go, that is, they come into being and they cease to be. To put it another way, it becomes either necessary or unnecessary to resolve them in order to decide on the proper course in a given situation. The formal statement of problems may persist unchanged as such, but the same cannot be said for problems themselves. Consequently, no philosophy can be understood without its circumstance, and to forego the latter is to reduce a mode of thought to a mere abstract outline. To be sure, such outlines are not only valid but indispensable as well. But they must be understood for what they are: as outlines and as abstractions. To mistake them for reality is to render any understanding impossible.

Therefore, we must include the entire history of philosophy in our consideration of a particular form of thought, and any philosophical utterance must be weighed in our understanding against this total background. This is a procedure based not on whim but on the realization that this history is an ingredient of our own circumstance and that philosophy is meaningful only within its context. We are our own masters only insofar as we know our own past; otherwise our best efforts amount only to remedy and fiction.

But these statements suggest an unavoidable question. Does not such concern for the past mean simply that we end up reveling in it? Are we not then dealing with pure history and not philosophy? The tendency is to think in terms of what in recent years has been called quite hastily and very mistakenly "historicism." In its strictest meaning, the vogue of historicism betrays a certain satisfaction that derives from history, like a delectatio morosa (morose delight) in historical forms washed up on our present shores like the remains of shipwreck. But if we take a closer look at things, we see that historicism is really untrue to history. How is this possible? First of all, history does not stop; by its very nature it is urgency and presence. The historical past is historical only insofar as it presents willy-nilly the present. Thus, any attempt to dwell in the past forms is antihistorical. Interpreted in this way--which is not to be confused with the awareness of the historicity of human life-- besides revealing basic deficiencies, historicism is a denial of itself, for it overlooks the deeper nature of history.

Furthermore, in Aristotle's words, "Philosophic knowledge cannot forego the point of view of truth" (τὴν φιλοσοφίαν ἐπιστήμην τῆς ἀληθείας).[39] Philosophy is not merely a pleasant exercise in comparing opinions; it is a matter of knowing what the truth is and of knowing how to respond to the reality of things. Philosophy aspires to know in the fullest meaning of the term. But this injunction does not imply what Dilthey called the "absolutism of the intellect." For thought, which is capable of apprehending reality, can never claim an exhaustive knowledge of all reality. This fact is always apparent in any knowledge of reality, precisely because it is real and therefore includes perspective as an element of its reality. A true view of things reveals what things are, but it does not reveal everything they are. Rather, the reality viewed is only that which can be seen from a certain perspective. Naturally, there can be no view taken from nowhere. Strictly speaking, the expression "true view" is redundant. Any view is true. What may not be true is the intellectual structure that I add to my view or substitute for it. Moreover, a "true view" may become false when I remove it from its perspective, or when I mistake it for a universal and exhaustive view of reality instead of what it really is: a view as partial as it is true. To absolutize my view and to insist that it is reality itself is to invalidate it and to condemn its partial truth to falsification insofar as it attempts to usurp other compatible or conflicting truths revealed by other possible perspectives. All intellectual absolutism aims more or less consciously at usurping the "point of view" of God--and this aim is far from being limited to Hegelian thought!

We should not consider these facts to be overly trivial simply because they are so obvious. The situation of each person is such that his intellectual action is determined by a strictly personal perspective. No man is the same as any other man or any period the same as another period. Every point of view reveals a dimension of reality that it alone can see, and yet it cannot see other dimensions that are equally real. Nevertheless, without this point of view, that dimension would have remained hidden and ignored. This explains why no philosophic view is the only one, and this is why also, insofar as they represent points of view and not ideological structures, different views are compatible with one another just as different dimensions of reality are compatible. Tout ce qu'un homme a vu est vrai (All that a man has seen is true), as Father Gratry was fond of saying. But this alone may be misleading in that it suggests an eclecticism that is not intended; for it does not mean simply that a certain view corresponds to a certain portion of truth and that to see the whole truth we need only to gather together these partial visions. Philosophic points of view are not in any way interchangeable; they are strictly qualified by their place in history.

What the seventeenth century saw coult not be seen by the thirteenth, nor was the thirteenth-century view possible in the fourth century B.C. Each moment rests on all previous ones, which function as elements of the present situation. At every moment the being of man comprehends what he has been at all stages of

the past, and the same thing happens in history. There is, then,
a historical coordination of the different philosophic points
of view, and this coordination is determined by the internal
articulation of history. Therefore, these philosophic points
of view act as elements of my particular point of view in a
historical, rather than eclectic manner. Only in this way can
each person remain true to his time.

It is literally impossible for me to read an ancient writer
without attempting to relate him to my own situation: just as
I can never fully immerse myself in his world, neither can I
abandon my own, try as I may. Even in the ideal example, where
all the elements of his world could be reconstructed, it would
still be necessary to add the basic structure of my own time, and
this would in fact create an entirely different situation. Hypo-
thetically, I may know everything that an ancient writer knew,
but I cannot forget what I know and what he could not know.
This is why it is impossible for philosophy to repeat itself.
I cannot read the same text that Plato wrote and his contemporaries read, for the same pages appear in different and unique
ways throughout history. Strictly speaking, there is no single
Plato but rather as many Platos as there are readers in different
historical situations.[40] My perspective joins and encompasses
all past views. The famous statement Vetera novis augere et per-
ficere (The new increases and perfects the old) is plausible if
it is correctly understood in its complete meaning: OMNIA vetera
QUA VETERA, scilicet HISTORICE (EVERYTHING old, INSOFAR AS IT IS
OLD, is clarified HISTORICALLY). This brings us to the question
of the appearance of scholasticism in our world.

12. Scholasticism in Our Situation

From our present point of view, scholasticism appears to be a
splendid portion of the past that constitutes our present reality.
It is, therefore, an element of our situation and hence an unavoidable part of our very being. We shall not repeat the mistake of
rationalism in this respect. Scholasticism is something that
happened, and inasmuch as this is so it has a present reality
in that form of being we call "historical."

Let us be more specific. Scholasticism was a historical
phenomenon, and as such it was conditioned by a certain set of
circumstances. These included a Christian "world," the prevailing authority of a theology and (since the thirteenth century)
a philosophy, and a causal relationship between them. The question remains unanswered as to whether medieval man could have
responded to the situation in which he found himself de facto
with something other than scholasticism. This question would
have to be answered before the history of the Middle Ages and of
scholasticism itself could be understood in the deepest sense.
That is, scholasticism will not be fully understood until it is

seen as merely one of the historical possibilities open to the
men who created it, and until historical reason reveals why it
was this possibility and not some other that came to be realized.

If at this point we compare the circumstances under which
scholasticism arose with those of our own time, we find that
they are almost exactly inverse. This fact lends heightened
interest to the present situation. Today we live in a world
that is not Christian. By this I mean that it is not a matter
of individual Christians or Christian people. Regardless of the
number of individuals who may profess to be Christian or even if
all men were Christian, this would not mean that the world itself
is Christian, for by Christian world we mean a system of certain
prevailing customs and usages. Hence it is possible to imagine
a Christian world in which many men are not Christian at all or,
on the contrary, a non-Christian world in which many individuals
profess Christianity for specific and personal reasons and not
because Christianity is the prevailing belief in a social and
impersonal sense. We are inevitably immersed in a social system;
we do many things not because they seem good or bad to us but
simply because they are considered the right thing to do. We
have no personal commitment to the social usages that constitute
our "world" in the sense described, but this was possible and
indeed occurred on many occasions in the Christianity of the
medieval world. On the other hand, when the world is not Christian, men who profess Christianity as a religion do so in a completely personal way. Such was the situation of all primitive
Christianity down to the time of Saint Augustine in which, during
the first three centuries, it shaped its existence in a pagan
world. Therefore the fact that our world is not Christian is not
necessarily a deplorable condition when considered from a religious
point of view. The problem arises, though we cannot go into it
at this point, when the world not only adopts a non-Christian
attitude but also, and with increasing frequency, demonstrates
an anti-Christian attitude in its social structure. Furthermore,
both in numbers of adherents and especially quality of faith the
professed Christianity of contemporary man is often deficient
from a religious point of view.

In the second place, there is at present no single predominant philosophy. At best--and even this is uncertain--there may be
an established philosophic "tradition." But this is a far cry
from the predominance of a particular philosophy, such as we find
in the thirteenth century. As for theology, it is totally without
social visibility and is preserved nowadays only within ecclesias-
tical groups who are themselves subjected indirectly to the pressure of society. In other words, theology matters to ecclesiastics
simply because of their profession. Yet at the same time this
allegiance must contend with the fact that these same men also
belong to "our" world. On the other hand, other disciplines,
such as science and technology, do prevail today. Contemporary
man holds on to the belief that scientific knowledge is effective

and that the machines it produces really work. Finally, philosophy appears to men of our time as a need for immediacy and for
the radical consideration of problems. It is viewed as a decisive
effort to reveal reality in its unvarnished state, free of the
interpretations and theories normally lying between it and us
and frequently mistaken for reality itself. Consequently, in
several essential ways, our situation is the very antipode of
the world in which scholasticism was possible and necessary.

Yet this very inversion of situations lends a peculiar
interest to scholasticism. We understand a certain reality only
by comparing it to others. For this reason, perhaps nothing will
aid us more in understanding our own historical circumstance
and the current meaning of philosophy than an adequate consideration of scholasticism in the medieval world. Moreover, we are
now leaving the so-called Modern Age behind us. It may well be
that future histories will end the chapter on the "Modern Age"
around 1900. And since willy-nilly we are prisoners at many
levels of the forms of life represented by "modernity," it be-
hooves us to make contact with other ways of life that are not
"modern." This is why we must consider medieval and ancient
human modes, not so as to repeat them--to attempt to do so would
be as naïve as it is impossible--but rather so as not to fall
back anachronistically into ways already tried and which belong
to the past, and, furthermore, so as to understand clearly that
the modern way of life is simply one among many possibilities.
A true knowledge of scholasticism can be an effective means of
transcending the "modern" ethos.

Considering the matter from another view, if we ignore the
historical reasons for an interest in scholasticism, we find others
nonetheless that are derived from the very intellectual form and
doctrinal content assumed by scholasticism. Above all, we find
a great deal of precision in scholasticism, although this precise-
ness is not always as great as it seems to be. In many cases,
this precision is due to a very elaborate terminology that should
be preserved and used to a certain extent, even though this cannot be done without reconsidering and applying it according to
each individual case. Philosophy must shun the vagueness that
always threatens it. "Depth" (the _Tiefsinn_ spoken of by Edmund
Husserl)[41] usually conceals a lack of clarity and theoretic precision. The scholastic disciplines of scholasticism and phenomenology have been in different ways schools of clarity and precision,
and without these qualities philosophy runs the risk of being
buried under nebulous notions where exact concepts are impossible.
We must not overlook the fact that, in general, scholasticism has
been exposed very little to errors and aberrations. This does
not mean that it does not contain its share of misconceptions.
In fact, its overall coherence and logic make its errors all the
more apparent. What is the reason for the essential soundness
of its concepts? First of all, scholasticism has never lost
sight of the content of revelation, and this has acted as a sort

of permanent corrective. Secondly, it has remained true to a
tradition and has proceeded with great prudence. Finally, scholastic thought has been the work of a school (schola), and its
ideas have always been hammered out in a kind of intellectual
collectivity. Almost always these factors have prevented scholasticism from going off on tangents, as has happened all too
often in modern philosophy. Sometimes such tangents are the
work of genius, but not even genius can justify them philosophically. No doubt the stability and soundness of scholastic thought
are offset somewhat by its undeniable propensity for "formaliza-
tion" and immobility, by its repetition of abstract and empty
formulas. Nevertheless, once this risk is overcome, philosophy
must scrupulously avoid abandoning itself to mere tangents of
any kind.

In considering the doctrinal content of medieval thought,
we find (especially in its less well-known and seldom-quoted
parts) certain elements that are of maximum interest from the
standpoint of twentieth-century philosophy. For deep metaphysical reasons that are seldom clearly understood--though often stated
and as often forgotten--the philosophy of our century needs to
know what man is. This need is much more radical than any prior
philosophical inquiry. Naturally, contemporary philosophy absorbs
and explains the findings of the past, and the surprising thing
is that quite possibly the most astute and precise consideration
of this theme is to be found in the scholastic theories of the
person. Originally these theories involved the study of the
divine persons, but inasmuch as these are neither visible nor a
part of our common experience, our knowledge of them is inferred
analogously from purely human data, from the concrete experience
of the persons we ourselves are. This is why the inquiry of the
Scholastics into human personality is of value both in a theological and an anthropological sense, insofar as personal being is
attributable to God and--primarily in the order of our knowledge--
to man. As an example, we need only cite Richard of Saint Victor.
As I have stated elsewhere,

> In Richard of Saint Victor the knowledge of human being
> and that of divine being are mutually clarifying. What
> experience teaches us about man allows us to infer--mutatis
> mutandis--certain things about the Divinity; and, inverse-
> ly, what reason reveals as proper to God serves to render
> understandable in the deepest sense the very being of man
> as a reflection of the Divinity. Quite possibly no other
> philosopher of the Middle Ages makes so conscious and
> astute a use of this method of alternating between divine
> reality and its human image and means.[42]

Nevertheless, the great amount of attention paid to scholasticism
during the past fifty or sixty years, generally motivated by a
concern for other topics and authors, has not benefited from this
essential trait.

Finally, there is another reason why scholastic philosophy is of urgent interest to us. At the heart of scholasticism lies the problem of what has been called "Christian philosophy," to which we shall now turn our attention.

13. The Meaning of "Christian Philosophy"

"Christianity marks the deepest division in the history of philosophy. The two great stages of Western thought are separated by it. But it would be erroneous to think that Christianity itself is a philosophy; for it is a religion, which is something quite different. Moreover, strictly speaking it is incorrect to think of Christian philosophy, if the adjective "Christian" is meant to define a characteristic of philosophy. We can speak of Christian philosophy only if we mean the philosophy of Christians as Christians, that is, philosophy as defined by the Christian circumstances in which the philosopher lives. In this sense, Christianity has played a decisive role in the history of metaphysics, for it has essentially modified the suppositions on which men base their lives, and this in turn has changed the vital circumstances in which men must dwell before they can philosophize. Christian man stands apart from the Greek, for instance, and his thought is different from Greek thought."[43] This somewhat summary and convenient notion of "Christian philosophy," which I offered elsewhere in explaining patristic and medieval philosophy, requires at this point a more complete explanation in the light of earlier considerations. But I shall not go into the details, must less into a discussion, of the controversy aroused some years ago concerning the notion and the historical reality of Christian philosophy as found in the positions taken by Gilson-Mandonnet.[44]

As we have seen, philosophy arises from a concrete set of circumstances. I do not mean by this that circumstances alone can explain philosophy, or that it emerges necessarily from a given situation. There is always a decisive interplay of freedom and chance. Even so, philosophy is conditioned by situation and exists only in view of it. With this in mind it is easy to imagine how much the fact that man is Christian affects his situation. His situation is essentially modified by his Christianity, and the philosophy that arises from a basis of Christianity will be intrinsically affected by that Christian circumstance.

But simply to be Christian is not enough, for, in the first place, one can profess Christianity in many ways. Moreover, a Christian may philosophize without reference to Christianity at all. This in fact happens whenever problems are treated that in themselves are totally removed from Christian concepts. This is why I have stated that Christian philosophy is that belonging to Christians as Christians. To put it another way, it is that philosophy of which one element is the presence of Christianity. But now a question arises as to the nature of that presence.

137

A Biography of Philosophy

First of all, the presence of Christianity exhibits a somewhat negative effect. For the Christian, discrepancy between the doctrinal content of his faith and the philosophical content of his thought will be an indication of error in the latter, and he will then set about to review his thought in a rational manner in order to discover that error. As a philosopher he cannot accept this discrepancy as proof of error but only as an indication of it, and it remains his philosophical task to reveal the error according to the philosophy itself. Secondly, as has often been pointed out, Christianity imposes the selection of certain problems; the Christian thinker prefers certain topics to the exclusion of others. But this fact should be understood in its total ramifications. It is not simply a question of greater or lesser interest in certain themes, but of something more fundamental. As we saw earlier, not every example of ignorance or discrepancy is a problem. Only that which we need to know poses a problem, and the philosophic problems of Christian man do not coincide with those of men in other situations. Thirdly, Christian man, thanks to his faith, knows from the first what to make of certain things that also hold an interest for philosophy. Yet the things we "know" by faith are not known in the strict sense; rather we "believe" them, as Saint Thomas Aquinas so clearly pointed out. And this brings us to the real question.

Naturally, the philosopher cannot bring the substance of his faith to philosophy, for faith and philosophy are different things. It might appear, then, that the philosopher ought to incorporate the content of faith into his philosophy and then justify the transmission in some rational manner. Yet, though this were valid in a sense, would it be philosophically valid? Evidently it would not. Philosophy has its own avenue, its own procedural and intrinsically systematic exigencies that preclude their being used to lend external support to extraneous notions. Apologetics is something infinitely respectable, rationally justifiable and valid, but it is not philosophy. This brings up the question of whether any influence of Christianity on philosophy may not indeed be extrinsic, whether, in other words, it makes sense philosophically to speak of "Christian" philosophy.

It seems to me that the influence of Christianity on philosophy is not only perfectly possible but is in fact real. But this influence is heuristic in nature. Christianity implies a certain intellectual apprehension of reality. The Christian, whether he is a philosopher or not, views reality through the nuances of that apprehension. This leads him to concentrate his view on certain specific points. In the case of the Christian philosopher, Christianity conditions his philosophic view, that is, it acts upon his perspective of the world. Leaving aside any reference to supernatural illumination or to mere lumen naturale, the Christian philosopher still sees things that the non-Christian does not see. This is what I refer to as the creative or heuristic influence of Christianity on philosophy. To put it another

way, Christianity acts as an element of the situation of the
Christian philosopher, placing him in a peculiar and unique
perspective that alone serves to open the way to a certain dimension or facet of reality. To me, Christian philosophy is any
philosophy, regardless of its method and intellectual principles,
that arises from the radical situation of the Christian and in
which the views of reality deriving from the Christian perspective
are articulated within a rigorously philosophical system.

But we must not overlook the fact that for Christian philosophy to exist, there must first be philosophy per se. This is
why, historically, Christian philosophy came into being rather
late. For this same reason, it was not due to chance that Christian thought first took the form of apologetics. Moreover, what
has been called Christian philosophy has not always deserved the
name: often it has lapsed into deficient modes of thought in
either of two ways: through a lack of philosophy or an insufficient basis of Christianity. Whereas in the Middle Ages philosophy often lacked independence in the sense that it was unfaithful
to its intrinsic needs, in the modern world the shortcomings, in
a variety of ways, have concerned the Christian situation. By
and large, modern philosophy has arisen with only marginal associations with Christianity, and in this sense it cannot be considered "Christian." Yet from another viewpoint, all Western
philosophy, beginning with the Church Fathers, is "Christian"
because Christianity is a basic ingredient of all the historical
situations experienced by men of the Western world during those
centuries.

This fact reveals another reason for contemporary interest
in scholasticism. By comparing it to modern philosophy in response to contemporary needs that transcend both modes of thought,
and by understanding its fate in history, we illuminate our own
situation. If, on the one hand, we find ourselves obligated to
vindicate the unilateral acceptance of that reality we call philosophy as a form of radical, universal, and autonomous certainty
regarding things, on the other hand, the Christian finds himself
in a situation somewhat like that of Saint Augustine regarding
the Ancients, or that of Saint Thomas Aquinas concerning Aristotelianism. The Christian beholds the splendid reality of modern
philosophy and, despite its being somewhat alien to Christianity,
finds that he must give an account of it. Nevertheless, as we
have seen, the situation of the modern Christian is much more
favorable because modern philosophy is much closer to Christianity
than Greek philosophy is.

Furthermore, as we have observed, in transforming his perspective Christianity allows the philosopher to see things in a
way that is his alone. When viewed from a Christian perspective,
modern philosophy is new and different from what it has usually
believed itself to be. The primary task that looms before the
Christian mind of today is the absorption into his peculiar out-
look of the whole philosophic past. In so doing he will, for

the first time in history, have the necessary basis for a sufficient form of Christian philosophy. For, strictly speaking,
Christian philosophy has never yet been more than a mere postulate.

We understand a historical reality only when we see it within itself, as something rooted in real life and in a specific
situation. On the other hand, the historical exists for us only
insofar as it is present in our lives as a part of our own situation. At the same time, we are capable of understanding something
only from our particular point of view, by projecting ourselves
from our own frame of reference to the situation we would understand. This process is known as hermeneutics. This is what I
have attempted to show regarding a certain historical reality,
scholasticism, which hitherto has been the favorite concern of
all forms of anti-historical thought. Our purpose, as our chapter
title announced it, was to view scholasticism in its own world
and in ours.

CHAPTER VI
Suárez in the Perspective of
Historical Reason

1. The World of Suárez

On January 5, 1548--in the same year that Ejercicios espirituales
(Spiritual Exercises) of Saint Ignatius of Loyola was published--
Francisco Suárez, the foremost figure in Spanish philosophy until
our time, was born in Granada. In that same year Giordano Bruno
was born, and in the preceding year, Justus Lipsius, Cervantes
(whose life, except for being a year ahead, coincides with that
of Suárez), and Mateo Alemán. To this same generation belong also
Tasso, Vicente Espinel, Lyly, and finally Tycho-Brahe.

The profile of the two generations bordering Suárez's is
quite significant, and a comparison of all three will tell us
much about two key aspects of Suárez's life: his possibilities
and the direction of history in his time. The preceding generation boasts of such names as Bodin, Montaigne, Scaliger, Charron,
William Gilbert, Luis de Molina (the Tridentine theologian and
author of the doctrine of semi-prescience), Mariana, and Saint John
of the Cross. The generation following that of Suárez includes
Góngora, Lope de Vega, Christopher Marlowe, William Shakespeare,
Francis Bacon, the skeptic Francisco Sánchez (author of the
famous Quod nihil scitur [For Nothing Can be Known]), Campanella,
Galileo Galilei, and Johannes Kepler.

It is a well-known fact that until this time, with the possible exception of the prescient and promising genius and insight
of Nicolaus Cusanus, there had been no original and important
philosopher since William Ockham in the middle of the fourteenth
century. This means that Europe lived for two centuries at the
very least without philosophy; or to be more precise, she lived
either from a philosophy--the holdovers from scholasticism--that
was not her own, or from unsuccessful attempts to formulate another,
as in the case of humanistic thought. This situation gave rise
to three kinds of intellectual life that attempted to fill the
philosophical void and in which the entire Renaissance came to
a crisis. The first of these is the proliferation of scholastic

treatises, endless commentaries on the Summa Theologica and
Classical commentaries of Saint Thomas Aquinas. The second is
erudition, the normal result of the knowledge characteristic of
humanism. The third is the inevitable consequence of the first
two: lost in a dense forest of opinions, discussions, and information of all kinds, man in 1500 finds himself headed inexor-
bly toward scepticism. Montaigne, Charron, and Sánchez typify
the man who, unable to find certainty within a welter of knowledge, withdraws unto himself to consider his own uncertain and
melancholy reality. "I myself am the subject of my book," declares Montaigne at the beginning of his Essais. And he goes
on to say: "Certainly man is a marvelously vain, diverse, and
inconstant subject; it is hard to make any constant and uniform
judgment about him.* This is why Montaigne fills his book with
stories in which the many undulating facets of this mutable
human reality are shown over and over again.

In only two disciplines, physics and politics, does reason
function with a measure of autonomy and effectiveness, and only
in them is it capable of any certainty through the use of mathematical reason and reason of the state; in other words, it achieves
certainty through the technique of dealing with devices and celestial bodies and through the ability to manipulate men. Copernicus,
Gilbert, and Tycho-Brahe pave the way for the maturity of Galileo's
scienza nuova; whereas Machiavelli, Vitoria, Mariana, and Bodin
represent the first stages in the science of the modern state.
Both sixteenth-century attempts to found a philosophy before it
was possible to do so are based on these two intellectual traditions. Giordano Bruno and Francisco Suárez, both born in 1548,
are the only outstanding philosophers of the Modern Age before
Francis Bacon and René Descartes. And their basic work contains
the realization of the two possibilities open to them at that
particular juncture of history. Their radical differences of
temperament and attitude only serve to reveal more clearly the
common historical situation, their "world," against which both
react.

Both Bruno and Suárez were men of enormous erudition and
quite familiar with the thought of the past. As Dominican and
Jesuit, respectively, their early preparation was purely scholastic and especially Thomist, but in reality their philosophical
range extended from the Greeks to their contemporaries.

Giordano Bruno's reaction to the wealth of inherited opinions
and doctrines was not expressed as an attempt to innovate. Throughout his life he was guided by a central idea, or better an emotion,
which he tried to articulate conceptually. He was the first European in whom the discovery of Copernicus had full vital and hence
philosophical repercussions. Previously, it had had little effect
beyond astronomy itself; now Bruno invokes the "noble Copernicus,"
whose writings had moved his spirit from his youth. In Giordano Bruno
the new astronomical image of the universe ceases to be mere "theory"
and becomes a radically new way to live reality. The infinite

universe, identified with God, was the idea by which Bruno lived. "This," he states, "is the philosophy that opens the senses, answers the spirit, magnifies the understanding, and reduces man to that state of true bliss which he may attain as a man."* Bruno's philosophy is really but an attempt to intellectualize this belief, the esthetic magnificence which he feels so deeply.

In order to do so, Bruno turns to philosophical tradition, that represented by Nicolaus Cusanus and Raymond Lull; but he also considers the Scholastics, Neoplatonists, Presocratics, and, most of all, Aristotle. The two principal ideas by which he attempts to explain reality are universal animation--all forms are manifestations of soul, and the world itself is a holy, sacred, and venerable living being--and the plurality of worlds. And unlike his remote teacher Cusanus, who astutely avoided it, Bruno is unable to skirt the question of pantheism and gives in to the temptation to resurrect the doctrine of dual truth taught by the Latin Averrhoists.

The minion rather than the master of his idea, driven by a formidable storm of hatreds and passions, Bruno wandered over the whole of Europe: Italy, Switzerland, France, England, Germany, and finally Italy again, where in 1600, after an inquisitorial process lasting nearly eight years, the restless and tormented flame--more of heat than of light--of what had been his tempestuous life was snuffed out by other flames on the Field of Fiore.

Having chosen the other of the two roads open to Suárez and Bruno at birth, Suárez was to live seventeen years longer.

2. The Attitude of Suárez

Francisco Suárez was descended from an old and noble Castilian family that had been known since the beginning of the twelfth century. As a child he had been destined for the Church. (Six of the eight brothers in the family entered the Church.) In 1561 he went to study in Salamanca. In 1564, a year after the end of the Council of Trent, he was among fifty candidates seeking acceptance in the Society of Jesus. Only Suárez was rejected, after his examination showed him to be of questionable health and intelligence. He refused to resign himself to the decision but went instead to Valladolid, where he presented himself to the Provincial Superior of Castile. A second examination was equally negative, but the Superior decided to admit him anyway. Returning to Salamanca, Suárez encountered great difficulty in his course in philosophy. He did not understand the material and took hardly any part in the discussions. He revealed the situation to the Superior and asked to be reassigned to more modest tasks, inasmuch as his only aim was to serve God and attain salvation. But the Superior advised him to persevere and have confidence. A short time later Suárez overcame his problems and went on to conclude his studies triumphantly, both in philosophy at the Jesuit school and more so in theology at the university.

In 1571, the year of the Battle of Lepanto, Suárez was named professor of philosophy at Segovia, where he took his orders. Until 1580 he taught there, in Avila, and in Valladolid. Still, his life was not free of unpleasantness; he was accused on several occasions by those who found his doctrine and his way of teaching suspect. He was always willing to give up his professorship, but he also declared that so long as he held the chair he could not change his method. What was there in Suárez, so rigorously orthodox, disciplined, and obedient, to arouse this opposition and distrust? It may be that the answer to this question will explain the odd difficulties he experienced early in his studies.

Discounting his evident lack of precociousness (not at all surprising in philosophy), the question arises as to whether his fellow students understood philosophy as well as might be supposed. It seems more likely that having mastered the art of scholastic argumentation and knowing the "rules of the game," they were skillful in the manipulation of theses whose real meaning escaped them. Possibly Suárez failed to understand the courses and the arguments precisely because he understood what they were all about, because he knew the problems and difficulties. Just what was the method of teaching in that time? His biographer Bernardo Sartolo gives us sufficient information: "In that time the falseness of opinions taught was concealed all the more for not having been examined. Certain supposedly firm and unassailable principles were established that a blind faith revered as maxims of philosophy and secure deities of reason; and the mere questioning of their truth would have seemed an act of irreverence."* This method of teaching was called leer por catapacios (reading by rote). In other words, learning amounted to the mere repetition of opinions and the manipulation of scholastic tradition as a repertory of inherited maxims or sentences without any necessary connection with reality. As Suárez himself admits, what amazes and alarms others about him is ". . . my method of reading, which is different from the usual. The custom here is to learn by rote, reading things because of tradition rather than examining them deeply and tracing them to their sources, which are divine and human authority and reason, each in its order."[1]

These remarks hold the key to Suárez's attitude. In the face of the predominate social presence of scholasticism in the schools and universities, the first temptation of a philosopher would be to renounce it, to turn his back on it, to clear his mind and seek truth directly. This was the attitude taken by Giordano Bruno who, in turning away from scholasticism, also came upon the discovery of Copernicus and made it the point of departure in his inquiry. Suárez's case is different. Full of respect for theology--we must not forget that he was first and foremost a theologian--and mindful of the content of revelation and its intellectual interpretations, he found that he needed to understand the secular tradition that was being taught routinely and inertly by rote. A teacher by profession, vocation, and obligation, he discovered that he had to delve into the whole of scholasticism in order to explain it. His procedure, his "method of reading," was to view scholasticism against two fundamental data from which inquiry had to begin: revelation and the reality of things as revealed by human reason. In short, whereas the philosophical task of Bruno was to innovate, that of Suárez was basically to rethink.

This fact influenced all of Suárez's work. It is first apparent in its external form, and later we shall see that it acted also in the content of his thought. As his prestige continued to grow, Suárez left for Rome where he taught theology for five years. Returning to Spain, he taught for a time in the University of Alcalá, but his presence there was not welcome. He returned to Salamanca, where opposition to his method and doctrine sprang up even more violently than before. Indeed, it grew so heated that he and his disciples had to suspend their classes. However, during these same years, his authority was established and in 1590 he began to publish. In 1593 he resisted the urging of Phillip II that he accept a chair in Coimbra, but in 1597 he had to yield to Phillip's insistence. Thereafter, with only brief intervals away in connection with the publication of his works, Suárez taught in what was then the most philosophically important university in the Peninsula. He died in Lisbon in 1617 after accomplishing a work that for the most part has yet to be understood. "I did not believe that dying was so sweet," were his last words.

Suárez's published works, begun late in his career, are but the culmination of his pedagogical tasks. His books are the explanatory outline of his courses, treatises in which he systematizes his lessons with a view to the needs of his students. In a word, they are study plans designed for university classes. Following publication of several theological treatises--De incarnatione verbi (On the Incarnation of the Word), De mysteriis vitae Christi (On the Mysteries of the Life of Christ), De sacramentis (On the Sacraments)--in 1597 the Salamancan presses published his outstanding philosophical work: the two huge volumes of his Disputationes metaphysicae, a work that in many respects, as we shall presently see, is one of a kind. Other theological writings followed and in 1606 he published his De Deo uno et trino (On God One and Triune). His juridical work, De legibus ac Deo legislatore, appeared in 1612, and the following year, the last of his works to be published in his lifetime, Defensio fidei catholicae et apostolicae adversus anglicanae sectae errores (In Defense of the Catholic and Apostolic Faith against the Errors of the Anglican Sect), written to refute the book by King James I of England, was published. He left many unpublished writings, and in all, his work comprises twenty-seven volumes. His is the most important work in scholastic thought since the fourteenth century with its brilliant English Franciscans Duns Scotus and William Ockham. This brings us to the question of the philosophical significance of Suárez's thought.

3. Method

I stated earlier that the philosophical task facing Suárez was to "rethink" the whole of scholasticism. But to "rethink" implies thinking over what other men, in other situations, have already thought. Thought in this sense is possible only through an essential, twofold change in one's point of view. First, the thought of the past can be considered only from the standpoint of one's own situation, from the system of beliefs, ideas, problems, and projects in which one lives; second, the comprehensive study of doctrines of differing periods and tendencies leads to a comparison of them and thus to the expectation of a new reality, expressed in their relationships, that surpasses the original thought, influencing and modifying its content. In summary, the task assumed by Suárez called for a new method, a way to gain access to that new reality that was to be the theme of his inquiry.

Suárez was a man of the Renaissance. The replacement of the medieval world by a Europe composed in the West at least of nations (Spain, Portugal, France, England); the juridical problems resulting from this new structure and dealing as much with the idea of the state as with the relationships among countries; the questions stemming from the discovery of the Americas and the East Indies (legitimacy of conquest, rights concerning the new lands, dealings with native peoples); the theological and political difficulties brought about by the Reformation, Anglicanism, and the wars of religion--all these factors qualified the situation in which Suárez lived, a situation that was vastly different from that of the medieval Schoolmen. There was another element in Europe that unfortunately was quite alien to the great Spanish scholastics of the sixteenth century: modern natural science and its mathematical vehicle. This fact was to have the most serious consequences for philosophy and, indeed, for the history of all Europe.

In order to give an account of scholasticism in its entirety, it must be considered from a new perspective, and its traditional forms--theological treatises, quaestiones, and above all, commentaries--must be examined in the light of its true intellectual principles. This necessitates a cognitive basis that will allow for a demarcation between philosophy and theology. Even as early as Saint Thomas Aquinas a careful distinction was made between the two disciplines, and with Duns Scotus and Ockham their separation was accentuated. But only in the sixteenth century did they come to be treated in works as independent topics. This period saw the rise of "courses": the Jesuits of Coimbra, under the influence of Fonseca with his Cursus Conimbricensis (Coimbran Course); the Carmelites of Alcalá and their Cursus Complutensis

146

(Course of Alcalá); the Salamancans; and in the seventeenth century, Arriaga and Juan de Santo Tomás. Heretofore, philosophy and theology had been, strictly speaking, indiscernible within scholasticism, for it dealt with philosophical questions stemming from, and rooted in, theological problems. Yet these courses, which grew out of an awareness of intellectual and pedagogical needs, fell short of a complete illumination of the question. It was left to Suárez to undertake this task with sufficient knowledge and an adequate method.

It bears repeating that Suárez was primarily a theologian and, what is more, a professor of theology almost all his life. He was not <u>primo et per</u> se a philosopher, and still less an "investigator"; he was a teacher. When he began to write his aim in so doing was to publish an explanation of theology so that his students could save time and effort, as well as avoid the risk of misinterpreting his lessons, by having a treatise on hand. We should bear in mind, further, that Suárez decided to write only at the insistence of his superiors. He had no pretensions as a philosophical author who had decided to publish his intellectual discoveries; rather, his task as a writer was but a <u>ministerium</u> closely tied to his teaching duties. He was obliged to clarify things in order to be able to teach; his publications were simply the written version of his lessons, nothing more.

Nevertheless, he discovered that he could not be what he wanted to be--the perfect theologian who inquires deeply into things and traces them to their sources--without previously having established the proper <u>metaphysical</u> foundation. He saw "as clear as day" (<u>luce clarius</u>) that <u>divine</u> and supernatural theology requires human and natural metaphysics. This is why Suárez had to interrupt his initial labor as a theologian in order to take up metaphysics. And in fact, his fourth treatise, <u>Disputationes metaphysicae</u>, was to become his principal work. Suárez wrote the <u>Disputationes</u> for a theological reason: they are a prerequisite and prior foundation of a true and serious theology.

What exactly are the <u>Disputationes metaphysicae</u>? To begin with, leaving aside the <u>Sapientiale</u> of the thirteenth-century English Franciscan Thomas of York, whose scope and meaning are quite different from those of Suárez, the <u>Disputationes</u> constitute the first treatise on metaphysics written <u>since Aristotle</u>. Furthermore, if one bears in mind that Aristotle's <u>Metaphysics</u> is not, in the strict sense of the word, a <u>treatise</u> on metaphysics, then the work by Suárez is absolutely the <u>first</u> ever on the topic.

Suárez proceeds as a philosopher in the <u>Disputationes metaphysicae</u>, but he does not lose sight of the fact that his philosophy must be "Christian" and therefore the servant or minion of theology. For this reason, he is obliged to pause from time to time in order to consider certain theological questions, not so as to treat them <u>in extenso</u> but to point out to the reader "as though with his finger" (<u>veluti digito</u>) how the principles of metaphysics must be referred and adapted to theological truths.[2]

Thus we find in his work a movement to and fro, a dual occasional relationship, chatacteristic of all scholastic thought: a progression from theology to philosophy in order to reach the groundwork of the former, and a reverse movement from philosophy to theology in which philosophical principles and enlightenment are bestowed on theology in order to imbue it with the nature of a true science.

First philosophy (prima philosophia) explains and confirms the principles that comprehend "all things" (res universas) and, for this very reason underlie "all doctrine" (omnem doctrinam).[3] Any doctrine as such, including theology insofar as it claims to be a science, is grounded in metaphysics, which enjoys absolute priority insofar as method is concerned. The reason for this priority is that the adequate object of metaphysical inquiry is being to the degree that it is real being (ens in quantum ens reale [being insofar as it is real being]);[4] and God Himself is the object of metaphysics, for "God is an object naturally knowable by some means" (Deus est objectum naturaliter scibile aliquo modo).[5]

These clear underlying relationships, so necessary to explain the principles of sciences, had been obscured by the traditional method of the Scholastics, who, according to Suárez, expounded indiscriminately on both theologies: theology sensu stricto, or supernatural theology, and natural, or metaphysical, theology. Over against this position, Suárez had to do what had never been done before: elaborate, distinctly and separately (distincte, ac separatim), a treatise on metaphysics.[6]

But this presents the question of Suárez's modus operandi. What is the structure of his philosophical work? Such questions involve literary genres, which are essentially tied to the content of philosophy and indeed to its very meaning as a human concern. At the same time, for better or worse, the key to the influence and eventual fate of Suárez is found in the form of his metaphysical work.

Suárez was obliged to delve into the accumulated knowledge of a multisecular tradition, for it constituted an essential dimension of the problem. The complexities and masses of opinions accumulated by scholastic thought, especially during the preceding four centuries, presented an overwhelming task and were the primary cause of the uncertainty surrounding the scholastic tradition. Some form of simplification was essential, as the entire Renaissance felt. But whereas the humanists decided to reject the excessive and problematic scholastic tradition, Suárez chose a more difficult solution: to clarify that tradition. Of course as a theologian he could not throw the past overboard, inextricably tied as it was to dogma, even in purely philosophical questions. Suárez could not, therefore, simply confront things without reservation; rather, as is essential to all scholasticism, he had to proceed by considering opinions. Suárez's task was to choose the "true sentence" or opinion from among those at his disposal, but to choose it in view of things. This was Suárez's contribution, made against a background of routine rote memorization, morbid delight in terminology, and the farrago of the commentaries, which, as Leibniz stated, wastes the most precious gift of all: time.

This explains why Suárez had to write the Disputationes: his task was to discuss the past, to clarify traditional opinions by weighing and comparing them with reality as it manifests itself to experience or reason, in order to attain a higher certainty than that offered by tradition. For in the absence of such certainty, the very multiplicity of those opinions had become the cause of the most radical uncertainty. This explains also why Suárez was very careful to include among the sources of truth "sacred and human authority and reason, each in its order."

With few omissions, the names constantly cited and used by Suárez were those that constituted the history of philosophy and theology up to his time. Grabmann's minute recounting of his sources reveals the enormous range of Suárez's learning. If ever there was a man who was not unius libri (of one book), that man was Suárez. From the Greeks, Aristotle and commentators, Plotinus, Proclus, and Plutarch, to the contemporary Scotists, Ockhamists, and Averrhoists of the sixteenth century, all manner of thinkers, pagan, Christian, Arabic, and Jewish, appear in his writings. There is only one serious and important omission, but one that is quite understandable for several reasons: the physico-mathematical thought that had been gaining ground since the fifteenth century and was to mold the mature forms of modern philosophy, beginning with Bacon and Descartes. The absence of this form of thought introduced an anachronistic element into the philosophy of the great sixteenth-century Spanish thinkers, and although they were personally outstanding men, it decisively affected the fruitfulness of Spanish thought as well as the subsequent course of European philosophy. Indeed, it would be difficult to measure the serious consequences it has had on the history of Spain over the past three centuries.

But here a new question arises: in what perspective do these thinkers appear in the philosophy of Suárez? In the first place, they are invested with a peculiar simultaneity. The opinions of the authors cited are situated in the present, making up a repertory of contemporary views that create uncertainty by their divergence and thus pose the problem confronting Suárez. This amounts to a kind of atemporal dialogue among the interlocutors of different periods, each one of whom preserves intact and undiminished his claim to truth. Yet a special role is reserved for two figures: Aristotle and Saint Thomas Aquinas. They appear invested with a special "authority," the meaning of which should be clarified. Opinions are not valid simply because they originate with Aristotle or Saint Thomas or because Suárez might swear in verba magistri that they were. The task assumed by Suárez is to rethink tradition in view of things, and this formula--which could be the most abbreviated summation of his philosophy--has no limits and makes no

exceptions in favor of any author. The authority of Aristotle
and Saint Thomas alluded to earlier is evident in the fact that
in cases where their opinion does not seem correct, instead of
rejecting it outright, Suárez appeals to a secondary criterion
of fundamental significance. Let us examine his method.

It consists of an elementary hermeneutics that attempts to
reconstruct what the philosopher tried to say from what he actually
said. This means that instead of adhering strictly to Aristotelian
or Thomist affirmations, Suárez delves into the context of statements and seeks therein the reasons for the author to say certain
things that are literally false but are true within the larger
setting of their complete thought. A case in point is the discussion of whether metaphysics is also a science of the accidental,
in the face of Aristotelian texts affirming that it deals only
with substance; or again, when Suárez examines the opinions of
Aristotle and Saint Thomas and tries to reconcile their apparent
contradictions on whether it is easier to know the universal or
the singular; or, to cite yet another example, concerning the
problem of whether wisdom is more noble and certain than the habit
of principles. Even in cases of the widest discrepancy, Suárez
has reservations about attributing an erroneous opinion either to
Saint Thomas or to Aristotle. Thus, when he posits the thesis
of the difference between essence and existence, he adds: Haec
existimatur esse opinio D. Thomae (This will be judged to be the
opinion of Saint Thomas).[10] The meaning of this is clear: given
the general assumption of the truth of Aristotelian and Thomist
thought, each in its proper order, an effort must then be made
to interpret each specific thesis in the light of the entire system of postulates. In this way, the truth of each thesis may be
effectively understood or the reasons for its error explained
and revealed. The fact should be emphasized that this is an exceptional and restricted use of this kind of hermeneutics in
Suárez, though by the same token its presence in his work cannot
be denied.

What would have been the structure of the Disputationes
metaphysicae had Suárez applied this method generally and deeply?
The answer is that he would have been led inexorably to a consideration of the relationships of the diverse opinions to one another.
I mean real and not merely logical relationships. To put it
another way, Suárez would have had to inquire first into the
genesis of such opinions within the different ways of viewing the
reality of things, and second, the origin of those same points
of view as they are conditioned by other views. In short, he
would have had to replace an atemporal and simultaneous consideration of doctrines with a historical approach. Undoubtedly, this
would have led to the intrinsic perfection of the metaphysics of
Suárez, for then and only then would he have really been able to
account for the philosophic past by justifying it in a radical
way within its own thought. In so doing, he would have remained
absolutely true to his personal aim of philosophizing in view of

150

things, because such a perspective would have meant a consideration of traditional doctrines not for their tradition but for
their reality.[11]

Elsewhere I have discussed the characteristics of Suárez's
philosophical method, insofar as it arises from his actual situation. In summary, the most salient features of his approach are
the following:

(1) The methodic separation of philosophy from supernatural
or revealed theology.

(2) The priority of metaphysics as a foundation.

(3) The order of theology and philosophy whereby the former
stands as the end toward which the latter strives.

(4) The occasionalistic relationship between theology and
philosophy, which determines the area of philosophical problems
and articulates the interest shown in various questions according
to a theological perspective.

(5) The mediacy of this dind of philosophy, which treats
the accumulated opinions on the Aristotelian-scholastic past in
order to ascertain the "true sentence" or opinion.

To these points we can now add:

(6) the simultaneous and atemporal, rather than historical,
consideration of the philosophic past, with only isolated examples
of a historically oriented hermeneutics.

The preceding are the salient procedural features of the
metaphysical thought of Suárez. They arise from the convergence
of the historical situation, insofar as it deals with inherited
modes of thought, and his personal aim, which transforms the historical into the real setting of an individual human life. And
these features have in turn helped to shape the subsequent fate
of Suárez in the centuries following his death. Finally, we must
now inquire as to that fate.

4. The Historical Fate of the Philosophy of Suárez

If one looks closely, it would seem to be an ironic fate. For
the fact is--perhaps somewhat overstated--that for two centuries
Europe has learned metaphysics from Suárez, but not the metaphysics
of Suárez himself.

At the end of the sixteenth century, when Suárez published
the two huge volumes of Disputationes metaphysicae, in which he
summed up with marvelous precision and clarity the labor of two
millennia concerning prima philosophia, he not only formulated a
repertory of personal solutions but at the same time asserted his
indisputable mastery of the field. Catholics and Protestants,
whether Scholastics or not, all turned to this admirable intellectual monument. Notice that metaphysics prior to Suárez had assumed
one of three forms:

(1) that characteristic of the work of Aristotle, that is,
a series of related but independent inquiries that deal for the

most part with the vindication and justification of what Aristotle calls the "sought-after science" (ητουμένη ἐπιστήμή), but which are arranged in an uncertain and problematic order;

(2) that adopted in the commentaries--Greek and medieval--on the Metaphysics of Aristotle in which strict textual adherence leaves no room for any autonomy; and

(3) that appearing in particular inquiries on specific points in which the question of metaphysics per se does not arise.

It should be clearly understood that I am speaking here only of metaphysics as a discipline. Only in Suárez are the lines drawn of a metaphysics that is not Aristotelian, regardless of how much it owes to Aristotle.

In the fifty-four disputations, Suárez poses the problem of the nature of metaphysics, and having established an adequate notion of it, he proceeds to study the concept of being, its passions and common principles, and the theory of causes. In the second volume of his work, he divides being into infinite and finite categories and studies in turn the Creator and the creature, including a minute ontological analysis of the latter. For the first time, the so-called metaphysical science assumes a systematic and explicit structure that transforms it into a discipline in the most literal meaning of this term. For this reason, all the metaphysicians of the seventeenth and eighteenth centuries learn metaphysics from Suárez, or from works that are closely based on his thought, and in this sense they are all his disciples.

But they did not learn the metaphysics of Suárez! As we have seen, it was largely a question of scholastic metaphysics bearing the permanent stamp of medieval scholasticism in the form of an occasionalistic relationship between theology and mediacy. However, scholasticism fell into obvious decline after the death of Suárez. The very value and soundness of his work clearly revealed the historical necessity of that decline. Without the Spanish theologians of the sixteenth century--above all, without Suárez--one might think that the cause of the passing of scholasticism was the mediocrity of its spokesmen. But Suárez is comparable to Saint Thomas or to Duns Scotus and is not inferior to the great figures of his time. Nevertheless, we find no abiding traces of his thought in scholasticism, which degenerated into sterility a few years after his death. But what was the situation of philosophy beyond scholasticism?

Let us recall several dates. Suárez published his Disputationes in 1597, the year that Bacon's Essays appeared. in 1609, Kepler's Astronomia nova or Physica caelestis (Celestial Physics) was published; in 1620, three years after Suárez's death, Bacon's Novum organum; in 1625, Huig de Groot's De jure belli ac pacis (On the Law of War and Peace); 1628, Harvey's De motu cordis et sanguinis (On the Motion of the Heart and Blood); and 1632, Galileo's Dialogo dei massimi sistemi (Dialogue on the Maximum Systems). Descartes published his Discours de la méthode in 1637, followed by Meditationes de prima philosophia (Meditations on First Philosophy

in 1641, and Principia philosophiae (Principles of Philosophy)
in 1644 (in other words, his works appear in the order of method,
metaphysics, and physics). These dates mean that in the fifty
years following the publication of Disputationes, modern philosophy and natural science came into being with an incomparable
surge of activity and a new method, i.e., a new way of approaching reality, that was the theme of the time. And since philosophy is always a method, modern philosophy reached its maturity
with Cartesianism, after a period of productive gropings, and
henceforth it was to be a rigorously new philosophy, very different from scholasticism and therefore from the thought of Suárez.

The metaphysical knowledge of Suárez was to be utilized in
its entirety, but from another set of assumptions and from another
perspective. In universities all over Europe until well into the
eighteenth century, Suárez was read and studied, and editions of
his works multiplied. But as philosophy was being created in
those centuries, it was rooted in an inspiration alien to Suárez's
thought. Even in cases of apparent loyalty to his teachings,
Suárez falls victim to the system of learning by rote that he
tried to abolish from Spanish universities during his lifetime.

We should be mindful of the fate of literary genres themselves,
for they betray an intimate connection with thought; more specifically, they concern the fundamental nature of thought: its style.
Suárez was almost an encyclopedia of knowledge. His Disputationes
contain over ten thousand pages written in small script in double
columns. He wrote at a time when "macrology" was giving way to
an era of conciseness. The important works of the period, those
of Galileo, Bacon, Descartes, and Leibniz, are quite brief, and
the works of the last two mentioned are mere pamphlets. Leibniz
was able to condense his metaphysics, Discours de métaphysique,
to fifty pages in octavo, and in his old age, twenty were excessive
for his Monadologie. "Más obran quintas esencias que farragos"
(Quintessences are more effective than farragoes), remarked the
Spaniard Gracián, who on occasion could speak for his age.

All this has reduced Suárez to little more than an unknown
voice today. At the beginning of the work cited earlier, Arboleya
confesses that: "Hardly any real knowledge accompanies the mention of him today. Suárez is as obscured by the brilliance of
his fame as others are by the mists of oblivion. Everything has
yet to be discovered about him."[12] As to this, one task stands
out above all the rest: the need to understand him from the historical perspective in which he is really situated, and to see in
him the final maturity of scholasticism as it reaches its perfection and conclusion at the same time. Because to see him in this
light means that the truth that it was given to him to discover
from his unique and irreplaceable point of view can be preserved
by integrating it with the march of philosophy down to our time.
To put it another way, this means clarifying the reasons--the historical reason, if you will--that motivated Francisco Suárez to
assume the task of thinking and writing his Disputationes metaphysicae.

A Biography of Philosophy

In this chapter I have proposed simply to bring to mind some of
the problems implied by that urgent philosophical task.

CHAPTER VII
Modern Metaphysics

1. The European Mind in the Seventeenth Century

There is no single date marking the beginning of the Modern Age in Europe. From the breakdown of the medieval unity in the fifteenth century until the time when the modern world was really its own master, nearly two hundred years passed. It is such a long span of time that the expression "Modern Age" is somewhat ambiguous. The elements that went into its formation appeared only gradually on the surface of European history. Indeed, segments of the medieval world coexisted with the more recent creations of fleckless modern origins. The persistence of medieval values was so noticeable in some countries, such as Spain, that the very existence of the Renaissance was problematic. It is commonly supposed that the Middle Ages lasted until almost the dawn of the eighteenth century in these countries, though this is true only to a limited degree and only in certain facets of life.

The transition from the medieval world to the modern is first apparent in three vital areas: art, politics, and religion. Renaissance art, especially in Italy and Flanders, the formation of Western nationalities and their subsequent colonial and ultramarine expansion, and the Protestant Reformation followed by the Catholic Counter Reformation culminating in the Council of Trent, are the great historical facts that bring about the change from one era to another. Furthermore, all these events take place approximately between the last years of the fifteenth century and the first half of the sixteenth. Let us point out some dates: 1474, the union of Spain; 1483, the death of Louis XI of France; 1485, Henry VII of England begins the Tudor dynasty; 1556, the abdication of Charles V of Spain; 1558, the beginning of the reign of Elizabeth I of England; 1517, the ninety-five theses of Luther; 1531, the separation of the Anglican Church; 1540, the founding of the Society of Jesus; 1545-1563, the Council of Trent.

In science and philosophy, the matter is more time-consuming and complex. Of course the sway of scholasticism is soon left behind. But it is one thing to leave something and another to reach something new. From the nominalist physicists until Galileo and Newton and from William Ockham until Descartes and Leibniz, the European mind needs more than two centuries to formulate a new kind of knowledge about things. Ockham, the last great medieval philosopher, died around 1350, and it was not until 1534 that Copernicus' treatise De revolutionibus orbium caelestium (On the Revolutions of Heavenly Bodies) appeared--and even this was only the first step in modern physics--and not until 1609 was a second and still immature step forthcoming in Kepler's Physica caelestis (Celestial Physics). The nuova scienza (New Science) was not formulated until somewhat later when the great works of Galileo were published. His Il Saggiatore (The Archer) appeared in 1623; Dialogo dei massimi sistemi (Dialogue on the Maximum Systems) in 1630; Discorsi e dimostrazioni matematiche intorno a due nuove scienze (Mathematical Discourses and Demonstrations Concerning Two New Sciences). The title alone of the latter work is quite revealing: "Mathematical Discourses and Demonstrations Concerning Two New Sciences." However, modern natural science did not really come into its own until 1687 with the publication of Newton's Philosophiae naturalis principia matematica (Mathematical Principles of Natural Philosophy). In philosophy, Descartes' Discours de la méthode (Discourse on Method) dates from 1637 and his Méditations from 1641. The Discours de métaphysique, which signals the maturity of Leibniz, was published in 1686 (probably).

To reiterate, then, two hundred years are needed for the new era to come into being, and this must be extended to three centuries if we have in mind the full maturity of the modern mind. Although the thought in those intervening years is no longer medieval, neither can it be said that it is modern philosophy. In reality it is not modern at all but is rather an attempt to revive the least substantial portions of Classical thought. Finally and foremost, except for isolated and exceptional examples, the thought of those centuries hardly deserves the term philosophy, if the latter is taken to mean, in fact, an authentic metaphysical knowledge of the nature of things.

Yet the more one insists on the evident discontinuity among the stages of philosophic maturity, the more clearly a new problem arises. In all ages, at least in the Western world after Greece, i.e., in Mediterranean antiquity and in Europe, life has always been oriented by some philosophy that in a very real sense appears as an ingredient of that life and therefore as a necessary factor in understanding both life and historical reality. The periods that we consider to be "intermediate" or "transitional" are from the historical point of view as substantive as the others. This means that the philosophy ideated by these periods, the philosophy they live by, requires an explanation, and without a sufficient knowledge of such philosophy, we cannot fully understand historical reality. This point was brilliantly expounded by Ortega in

his prologue to the Spanish translation of Bréhier's History of
Philosophy. Yet from time to time man does modify the nature of
his vital dependence on a philosophy. It should be recalled that
philosophy is a reality that made its appearance at a specific
time and place: along the Ionian coasts in the seventh century B.C.
Furthermore, since then it has existed only in certain cultural
circles and not in others. It is possible that the philosophy
on which a certain historical period bases its life is not really
its own thought. Finally, besides this possibility, it may be
that the philosophy in question is inadequate as philosophy, i.e.,
insofar as it represents an attempt to reach a clear understanding
of reality. This establishes very different categories among philosophical systems that are quite apart from any intrinsic apprais-
al of such philosophies. Similarly, the conditions under which
philosophies exist also have a decisive effect on the corresponding historical periods, for it is one thing to possess a system
of philosophical convictions conceived according to the circumstances
of one's own life and based on a primary metaphysical understanding
of reality (to use an expression that is perhaps vague and inadequate but that refers to a most concrete reality), and altogether
another thing to adopt ideas that are alien and hence somewhat
unwieldy and imperfectly suited to a situation that is in turn
automatically oriented and modified by this very fact.
     This is the difference we find if we compare the period from
the fourteenth to the sixteenth century to the intellectual situation of the seventeenth. In the earlier period there is no system
of congruent ideas arising from an original mode of thought. Instead,
men live in the wake of a past tradition in which are commingled
revivals of antiquity with hints--but no more than hints--of new
intellectual directions. In the second period, science and philosophy display an incomparable self-assurance and enjoy a unified
and effective body of doctrine of reality. But it would be a
serious mistake to interpret thought after Ockham and before
Galileo and Descartes as a "preparation" for the second period.
Such a progressive notion would hinder our understanding of the
period and it would deprive that philosophy of its substantive
value that must be considered apart from its strictly intellectual
qualities. This is not to deny that certain ideas of this period
turned out to be necessary antecedents of the nuova scienza or of
rationalistic philosophy. Later thought can so interpret them,
and this is a perfectly legitimate and necessary way of viewing
them provided that such an interpretation is not exclusive, or
for that matter even primary, but is preceded by an adequate
understanding of the ideas themselves, as viewed from the perspective of their time. Only a few thinkers whose thought is especially
innovative--albeit also fragmentary--and who are perhaps of most
interest to us today, can be understood as representing the first
intuition and indication of the great ideas that will dominate
and direct philosophy in the seventeenth century. Such men, for
instance, as Copernicus and Nicolaus Cusanus, among others, must

be studied in the light of these ideas.

At this point we may ask what philosophical elements the great metaphysicians of the seventeenth century found in their circumstances and in their immediate past; and, secondly, we may inquire as to the degree and kind of influence exerted by these elements on the development of their own philosophy. These questions then lead to a third: what are the stages and problems of the metaphysics of the baroque period?

The greater volume of teaching and philosophic production at the beginning of the seventeenth century was still scholastic in content. The decline of scholastic authority and hostility with which Renaissance men viewed it should not cause us to forget this fact. The philosophy habitually written and taught in the universities was first of all the scholastic thought of Saint Thomas, Duns Scotus, or Ockham, and secondly the varieties of scholasticism presented by the Hispanic thinkers, Juan de Santo Tomás, Fonseca, or Suárez, for example. Descartes studied scholasticism at La Flèche, and Malebranche received a similar education at the Collège de la Marche. This was true even in Protestant circles: Leibniz spent his youth in the study of the Schoolmen before going on to the modern writers.

Scholasticism lies behind all rationalistic speculation and there are constant references to it. Very often Descartes uses the terminology of l'école when he wishes to render his thought understandable to the masses of his readers. As for Leibniz, his allusions to scholasticism are more explicit and concrete, no doubt because it was more remote from contemporary readers. In fact, during the fifty years that separate the two thinkers, scholasticism was largely, though not completely, replaced by Cartesianism. One need not look beyond orthodox Catholic thought to find this evident Cartesian influence; it is apparent, for instance, in the work of Bossuet and perhaps still more so in the Traité de l'existence de Dieu (Treatise on the Existence of God) of Fénelon.

But within scholasticism itself, two phases differing even in chronology must be pointed out. One of these is what can properly be called medieval and refers to nominalism before Ockham. It was against this version of scholasticism that Renaissance humanism reacted so strongly. Its last important representative was Gabriel Biel (1425-1495?), but scholastic influence both before and after him was slight. The second phase of scholasticism was Renaissance in character and, therefore, to a degree modern. Such was Spanish scholasticism with corresponding repercussions in Portugal and Italy. In a sense it involved a reaction against humanism and dealt with the problems of the Renaissance (the matter of Indians, the rights of peoples, the modern state, the Protestant Reformation, etc.). As a mode of thought, it was very fertile and had a decisive influence on rationalistic philosophy. Its leading thinkers, most of whom were Dominicans and Jesuits, include

Francisco de Vitoria (1480-1546), the Tridentine theologians
(Soto, Melchor Cano, Carranza, Bañez, Láinez, Salmerón, among
others), and finally the three philosophers mentioned earlier:
Pedro Fonseca (1548-1597), the Portuguese commentator on Aristotle;
Francisco Suárez (1548-1617), the most original metaphysician of
modern scholasticism; and Juan de Santo Tomás (1589-1644), the
contemporary of Descartes. These thinkers exerted a very real
influence on the rationalistic philosophy of the seventeenth
century, and taken as a group, they are reason enough to turn
attention--as did Leibniz--to the thirteenth-century Scholastics.

Furthermore, we must consider the reaction against scholasticism that took the form of "humanism." It began in Italy and
was represented as early as the fourteenth century by Petrarch.
The movement reached its maturity in the Academies such as the
Platonic school of Florence (1440) with Marsilio Ficino and,
among others, Pico de la Mirandola and Johannes Bessarion; and
with the Aristotelian adherents (Hermolao Barbaro, Pietro Pomponazzi).
This tradition continued until the first half of the seventeenth
century with Niccolò Machiavelli (1469-1527) and Tommaso Campanella
(1568-1639), or with Bernardino Telesio (1509-1588), who represents
a trend toward the philosophical study of nature. The entire active
and extensive humanist group (Erasmus, More, Montaigne, Ramus, Vives,
etc.) was opposed to medieval philosophy and attempted to surpass it.
But these men could offer only superficial thought rooted for the
most part in the supposed restoration of Greco-Roman philosophy.
Indeed, from the standpoint of philosophy, the most noteworthy contribution of the movement was its revival of ancient systems that
would have a deep impact on the metaphysical and moral thought of
the seventeenth century. Yet Aristotle and even Plato were soon
relegated to a secondary position in favor of late Classical philosophies such as Stoicism, Epicureanism, and Scepticism. Seneca,
Cicero, Epicurean atomism as revived by Pierre Gassendi (1592-1655),
Pyrrhonism, which influenced the European mind from the sixteenth
to the eighteenth century--these were the Classical tendencies that
impacted on the thinking of the new era. "The three philosophies,"
wrote Ortega, "like three fates as godmothers, hover around the
cradle of Cartesianism and therefore around the whole of classic
European rationalism."

Finally, by the fourteenth century, a mystic movement branched
off from scholasticism, especially in Germany, Flanders, and France.
First represented by Meister Eckhart (1260-1327), continued in the
fourteenth century by Johannes Tauler (1300-1361) and Jan Ruysbroeck
(1293-1381), and in the fifteenth by Dionysius the Carthusian and
Jean de Gerson (1363-1429). In the sixteenth century we find a
German Protestant branch of considerable impact (Sebastian Franck,
Weigel, Jakob Böhme) as well as the flowering of Spanish Catholic
mysticism, especially in Saint John of the Cross and Saint Theresa
whose influence can be found even in Leibniz.

Although various implications make it hard to draw exact boundaries, the ideologies treated merit consideration as vestiges of

medieval thought or as more or less intelligent and mature attempts
to evolve a system of ideas suitable to the new era. At this
point we must turn our attention to the intellectual elements
encountered by the men in the seventeenth century that they must
interpret as "antecedents" of their own thought and as the first
indications of modern natural science and rationalistic philosophy.
All these elements bespeak a common concern: the orientation toward the problem of the external world. Furthermore, they are
overshadowed by the common question of the method whereby knowledge
may be attained. In more concrete terms, this mode of thought
arises from the exclusive exercise of reason and hence follows
the philosophical patterns first laid down by Duns Scotus and
Ockham. Their method may be described as the tendency to apprehend reality by means of mathematical concepts, sub specie mensurae.
This means that the two philosophical topics of that time are the
world and the mind which conceives of that world mathematically.
These concerns lead in turn to the problem of the infinite and
thence to God--that is, to questions beyond the capability of the
intellectual systems set up to treat them. Consequently, the
thought of that time is constantly beset by the danger of pantheism,
and it is not until the very end of the century that such themes
are placed in their proper perspective.

Owing to somewhat uncertain and overlapping characteristics,
three tendencies, rather than three groups, must be pointed out
among the thinkers of this period. The first of these is speculation about the world based on notions that are often irrational
and even magical. To this trend of thought belong Paracelsus,
Agrippa von Nettesheim, and perhaps Leonardo da Vinci. Over against
this kind of thought, which we might call a natural science without
method, we find the beginnings of the nuova scienza, which is characterized by a constant and formal appeal to the mathematical method.
The most outstanding adherents to this mode of thought are Kepler
and Copernicus, both of whom help pave the way for Galileo. Finally,
we discover philosophy sensu stricto, eminently represented by
Nicolaus Cusanus (1401-1464) and Giordano Bruno (1548-1600). In
embryonic form, several of the principal themes of later philosophy
are found in their work; and they reappear in Spinoza and Leibniz
and even in German idealism. These topics include the problem of
the relationship of God to the world, the idea of the infinite,
and a new monadic conception of the individual that involves a
profound alteration in the notion of substance.

Finally, almost simultaneous with the triumph of Galilean
physics and Cartesian philosophy, English empiricism comes to the
fore with Francis Bacon, whose Novum Organum was published in 1620.
It continues with Thomas Hobbes (1588-1679), who greatly influenced
political studies, and is maintained by his followers until its
culmination in John Locke (1632-1704). The latter signifies the
maturity of empiricist philosophy in the Islands, just as Leibniz,
who must deal with empiricist doctrines, represents the plenitude
of Continental rationalism.

Such are the elements encountered by the great seventeenth-century philosophers in their intellectual circumstance. They live in a highly complicated world of ideas and from it they receive the most disparate of influences which they must place in some orderly perspective. As he begins modern philosophy in the true sense of the word, Descartes achieves a kind of magical simplification of these influences. And through this transformation he seems to emerge as a philosophical Adam, as it were, who begins afresh and knows no past. But let us not be deceived by appearances; beneath this seeming absence of earlier postulates in Cartesian philosophy lies a multitude of ideas briefly summarized above; the same ideas appear in more explicit form in the work of Leibniz.

2. The Genesis of Modern Philosophy

As we have seen, the two general tendencies of Renaissance philosophy were either to continue the scholastic tradition with its medieval forms and its propensity for mere exegesis of great works, or to break with the medieval past and with Aristotle, who was considered the source of scholastic thought. Both tendencies were really insufficient and held no lasting promise. Despite the genius of individual thinkers, Spanish scholasticism declined rapidly and after the death of Suárez, or at the latest, after the passing of Juan de Santo Tomás, it quickly lost all philosophical authenticity. It was too closely linked to traditional forms, to the repertory of problems belonging to the Middle Ages, and to the solutions proposed for those same problems. Consequently, it lost contact with reality. Its gravest error, however, lay in its tendency to hold that all important questions had already been resolved, for which reason it turned a deaf ear to the whole range of true problems and renounced the spirit of real philosophical investigation. Instead, it preferred mere commentary and the polemical defense of a body of doctrine handed down generation after generation. Eventually, even those dedicated to its preservation and transmission lost sight of its original purpose.

On the other hand, the humanistic thinkers who rejected scholasticism in favor of Classical philosophy forgot that medieval thought, throughout its history, had been nourished by the Classical writers. The Schoolmen had found inspiration not only in Aristotle (whose influence, after all, was somewhat late in exerting itself) but also in the Humanists' favorite thinkers: Plato, the Neoplatonists, and the Stoics. This means that the continuation of Greek thought is much more real in the Church Fathers and the Schoolmen than in the Platonic philosophers of the Renaissance. Furthermore, the latter did not really attempt to reach a direct and deep understanding of Classical thought but were quite satisfied with its more superficial and literary aspects. Finally, the position of the humanistic thinkers regarding scholasticism

itself was unsatisfactory. To begin with, by scholasticism they
generally meant the thought of the fourteenth century, i.e.,
scholasticism when the movement was in its period of decadence,
and they were simply not familiar with its development by its
most illustrious representatives. Secondly, the humanists considered
it in toto, reducing it arbitrarily to Saint Thomas and his commenta-
tors--an error also made, frequently, by the adversaries of humanism--
and overlooking the wide variety of medieval philosophy. Finally,
after taking as a justified point of departure the abuse of formal
logic and the erroneous presentation of questions dealing with
physics, the opponents of Aristotle and scholasticism condemned
them without appeal and without taking the trouble to know them.
They viewed the whole of scholasticism as a kind of opaque mass
interposed between the twin clarities of the Classical world and
its Renaissance revival.

   This twofold manner of considering the question did not end
with the seventeenth century. Even today we can find many examples
of both positions. Let us examine two of them: the first in
Bordas-Demoulin (Le Cartésianisme ou la véritable rénovation des
sciences [Cartesianism or the True Renovation of the Sciences],
pp. 1-4), and the second in Jacques Maritain (Antimoderne [Anti-
modern], pp. 99-106). Bordas-Demoulin says:

   Modern men, like the ancients, have not philosophized as
   soon as they first attempted to do so. In fact, it has
   taken modern man four times as long as the ancients. The
   attempts of the ancients took two centuries, from Thales
   to Socrates; modern men have required eight, from Alcuin
   to Descartes. It is true that seven of those centuries
   were absorbed by scholasticism and scarcely one was left
   for the speculations of Telesio, Bruno, Campanella, Ramus,
   and Bacon, all of whom attempted to innovate. Now then,
   far from opening the door to philosophy, scholasticism
   served only to close it; for it casts thought out of
   itself and buries it in words, whereas the object of
   philosophy is to turn thought in on itself. It was in
   spite of scholasticism that Saint Thomas, Saint Bonaventure,
   Saint Anselm, Henry of Gant, and Albertus Magnus understood
   certain things, and this was especially true in the case
   of Roger Bacon who gave the first indication of reform
   two centuries before Telesio. They were secretly excited
   by Christianity, the spirit of which gave them strength,
   although the theocracy in which it was enveloped tended,
   along with scholasticism, to stifle them. No doubt scholasticism represents an attempt to philosophize, but the
   effort is counterproductive because the Scholastics turn
   their back on reality and truth. With each advance it
   only sinks deeper into darkness, and with Duns Scotus it
   falls into a bottomless pit of subtleties. However, the
   human spirit, strengthened by Christianity, becomes

aware of its power and attacks scholasticism as it does feudalism.[1]

In other words, Bordas-Demoulin believes scholasticism to be a fruitless effort that hinders the emergence of true philosophy, and it is only in spite of it that medieval philosophers discover the truth. But we should especially take note of the fact that far from opposing scholasticism with anti-Christian views, he believes it to be the antipode of Christianity itself, which had acted as a stimulus to medieval thought. Bordas-Demoulin's position, therefore, is contrary to the opinion, as common as it is abusive, that identifies scholasticism with Christian philosophy.

In contrast, Maritain writes:

> Now then, what is the attitude of Thomist thought regarding so-called modern thought? In order to answer this question properly, a distinction must be made between modern science and specifically modern philosophy. Furthermore, within the latter, we must also differentiate between the spirit that moves it and the substance of truth that it potentially contains. . . . We reject the spirit of modern philosophy, its specific principles, its general orientation, and its ultimate aim. From it we would retain only useful lessons. . . . Today only Saint Thomas appears as the representative par excellence of Christian philosophy, and because only he encompasses in his principles all the universality, all the breadth, height, and depth of Christian thought, only he can effectively defend it against errors that would be unamenable to any palliative. Modern scholasticism can take pride only in humbly imitating him and not in rethinking his doctrine according to contemporary modes. Instead, it should reconsider the problems of our age in the light of Saint Thomas' doctrine. . . . Aside from these reservations, modern philosophy is quite useful to thought because of the very errors it contains; for in order to refute them, one is constantly obliged to delve deeper into truth, to define its principles, and to clarify new aspects. . . . It behooves scholastic philosophy to assimilate, rectify, and balance everything; and to put into clear perspective those intellectual intentions that modern philosophy had corrupted. This is the only acceptable manner of reaching an accord with modern philosophers.[2]

Maritain takes a view completely opposite to that of Bordas-Demoulin. In essence and on the whole, he believes modern philosophy to be an error that must be refuted, though certain particles of truth may be gleaned from it. The only true philosophy is scholasticism, and Saint Thomas is its most authentic spokesman and must be

humbly imitated. But the most important fact of this imitation
is not that Saint Thomas needs to be reconsidered in the light
of present conditions but rather that those very conditions must
be appealed to his philosophic postulates, principles, and modes
of thought. No clearer and more incisive expression can be found
of the two positions that contended with each other until the advent of seventeenth-century philosophy. Furthermore, we see
clearly that neither view gives ground in the arena of their
dispute.

Between the years around 1600 and our time lies the corpus
of modern philosophy, the first stage of which (from Descartes to
Leibniz) consists of surpassing the older, opposing views that
scholasticism is either all error or all truth. It is true that
Descartes, "that great effacer of his own past," appears to be
almost without ties to his philosophical tradition; and although
in a sense his efforts disguise rather than destroy those ties
(larvatus prodeo), they have allowed a "Renaissance" interpretation
of his thought, that is, a view that his work represents a radical
innovation and a complete break with the past. Bordas-Demoulin
so interprets Descartes, as we have seen, as does Hamelin in his
classic book Le Système de Descartes (The System of Descartes),
p. 15: "Descartes comes directly after the Ancients, almost as
if nothing separated them from him except the physicists." Yet
ninety years earlier Father Gratry pointed out Augustinean and
scholastic influences in Descartes and indeed in all seventeenth-
century philosophy. More recent studies (cf. A. Koyré, L'Idée
de Dieu chez Descartes [The Idea of God in Descartes] and the
studies of Etienne Gilson) have found supportive evidence for this
same thesis. Descartes is immersed in a tradition that stretches
from the Ancients to Duns Scotus and includes Saint Augustine,
Saint Anselm, Saint Bonaventure, and Saint Thomas, to name only
the most outstanding figures. The problems treated by Descartes
grew out of scholasticism and were brought to the fore by the
nascent physics of the time. The latter influence leads him to
stress its innovative and antischolastic stand while rejecting in
his philosophy both the method and the literary genres of medieval
speculation. Descartes' method is new; he strives ". . . to guide
reason well and to seek truth in the sciences." He does not possess the truth he seeks, for it is submerged in ignorance and
doubt. For this reason, he cannot write a Summa or even Quaestiones
disputatae. Neither is he willing to use the whole syllogistic
apparatus of logic. His aim is knowledge and ". . . as for logic,
its syllogisms and most of its other instructions serve more to
inform another of what one knows or even as in the case of Lully's
art, to speak without judgment of those things one does not know,
than to learn what is unknown" (Discours de la méthode, 2nd. part).[3]
At first it seems that Descartes plans simply to write a short
autobiographical discourse, offering rules for his new method
and giving examples of results he has obtained by its application.
However, when he decided to offer a more mature exposition of his

philosophy, Descartes wrote his Méditations, a short, intimate, and simple book that, like his Discours de la méthode, betrays no connection to the medieval Summas and even less to scholastic Commentaries; yet we note that it bears the same title as works by Saint Augustine, Saint Anselm, and Saint Bernard.

Furthermore, in continuing in this tradition, which can be traced through the Franciscan thinkers after the thirteenth century, Descartes veers toward the religious, practical, and moral conception of theology as it appears in the Nominalists and hence in the mystical writers mentioned earlier. In the first part of his Discourse, Descartes clearly states his attitude toward theology: he admits to a reverence of it and hopes, "like any other man," to reach heaven. But the ignorant as well as the learned are admitted into paradise, he observes--echoing the theme of devotio moderna that can be traced to Thomas à Kempis--and, therefore, theology is really unnecessary in the final sense. Moreover, inasmuch as it lies beyond the natural forces of man, Descartes foregoes theology entirely. This line of reasoning, Augustinean and mystic in origin, leads Descartes back to the intimacy of self and causes him to base his entire philosophy on the principle of cogito, ergo sum, on the immediate fact of the existence of the thinking ego.

The post-Aristotelian philosophies also exert a clear influence in Cartesian thought. Over against skepticism, Descartes attempts to establish an evident and incontestable form of knowledge, and he sets out to do so by choosing doubt itself as a starting point. Among the several reasons that lead him to universal doubt, he points out the plurality of contradictory opinions held by philosophers of all ages. This attitude in itself is Pyrrhonism. Yet Descartes is not content to stop at this point; rather, while he admits the validity of this view, he at once surpasses it by revealing the existence of truths that are not only undoubted but also undoubtable. As for Stoicism, its influence on Descartes is even deeper and indeed more positive. The entire moral concern of Descartes, in his correspondence with Princess Elizabeth as well as in the Traité des passions de l'âme (Treatise on the Passions of the Soul), is impregnated with Stoicism, and he reveals this influence in alluding to the De vita beata of Seneca. Likewise, the ethical thought traceable to Cartesian philosophy--that of Spinoza, for instance--clearly reveals Stoic antecedents. Furthermore, it would not be amiss to investigate carefully the imprint of the Stoa on the idea of nature appearing throughout the Cartesian movement.

Finally, the most visible tradition in the philosophy of Descartes is the naturalistic and mathematical thought of men such as Copernicus, Galileo, Huyghens, and Snellius, which derives remote but real influences from the Italians, Telesio and Bruno; from Nicolaus Cusanus; and even from the nominalist physicists. At times this influence has appeared to be the only one in Cartesian thought, though in the light of the less visible antecedents in

Descartes, we can now see that this supposition is erroneous. Nonetheless, its presence in his philosophy is so clear and unmistakable that it would be idle to dwell on it further.

Modern philosophy, therefore, really begins with Descartes, who based his thought on the general postulates of medieval philosophy. Thus, he reestablishes the continuity of thought in which the Renaissance believed but attempted to destroy. At the same time, he incorporates into his thought all the elements created and activated by the men of the Renaissance, and in this sense--albeit only in this sense and with the restrictions of scope previously noted--Descartes may be considered as representing a period of transition between two ages of philosophic plenitude.

Yet Descartes is but the beginning of rationalistic metaphysics. He inaugurates modern thought in a most positive way and reveals in his work the innovative characteristics of the new era. Following him, there is a deeper understanding of the intellectual background of the new philosophy. The generations immediately following Descartes fall under Jansenist influence, and their most outstanding thinkers, for instance, Antoine Arnauld, Blaise Pascal, and Pierre Nicole, betray an overriding concern for theology. Thematically they link traditional thought with Cartesianism. Indeed, certain of the Cartesian regulae are even incorporated into the logic of Port-Royal. With Bossuet and Malebranche the merger of philosophy with Augustinean and medieval theology is completed. As a matter of fact, the fusion is so complete and significant that it marks the beginning of a mode of French thought, represented especially by oratory, that modern philosophy has cultivated without breaking the ties that bind it to the entire medieval past. Saint Augustine and Descartes, together with the intermediate presence of Saint Thomas, seems equally a part of this vast movement. In Leibniz, finally, the older traditions reappear. However, their appearance is not merely implicit or factual but explicit and historical. Leibniz is the first to incorporate all contemporary influences by affirming and situating them within a certain perspective. He makes a clear attempt to weigh and judge the philosophical past, and he does this not so as to renounce earlier forms of thought but in order to include them in a higher and more advanced point of view. This is why he does not share the common disdain (evident since the fifteenth century) for scholasticism, but instead is bold enough to praise it from a distance and to refer to it as a common good in which he shares. For this reason Leibniz represents the mature summation of philosophical trends of the Renaissance and Cartesian thought from Cusanus to the Spaniards. It is not by mere chance that we owe to him the suggestive and disturbing concept of philosophia perennis, "perennial philosophy."

3. The Problems of Rationalistic Metaphysics

Were we to attempt to reduce to a single statement the whole
range of problems in seventeenth-century philosophy, we should
have to say that they lay in the efforts to clarify three questions,
the first two of which depend on, and derive their ultimate meaning
from, the third: the problem of method, that of substance, and,
thirdly, that of God.

(I) Method. Descartes' point of departure is doubt and hence
a fear of error. His aim is, above all, to apprehend some indubitable truth that will serve as a foundation from which to launch
the search for other truths. In this way, no room is left for
error. With Cartesianism begins the philosophy of caution, dominated by a fear of error rather than a zeal for knowing the truth.
Nevertheless, Descartes does wish to know, and to know of a certainty; for him, philosophy is "the search for truth by means of
man's natural light." In other words, philosophy itself is a
"method," a way or road leading to truth. Yet this method cannot
be simply a certain orientation of philosophical inquiry; rather,
it must afford an infallible rule for distinguishing the true
from the false, and it must also allow for a demonstration of
the supreme truths. Method, then, must become what it had always
been in philosophy since the time of Parmenides: an avenue leading to reality itself. And this is found primarily in what
Descartes calls "intuition," intuitus.

As Descartes writes in his Regula III, "By intuition I
understand . . . the conception which an unclouded and attentive
mind gives us so readily and distinctly that we are wholly freed
from doubt about that which we understand. Or, what comes to
the same thing, 'intuition' is the undoubting conception of an
unclouded and attentive mind, and springs from the light of reason
alone; it is more certain than deduction itself, in that it is
simpler. . . . Thus each individual can mentally have intuition
of the fact that he exists, and that he thinks; that the triangle
is bounded by three lines only, the sphere by a single superficies,
and so on."[4] This intuitus is what the unclouded and attentive
mind conceives through reason alone. The object of intuition is
naturae simplices (simple natures). Now these naturae are merely
views and contain no error whatsoever, inasmuch as error is a
product of judgment, that is, of the haste or bias with which one
affirms or denies something. Descartes states in Regula IV:
"Thirdly we assert that all these simple natures are known per se
and are wholly free from falsity. It will be easy to show this,
provided we distinguish that faculty of our understanding by which
it has intuitive awareness of things and knows them, from that
by which it judges, making use of affirmation and denial."[5] Earlier
Descartes has stated: "Only understanding is able to perceive
the truth."[6] And since things in the final analysis are composed
of naturae simplices, all understanding, even that reached through
deduction, is rooted in this primary intuition. This vision,

which is a contact, so to speak, with reality, is infallible.
This means that any vision or idea is true. As Descartes says:
"L'idée est la chose même conçue" (Idea is the thing itself con-
ceived).

Stated in another way, human reason is the instrument of
transcendence, and as such, it apprehends itself. But the importance of this fact is not that Descartes proposes to know things
by means of ideas but rather that ideas are themselves reality
observed; they are actually things in conceptual form. In this
way--but only in this way--Cartesian rationalism is also idealism.
The primary "simple nature" within our cognition is the "I" and
on it rest all other such "natures." Furthermore, Descartes
asserts that "Je ne suis qu'une chose qui pense" (I am but a
thing that thinks) and therefore my being consists of thinking,
in having cogitationes. Hence, things are really the ideas I
have of them. Later we shall see how not only the transcendence
of ideas but also the truth of these same ideas depend on the
Divinity.

This point of view is predominant in all rationalistic philosophy. In Malebranche the "vision in God" places the spirit,
whose natural abode is the Divinity, in the immediate presence
of divine ideas and hence of things. Substances and spirits and
their properties--in other words, all the things of this world--
are knowable by means of the ideas we have of them. An idea
offers knowledge of things and their properties as they really
are, and the possible deficiencies of understanding in such a
process arise not from the idea but from the mind. "Since the
ideas of things that are in God contain all the properties of the
things themselves, he who sees the ideas sees also all the properties of the things. Were the spirit infinite, it would see the
things that are in God in a most perfect way. The gaps in our
knowledge of extension, figures, and motion, are due not to any
defect in the idea but rather to our spirit which contemplates
them."[7] Man is defined by his participation in reason--animal
rationis particeps (an animal sharing in reason)--and this does
not refer to any particular cognitive faculty but implies that
man exists in a superior universal order of transcendence: "The
essential difference of man arises from his necessary union with
universal reason."[8] Within the same context he demonstrates even
more clearly how reason implies absolute reality itself: "Yet if
it is true that the reason which all men share is universal, if
it is true that it is infinite, if it is true that it is immutable
and necessary, then it is certain that it is in no way different
from the reason of God Himself. . . ."[9]

Bossuet in turn writes: "There is, then, necessarily something prior to all time and to all eternity and it is within this
previous eternal something that eternal truths subsist and manifest themselves to me. . . . Thus we perceive these truths in a
light greater than ourselves. . . . These eternal truths, which
human understanding discovers to be always the same, and by which

all understanding is determined, contain something of God, or rather, they are God Himself."[10]

In Spinoza, who carries the philosophical themes of the seventeenth century to their extreme form, idea is identified with reality: "The order and relationship of ideas is the same as the order and relationship of things."[11] For this reason he rejects the possibility of falsity of ideas, as ideas, and instead considers them to be necessarily true: "All ideas are true insofar as they pertain to God. Nothing positive in ideas will allow them to be called false. Any idea we hold that is absolute, that is, adequate and perfect, is true."[12] Hence ideas conicide with reality in a strict parallelism. For instance, Spinoza develops the concept to the point of saying that the soul is the idea of the body.

Finally, in Leibniz as we shall see later, ideas arise from the very structure of the monads, or human units, and are therefore innate in a radical sense. Nothing comes from outside the mind; an idea is not a passive impression of some external thing but rather has its active beginning in the mind. But Leibniz goes further and states that the very reality of the monad consists of its power of representation, of vis repraesentativa. The activity by means of which the monad reflects and represents the universe is not merely consecutive or incidental to its essence, not simply one of several possibilities, but rather constitutes its very essence. This means that idea envelops reality. Furthermore, the only external object revealed to the soul is God, and it is only through God--and not in God, as Malebranche thought--that we are able to see things. Stated in another way, the monad, with all its innate ideas, is created by God, and it is by virtue of this Divine creation that the truth of things is assured. In other words, the divine creation substantiates the reality of the universe that is consciously reflected in the thinking monad. The continuous action of God on the monad is the cause of ideas, and for this reason ideas lie necessarily in the realm of transcendence. (See paragraphs 28 and 29 of the Discourse on Method.)

These brief observations suffice to reveal the meaning of the rationalistic method. This method does not imply adherence to some mental technique, for it is not a simple cognitive process leading to truth; rather, it is the conviction that reason--as the seventeenth century understood it, i.e., as clear and distinct ideas--is the instrument that readily apprehends reality. An idea is the thing itself viewed. Hence, being consists of being idea, at least quoad nos (until us). And to reiterate, this is why rationalism is a form of idealism. Yet this is possible only because God assures the transcendence of ideas, i.e., their truth and their ideal reality. Thus we see that all systems of rationalism are based on a concept of God, and if these same systems deny the possibility of a natural knowledge of God, at least they experience a need to prove his existence as a guarantee of all truth. One may recall, for instance, the Cartesian argument of the Evil Deceiver,

the occasionalism of Malebranche, the identification of reality
with God (natura sive Deus [Nature or God]) in Spinoza, and the
harmony preestablished by God among the monads of Leibniz.

The foregoing concepts include the most important elements
of the rationalistic method, but in turn they give rise to serious
problems. When English philosophy, especially with David Hume,
questions the proofs of the existence of God (specifically the
ontological argument on which all Continental philosophy rests),
this idealism, already divested of its transcendent features, is
reduced to a system of mere impressions that allow opinions and
appearances but not an authentic knowledge of reality. This is
why the idealism of the seventeenth century appeared, to use a
Kantian term, "dogmatic" and why it would lead eventually either
to the skepticism of Hume or to a new inquiry along other lines
into the problem of being and knowledge. This is the task of
transcendental philosophy and specifically of Immanuel Kant in
his Critique of Pure Reason. But the real problem of rationalism
is contained in the thesis that idea is reality itself as seen
by us (L'idée est la chose même conçue [Idea is the thing itself
conceived] as Descartes put it so clearly), and it is from this
assumption that any adequate discussion of the problem must begin.

(II) Substance. Cartesian thought is substantialistic; the
modifications in the problem of being brought about by its idealism have not the slightest effect on the cardinal notion of
Cartesianism that being is substantive being. From the very beginning in Part IV of his Discourse on Method and just after he
discovers his fundamental principle of Je pense, donc je suis
(I think, therefore I am), Descartes interprets substantively
the reality of the "I" on which his philosophy is founded, and of
course he understands by substance that which is independent and
sufficient in itself to exist: "I knew . . . that I was a substance
whose entire essence or nature consists of thinking and that in
order to be, it has no need of any place nor depends on any material thing."[13] In a clearer and more thematic way, he defines
substance in his replies to the four objections to the Méditations:
"This is the very notion of substance, that which can exist by
itself, that is, without a need of any other substance."[14] And
to this independence is added, as a characteristic of substance,
the immanence of properties and attributes. As Descartes explains
in the definitions included in his response to the second objection:
"Everything in which there resides immediately, as in a subject,
or by means of which there exists anything that we perceive, i.e.,
any property, quality, or attribute, of which we have a real idea,
is called a Substance."[15] Following this line of thought in order
to define the different substances, Descartes turns to the nature
of the attributes that determine these substances. Thus, he
distinguishes between the substance of mind and extended substance:
"That substance in which thought immediately resides I call Mind. . .
That substance, which is the immediate subject of extension in space
and of the accidents that presuppose extension, e.g. figure, situation

movement in space, etc., is called Body."[16]
    Hence we see that Descartes takes the notion of substance
in the Aristotelian sense of ὑποκείμενον, as the subject of accidents, and it is characterized by the fact that these accidents
are predicated on it and not the contrary. Therefore, whereas
such accidental features are dependent on a supposition or subject
for their existence, the subject is "independent," or "absolute"
(χωριστόν). But we must not overlook the fact that in Aristotle
the notion or idea of ὑποκείμενον (substratum) is derived in turn
from the οὐσία (possession), the properties or possessions of a
thing, the repertory of its possibilities. This is the primary
concept of substance. Both these concepts of substance, as οὐσία
and as ὑποκείμενον, play a major role in the philosophy of the
seventeenth century and ultimately help to shape its deepest meaning.
    Now we can understand why Cartesian idealism brings about no
essential changes in the idea of being and why it affects only
the primacy, or hierarchy, of substances. Being is being qua
substance; it is a quality inherent in substance. The cogito
merely establishes the priority of thinking substance, mind, over
the extended substance, body. The basis of all reality is the
"I," which is thus converted into a primum, a πρώτη οὐσία (primary
substance), at least quoad nos (until us). Descartes is aware of
the difficulty inherent in the very assumption that substances
exist--that, according to his own definition, there are independent
substances having no need of others in order to exist. He explains
away this difficulty by appealing to the concept of "complete" and
"incomplete" substances, and after a rather laborious examination
of the objections and difficulties aroused by his thought, he comes
to a double conclusion. First, he holds that individual things
have no share in true substantiality, at least not in the absolute
meaning of the term. Substance is that which properly corresponds
to the res extensa (extended thing)--of which tangible and physical
things are parts--and to the res cogitans (thinking thing). Secondly,
absolute independence, enjoyed only by God, as a definition of substance is restricted and interpreted in the Cartesian view as independence from any other created substance. Nevertheless, these
restrictions were not upheld by rationalistic metaphysics.
    Spinoza, for example, abandons them very early. The Cartesian
roots of his thought are the most important and well-known elements
of those that had an influence on him. Cartesian philosophy serves
as a starting point for Spinoza, but he proceeds to develop it
along lines that contradict, as we shall see, the most profound
dimensions of Cartesianism. Following his trend of thought,
Spinoza comes to identify nature with substance, to affirm the
unity of the latter, and hence to hold that God and the world are
one. If we compare the definition of substance given by Spinoza
in expounding on Cartesian philosophy in his Principia philosophiae
cartesianae more geometrico demonstrata (The Cartesian Principles
of Philosophy Demonstrated Geometrically) (Part II, Definition II)
with his own definition found in the mature thought of his Ethics,

we see clearly Spinoza's progression from one notion to the other. In the first of these texts, he states: "We understand by substance that which in order to exist needs only the concurrence of God."[17] In the second (Ethics, Part I, Definition III), he adds: "By substance I understand that which is within itself and which is self-conceived, i.e., that which does not need the concept of anything else in order to form the concept of itself."[18] The Cartesian restriction (solo Dei concursu [only the concurrence of God]) disappears, and with it vanishes also the possibility of substance apart from God. This leads directly to Spinozan pantheism.

This becomes even clearer if we consider a passage from Spinoza's Cogitata metaphysica in which he defines creation (Quid sit Creatio [what creation is]): "We say therefore that creation is an operation in which only the efficient cause appears; in other words, a created thing is that which, in order to exist, presupposes only God."[19] Stated in yet another way, creation defines the nature of substance, and if that nature is the exclusive property of God (as Spinoza maintains in his Ethics), then creation is impossible. In his Cogitata Spinoza holds that accidents are impossible inasmuch as they lack substantiality: "From this definition it may be satisfactorily inferred that the creation of modes and accidents is inadmissible, for they would imply a created substance other than God."[20] At this point we understand the degree to which the conception of substance affects the very basis of Cartesian thought and by extension the whole of rationalism.

The problem of substance becomes especially acute in Leibniz. His theory of monads is a step in the transition from the notion of substance as ὑποκείμενον, or substratum, to that of οὐσία, or possession. Unlike Descartes and Spinoza, who base substantiality on a notion of independence, Leibniz holds that it consists of the activity that springs from the very essence of things. Furthermore, this activity is also realization and is not to be confused with mere potentiality. It approaches the Aristotelian idea of entelechy, a term Leibniz himself uses.[21] The monad contains its entire reality within itself; it is the source of its own transformations and activities, and it possesses a repertory of possibilities that are realized within its own confines. This is why it is substance, and its so-called independence is merely a consequence of this positive self-sufficiency. In a writing published in his Acta Eruditorum (1694), under the title De primae philosophiae emendatione et de notione substantiae (On the Emendation of First Philosophy and the Notion of Substance), Leibniz states:

> The notion of forces or "virtue" (which the Germans call Kraft and the French, force) . . . sheds much light on the understanding of the true notion of substance. For active force is different from the idea of potentiality commonly known in the schools. The active potential or faculty as the Scholastics understand it is merely an

immediate possibility of performing an act. Yet it
needs some external thrust or stimulus in order to
become an act. But the active force contains within
itself a certain act or ἐντελέχειαν (entelechy), and
it is an immediate step between the ability to act
and the act itself, inasmuch as it involves an effort.
Thus it is capable of converting itself into an operation. To do this, it has no need of external stimula-
tion but merely the suppression of any impediments.
This can be illustrated by the example of a heavy
suspended object pulling on the rope that holds it,
or by that of a taut bow.

Leibniz goes on to say: "This capacity to act is inherent in all
substance, and some action is always forthcoming from it."[22]
In his later writings Leibniz goes into more detail concerning the nature of substances and reveals more clearly his debt
to Aristotle. In his Système nouveau (New System), 3, he states:

In order to find these real units, I was obliged to
appeal to the concept of a formal atom. . . . It was
then necessary to recall and, to rehabilitate, as it
were, the substantial forms that are so scorned
nowadays. . . . I found that their nature consisted
of force, and from that it followed that something
analogous to feeling and appetite was involved.
Thus, they had to be understood much as we understand the soul. . . . Aristotle calls them primary
entelechies. I prefer to call them, perhaps in more
understandable language, primitive forces that contain not only the act or complement of possibility,
but also an original activity.[23]

In the final phase of his thought, expressed on Monadologie (1714),
he writes: "The natural changes in the monads come from an internal
principle, since an external cause could not influence their inner
structure" (Thesis 11). And he adds: "All simple substances or
created monads might be called entelechies, for they contain within
themselves a certain perfection (ἔχουσι τὸ ἐντελές) and a self-
sufficiency (αὐτάρκεια) that makes them the source of their internal
actions and causes them to be incorporeal automatons" (Thesis 18).[24]
For Leibniz, therefore, independence is based on autarchy.
A plenary state of being can only imply the possession of something.
Thus, just as the "free man" of whom Aristotle speaks (Metaphysics,
I, 2) exists by himself and no other., i.e., he is possessed of
something on which he bases his autarchy, so Leibnizian substance
needs no other; for it contains, imbedded in it for all time in
the act of its creation, the internal principle of its entire
reality. For this very reason, Leibniz reinvests substance with the
individual characteristic it had had with Aristotle (ἡ ἴδιος ἐκάστου,

"that which is proper to each thing") and postulates an absolute and irreducible pluralism. This view contrasts with the Spinozan unity of everything in God, but it is inherent in the Cartesian doctrine of res cogitans (thinking thing) and res extensa (extended thing), which, despite their duality, imply an underlying unity in that both were created by God.

Now we have the elements necessary to understand the great problem of the communication of substances that dominates seventeenth-century metaphysics. We have observed that idealism consisted primarily of affirming the priority of the substance of mind over extended substance and that it involved defining one or the other of these substances by means of antithetical and irreconcilable attributes (cogitatio [thought] and extensio [extension]). Cartesian dualism presents the problem of interaction between substances. This in turn brings up the question of whether knowledge is possible (and by extension, whether ideas may contain truth) and involves, among other things, the relationship of body and soul. Though his reasoning is not always clear and explicit, Descartes posits his argument on God who, as the Creator of both finite substances, links them together ontologically by having them form a single ens creatum (created being). This is the metaphysical meaning of the argument of the Evil Deceiver; it is an obligation to demonstrate the existence of God in order to be assured of his "veracity," or, to put it another way, in order to guarantee the correspondence of substances and, by extension, the truth of clear and distinct ideas.

Malebranche carries this notion to its ultimate consequences by advancing the concept of occasionalism, the continuous intervention of God that causes my ideas to coincide with the movements of extended substance. On the "occasion" of each alteration in either res, God produces a corresponding alteration in the other. Thus, any real communication between substances is precluded, and Malebranche turns to his erroneous theory of vision in God. According to this concept, we see all things in God and in His divine ideas. Malebranche tries to explain this view in a more satisfactory way in several passages of his Recherche de la verite (Search for Truth), and in doing so, he avoids the question of a direct view of the divinity. Despite his caution, however, he is led again and again to make erroneous statements.

Spinoza resolves the problem in a much more radical way by denying the plurality of substances, thus reducing communication among them to a mere parallelism. For him, all substance is one (natura sive Deus [nature or God]); extension and thought are only attributes of that universal substance, and individual things are mere modes, or modifications, that affect it according to a certain attribute. The extremes to which Spinoza goes in resolving the problem--denying the very assumptions from which it arises--reveal its cardinal importance in the rationalistic thought of the seventeenth century.

By way of contrast, Leibniz, who goes to the other extreme in

pointing out the individuality and multiplicity of things, cannot
accept a solution that consists of denying the problem itself,
as does Spinoza, nor does he believe in the constant intervention
of God. For to do so would be to argue for a kind of unending
miracle. Instead, he presents his rather odd theory of preestablished harmony, according to which God has created substances in
such a way that their subsequent development is harmonious and
everything happens as if real communication existed between them.
Each monad remains self-contained but its being consists of re-
flecting the entire universe, comme un miroir vivant (like a living mirror), by means of the representative power invested in it
and others like it at the moment of creation.

It is apparent that in the thinking of all the philosophers
discussed in this chapter so far, the solution to the problem
hinges on the Divinity; for the Divine makes possible the correspondence of the two rei in Cartesian and Occasionalist thought,
just as it is identical with universal substance in the thought
of Spinoza and just as it establishes the prior harmony of the
created monads. To repeat, rationalistic philosophy is ultimately tied to the problem of God, whose existence it is compelled
to demonstrate. If at this point we turn again to the problem
of knowing, it appears as a particular instance in the general
question of communication between substances. The possibility
of such communication is what allows the "I" to know things.
Likewise, from this point of view, the truth of ideas depends
on God, because only He can make it possible, in one way or
another, for the subject to see the reality that we conceive as
idea.

(III) God. The problem of God is predominant in seventeenth-
century metaphysics, and merely attempting to survey it adequately
would lie beyond the scope of this study. It is the central
theme of that century; as we have had occasion to show, it emerges
from the midst of other questions. At this juncture, however, it
is possible to give only that elaboration necessary to situate
the overreaching problem of the divinity within the philosophical
perspective of rationalism. I would refer those interested in
further discussion of the topic to another of my works, in which
I have dealt with it at length.[25]

The seventeenth century insists more on the demonstration
of the existence of God than on a knowledge of Him. A certain
amount of knowledge of the divine is necessary, of course, for
without it, the proof of existence becomes impossible. Yet once
that existence is demonstrated, rationalism ignores theology.
This is especially true of those thinkers who are strictly philosophical and most representative of the movement: Descartes,
Malebranche, Spinoza, and Leibniz.

Descartes, who is prone to subject things to doubt and to
construct his philosophy on unshakable evidence, begins with the
"I" as the principle of all philosophy. His primary purpose is
not to consider the theme of God. Rather than concern himself

175

principally with theology, he shares the view, common in the
waning years of scholasticism, that theology is a practical discipline dependent on revelation for its truth and hence beyond
the natural ken of man. Descartes writes in the First Part of
his Discourse: "I revered our theology and hoped like any other
man to reach Heaven. But having learned of a certainty that the
road to Heaven is no less open to the ignorant than to the most
learned, and that the revealed truths that lead to it are beyond
our intelligence, I had not dared submit them to the frailty of
my reason. It seemed to me that in order to examine them success-
fully, one must needs have some extraordinary assistance from on
high and be more than a man."[26] Descartes, therefore, rejects
from the outset any inquiry into the nature of God. Yet scarcely
does he begin to philosophize, hardly has he discovered a primary
truth--"I exist"--and a criterion by which to orient his inquiry--
"evident ideas are true"--than he finds himself in a situation
where he can go no further. If an Evil Deceiver were to delude
me when I see what appears to be evident and palpable things,
notes Descartes, then I should be unable to trust my clearest
and most distinct ideas. Under such circumstances, only the
evidence of the cogito would be valid: if "I" am deceived, then
I must needs "be." As for other truths, only the existence of
God allows me to be sure of them; only if there is some infinitely
powerful and good being who guarantees that my evidence is not
the deceit of a malign power, can those truths stand. Stated
in ontological terms, the truth of my own existence is known in
an immediate and immanent way and hence is strictly indubitable.
In order to know other things, however, I must look beyond my
self; I must transcend myself. And only God can reestablish the
ontological bridge between the "I" and extended things that idealistic Cartesian dualism has previously severed. For this reason,
although Descartes remains outside of theology sensu stricto, he
is nevertheless obliged to demonstrate the existence of God as
res infinita (infinite thing), the creator of res extensa and
res cogitans and the common source of being in the "I" and in
things as they converge in the form of ens creatum (created being).
Thus God exercises a liberating influence on man, causing him to
transcend his own being in order to discover the reality of things
other than himself. Such is the decisive role assumed by the
theme of God in Cartesian thought. The Cartesian proofs of the
existence of God (the idea of the Divinity and the ontological
argument), which for the present cannot be dealt with in any
detail, affect the central problems of philosophy.

The point of departure for Descartes in his attempt to
prove the existence of God is the reality of the "I" in comparison to the clear and lucid idea of the Divinity. Over against
my finitude and imperfection, I discover within myself the idea
of God as an infinite and perfect being in full and concomitant
possession of all the perfections that either I lack completely
or enjoy only in part. The elimination of personal limitations,

the elevation to infinite proportions of everything real, positive, and good within me, these are the procedures for reaching an idea of God. At the end of Meditation III, Descartes summarizes the ultimate meaning of his theodicy:

> This idea [of God] was born and produced with me from the moment of my creation, as was the idea of myself. And truly, it ought not seem strange that God, in creating me, should have instilled this idea in me as a kind of mark that an artisan stamps on his work; nor does this mark need be something different from the work itself. Rather, it follows that inasmuch as God created me, it is highly probable that in some fashion he made me in his image and likeness and that I am aware of this likeness, in which the idea of God dwells, by means of the same faculty through which I know myself. In other words, when I reflect on myself, not only do I realize that I am an imperfect thing, incomplete and dependent on something other than myself, and that I ceaselessly am drawn to and aspire towards something better and greater than I, but also I know that that on which I depend possesses within itself all the great things to which I aspire and of which I discover the ideas in myself. This perfect being does not possess these attributes as mere indefinite and potential perfections, but, rather, enjoys them fully now and forever. Thus, this being is God. The whole strength of the argument used here to prove the existence of God resides in the fact that I realize that my nature could not be what it is, that is, that I could not have an idea of God, if God did not really exist.[27]

Thus we see how deep are Descartes' roots in the Christian philosophical tradition, with its Augustinean and medieval heritage, a tradition that affords him a knowledge of God primarily by means of His image in the human soul, a tradition that runs from the in interiori homine habitat veritas (Truth dwells within man) of Saint Augustine, through the cubiculum mentis (cubicle of the mind) of Saint Anselm, to the Funken der Seele, or scintilla animae (sparks of the soul), of Meister Eckhart.

In the philosophy of Malebranche, who absorbs the essential doctrine of Descartes, the theme of God persists--indeed, it is carried to such extremes that almost all other topics disappear. Malebranche categorically denies the possibility of real communication between mind and objects, and therefore the possibility of any direct knowledge of the world. Yet he believes that the reality of God is revealed to us immediately and that only through this immediate reality can we derive a knowledge of things. Instead of an indirect and mediate view of God that implies going from

creation to Creator, as Saint Paul states: "For the invisible
things of him from the creation of the world are clearly seen . . ."
(Romans, 1:20), Malebranche holds that we see things in God, i.e.,
that our notion of things is mediate, our notion of God, direct:
"God is in the closest union with our soul by His presence, so
that one may say that He is the abode of spirits, in the same way
that space in a certain sense is the dwelling place of bodies.
Having postulated both things, it is certain that the spirit can
see what it is in God that represents created beings; for to the
spirit, this Divine quality is most spiritual, intelligible, and
accessible." He adds: "If we should in no wise see God, we
would see nothing."[28] The problem lies in the way we see God.
If we saw Him per speculum (by reflection), Malebranche would be
right; but he almost always interprets it otherwise, forgetting
that Deum nemo vidit unquam (No man has ever seen God).

Nearly all the seventeenth-century thinkers move within the
indeational context created by the Augustinean-medieval tradition,
on the one hand, and by Cartesian thought, on the other. This is
the ideological milieu of Pascal (Pensées), whose principal contribution is a knowledge of God based on a form of reason that
transcends mere ratiocinative raison. His is a reason that dis-
closes the first principles, but which is given the commonly
misunderstood name of coeur (heart). Herein also must be included
Bossuet (De la Connaissance de Dieu et de soi-même [On the Knowledge of God and Self]), who sees in God the "necessary being" who
is infinite in all ways--and therefore apart from the world--and
toward whom men strive because of a ressort caché, a hidden spring.
To this group belongs also Fénelon (Traité de l'existence de Dieu
[Treatise on the Existence of God]), who discovers in our most
truly human characteristic, reason, a hint of something that may
come to us, as though by loan from higher powers, illuminating
our minds like the light of the sun. This is what he calls raison
supérieur (higher reason). Reason, then, is a relationship between
God and us, and it permits us to proceed from an understanding of
reality to a knowledge of the infinite God. Finally, we must include Samuel Clarke (A Demonstration of the Being and Attributes
of God), who begins with the necessity of something that exists
throughout eternity. Clarke reasons that God is a self-existing
being, and since every being must have reason for being, God exists
necessarily.

With Spinoza, on the other hand, the problem becomes more
complex. Having rejected the substantial nature of thought and
extension as found in Descartes, and having reduced them to mere
attributes of a single, universal substance, Spinoza must then
reduce to one meaning the three terms nature, substance, and God.
Spinoza's procedure alters all the traditional relationships and
above all invalidates the meaning of the Cartesianism that lies
at the bottom of his own metaphysics. Whereas Descartes rigorously
separates the two finite substances and establishes the transcendent reality of God as the ontological foundation of them both,

Spinoza identifies them as the same substance and eliminates the differences separating them. Yet the most crucial fact is that Spinoza begins with a notion of substance; his own definition of it leads him to postulate the substantial oneness of things and to identify that substance with a notion of God as ens absolute infinitum (absolutely infinite being) (Ethics, I:VI). Spinoza devotes himself almost exclusively to meditations on God. Yet what might seem to be theology sensu stricto is really a metaphysical study of substance, as well as a rational consideration of nature. The distinctions made between natura naturans (creating nature) and natura naturata (nature created) reveal the inadequate efforts of all pantheism to escape its own consequences.

Such is the philosophical horizon appearing before Leibniz. His idea of substance as a self-contained monad makes the problem of God especially acute in his thought. Faced with multiple efforts of the past and present to resolve this great question, Leibniz takes a broad and comprehensive attitude. The two great proofs of the existence of God (which are closely related to each other) are based on the idea of God (the ontological argument) or on the existence of something (proof a contingentia mundi [by the contingency of the world]). Leibniz accepts both, but he also subjects them to fundamental modifications in an attempt to render them more meaningful and complete.

In the preceding pages I have attempted, with the greatest possible simplicity, to indicate the assumptions on which modern metaphysics rests. This clarification is necessary, at least to a minimal degree, in order to come to grips with the reality of that philosophy. As one considers the classic thinkers of a philosophical era, nothing can replace a direct, albeit partial, view of its metaphysical problems presented in all their original authenticity.

CHAPTER VIII

Physics and Metaphysics in Newton

1. Natural Philosophy

As we complete the tricentennial of Newton's birth, it is of
interest to consider for a moment the methodological bases of
his brilliant scientific system, on which European physico-mathematical thought has rested, in large part, for some three hundred
years. First of all, we should not lose sight of the fact that
Newton was not "only" a physicist, though physics was his primary
interest, and that the eighteenth century regarded his work as a
philosophy. Let us leave aside for the moment the way in which
the term "philosophy" was misused at that time and instead consider Newton's own claims and the scope he attributed to his principles of knowledge. The fact that his work was concentrated on
physics and that this meant in turn a close connection with mathematics should not cause us to forget that such activities were
but the "application"--to an uncommon degree, to be sure--of a
general method, an attitude, if you will, concerning the knowledge
of things. Strictly speaking, it is enough to understand with
some degree of accuracy the title of his principal work: Philosophiae
naturalis principia mathematica (Mathematical Principles of Natural
Philosophy). The adjective "mathematical" modifies only the word
"principles," while the subject of these principles is a certain
"natural philosophy." Now this expression, "natural philosophy,"
has never been the equivalent, and certainly not in 1687, of what
we understand physics to be.

    "Since . . . the moderns . . . have endeavored to subject the
phenomena of nature to the laws of mathematics, I have in this treatise cultivated mathematics as far as it relates to philosophy."[*]
In these words, at the very beginning of his work, Newton leaves
no room for doubt as to what he proposes to do in it. It is a
matter of gaining knowledge of natural reality. Yet his purpose
does not end there. Most of Newton's principles are valid only
in terms of such knowledge, but some are truly first principles
on which rests all real knowledge. Newton is therefore confronted

with a dual intellectual task. On the one hand, he must establish
the true principles of a knowledge of reality; on the other, he
has to determine the conditions of the objects of natural science
and reveal the most effective method of dealing with them. He
must provide, in other words, a positive setting for physical
science in the form of philosophical postulates that will serve
as its foundation. Let us observe how he approaches this double
problem.

2. The Inductive Method

Newton distinguishes two methods of cognition, analysis and synthesis, which correspond exactly to what philosophy has customarily
referred to as induction and deduction. Newton defines them as
follows:

> This Analysis consists in making Experiments and Obser-
> vations, and in drawing general Conclusions from them
> by Induction, and admitting of no Objections against
> the Conclusions, but such as are taken from Experiments,
> or other certain Truths. For Hypotheses are not to be
> regarded in experimental Philosophy. . . . By this way
> of Analysis we may proceed from Compounds to Ingredients,
> and from Motions to the Forces producing them; and in
> general, from Effects to their Causes, and from partic-
> ular Causes to more general ones, till the Argument
> ends in the most general. This is the Method of Analysis:
> And the Synthesis consists in assuming the Causes discover'd,
> and establish'd as Principles, and by them explaining the
> Phaenomena proceeding from them, and proving the Explana-
> tions.*

Which of these two methods is the more important? It would
have to be induction or analysis, of course, because all deduction
is based on a prior induction. Like Aristotle, Newton believes
the starting point in a deduction to be a general principle (the
premise of a syllogism) and that this principle is founded on a
previous induction which, beginning with individual cases, eventually leads to that principle. In the same context, he states:
"As in Mathematicks, so in Natural Philosophy, the investigation
of difficult Things by the Method of Analysis, ought ever to pre-
cede the Method of Composition."* And on a more explicit note
at the end of the Principia, he adds: "In hac philosophia experi-
mentali propositiones deducuntur ex phaenomenis, et redduntur
generales per inductionem" (In experimental philosophy, propositions are inferred from phenomena and are generalized by means
of induction).
    But this leads to the real problem: what is it that allows
us to go, by means of induction, from particular cases to universal

propositions? What is the basis of this inductive process, through which it is possible to move from effects to causes and to generalize the results obtained thereby. In reality, the very idea of nature lies behind the inductive process; yet this is not primarily "nature" in the sense of physical nature but rather the eternal mode of behavior and being of reality. Traditionally, nature (physis) meant an abiding and changeless foundation of the world: in pre-Socratic thought it was considered the substratum from which all things arose; in Aristotle, it was the principle of motion, that in which motion continued endless and unchanging; and in Renaissance physics it was understood as the constant mode of variation, as natural "law." In his Regulae philosophandi, at the beginning of Book III of Principia, Newton clearly formulates the basis for this kind of analysis as the necessary foundation for the inductive method in general:

> Rule I. We are to admit no more causes of natural things than such as are both true and sufficient to explain their appearances.
> Rule II. Therefore to the same natural effects we must, as far as possible, assign the same causes.
> Rule III. The qualities of bodies, which admit neither intensification nor remission of degrees, and which are found to belong to all bodies within the reach of our experiments, are to be esteemed the universal qualities of all bodies whatsoever.
> Rule IV. In experimental philosophy we are to look upon propositions inferred by general induction from phenomena as accurately or very nearly true, notwithstanding any contrary hypotheses that may be imagined, till such time as other phenomena occur, by which they may either be made more accurate, or liable to exceptions.*

In his explication of these four rules, Newton offers hints of their deeper meaning. He says, for instance, that nature is simple and does not admit of superfluous causes. It is always in harmony with itself (sibi semper consona). The argument of induction may not be evaded by hypotheses. In other words, having assumed the existence of nature, and in view of its unchanging mode of behavior and being, we are induced to proceed from particular things and phenomena to general propositions. And only a new fact, a new phenomenon, that reveals a new dimension of nature, can induce us to rectify our former conclusion or, ontrariwise, to strengthen it and give it universal validity.

Yet at first glance this would appear to be mere Baconian induction, based on the observation of a certain number of cases and, depending on the number of cases and the quality of phenomena tested, leading only to a greater or lesser degree of probability. However, despite the constant use of such induction in science, it seems that this is not what Newton has in mind. Rather, he discovers that substances reveal impenetrability, extension, movement, inertia, and hardness. From this discovery of such properties in accessible things, and without subjecting other substances to experimentation, he concludes that these same properties are common to all substances. Newton goes on to say that "this is the foundation of all philosophy" (Et hoc est fundamentum philosophiae totius). This is a matter that deserves closer scrutiny. Let us consider the problem of divisibility. We know that bodies are divisible, i.e., that their divisive and contiguous parts may be separated, because phenomena reveal as much. Moreover, we know by means of mathematics that their indivisible parts may be considered, by reason, to be divided into still smaller parts, but it is uncertain whether, in actuality, these parts can be so divided (per vires naturae [by the powers of nature]). Newton adds, however, that if it could be ascertained by even a single experiment that some indivisible part could in fact be divided, then we should conclude that all indivisible parts could likewise be divided indefinitely (in infinitum). In other words, a single case suffices to attribute a certain property to a class of objects. This means that it is not a matter of simple statistical probability but of real and essential induction. This becomes clearer if we consider a negative example: the fact that bodies have weight with respect to each other leads one to infer that all bodies attract one another in mutual gravitation, but by no means is it to be inferred, observes Newton, that gravity is essential to bodies (attamen gravitatem corporibus essentialem esse minime affirmo [But I hardly affirm that gravity is essential to bodies]) because gravity decreases as we move away from the earth. This means that gravity is not an immutably inherent property of a body but the result of a relationship between one body and another.

Such is, then, the deepest meaning of Newtonian analysis. We must not forget that the purpose of the English thinker was to cultivate mathematics insofar as it relates to philosophy. In Newton this analysis takes on a mathematical form--though it is by no means restricted to mathematics--and is the same "hidden" or "latent" analysis (analysis latens) that he refers to as the "method of fluxions." In short, it is infinitesimal analysis, and its source is found in the cognitive method that we have examined cursorily.

3. The Meaning of Modern Physics

We must now turn our attention to the position Newton takes concerning the problem of physical knowledge as well as the boundaries and methodological conditions of the science of physics. To begin with, he makes a distinction and division between the two concepts of cause and principle that, traditionally, from the time of

Aristotle had been united but were already beginning to diverge in the thought of Giordano Bruno. In Aristotelian philosophy, physics is the science of nature, and nature is the principle of movement, i.e., its real principle which is at the same time a cause (αιτία). Aristotle wishes to know what motion is and why things move. Newtonian physics, in contrast, aims not at the knowledge of causes but at the discovery of the principles of motion (for instance, the principle of gravitation or attraction). These Newtonian principles are not causes that explain the why of things. Neither are they hidden qualities in the Scholastic manner. Rather, as Newton says, they are "laws of nature," the unvarying way phenomena occur, and they reveal only how things constantly and invariably undergo variation. These principles may be inferred from observable things themselves; afterwards it can be shown that the properties of bodies and phenomena derive from such principles. In other words, phenomena and physical bodies may be explained according to this general behavior we call "law." But this by no means presupposes a knowledge of causes, for causes themselves may well remain unrevealed. If I say that motion under certain conditions will occur in a specified way, i.e., according to a certain physical "law" expressed mathematically as an equation, I am not making the slightest affirmation concerning the real causes of that motion. "And therefore," writes Newton, "I scruple not to propose the Principles of Motion above-mentioned, they being of very general Extent, and leave their Causes to be found out."

Newton discusses this viewpoint, in a more penetrating and precise way, in the concluding pages of Principia:

> Hitherto we have explained the phenomena of the heavens and of our sea by the power of gravity, but have not yet assigned the cause of this power. This is certain, that it must proceed from a cause that penetrates to the very centres of the sun and planets, without suffering the least diminution of its force; that operates not according to the quantity of the surfaces of the particles upon which it acts (as mechanical causes used to do), but according to the quantity of the solid matter which they contain, and propagates its virtues on all sides to immense distances, decreasing always as the inverse square of the distances. Gravitation towards the sun is made up out of the gravitations towards the several particles of which the body of the sun is composed; and in receding from the sun decreases accurately as the inverse square of the distances as far as the orbit of Saturn, as evidently appears from the quiescence of the aphelion of the planets; nay, and even to the remotest aphelion of the comets, if those aphelions are also quiescent. But hitherto I have not been able to discover the cause of those

properties of gravity from phenomena, and I frame no
hypothesis; for whatever is not deduced from the phenomena is to be called an hypothesis; and hypotheses,
whether metaphysical or physical, whether of occult
qualities or mechanical, have no place in experimental
philosophy. In this philosophy particular propositions
are inferred from the phenomena, and afterwards rendered
general by induction. Thus it was that the impenetrability, the mobility, and the impulsive force of bodies,
and the laws of motion and of gravitation, were discovered. And to us it is enough that gravity does
really exist, and acts according to the laws which
we have explained, and abundantly serves to account
for all the motions of the celestial bodies, and of
our sea.

It is generally known that modern natural science is born
of this attitude of renunciation, already apparent in Kepler and
Galileo and fully developed in the English physicist. No longer
will physics be a science of "causes" but rather one of "laws."
It will not claim knowledge of what things are and why they move
but will limit itself to knowing how they move. Therefore, the
correct response to the questions raised by physics will be a
mathematical formula that expresses the law of variation in a
quantitative way. This process in turn endows physics with its
positive nature and constitutes what Auguste Comte would consider
essential to true knowledge--which he would in fact call "positive"
knowledge. Yet Newton does not see things in the same way. He
believes not simply that a knowledge of things is precluded but
rather that such knowledge is not the aim of physics. His statements on the topic merely defer judgment (nondum assignavi, nondum
potui deducere [as yet I could not ascribe, I could not deduce])
and leave the task of discovering causes to others. What is the
significance of this attitude?

4. Physics and Metaphysics

Let us recall that at the conclusion of his Optics, in his definition of the analytical method, Newton states that by means of this
method one may go from effects to causes and, within the latter,
from particular to general causes and ultimately to the first
cause. The restrictions weighing on physics do not necessarily
extend to the general method of knowledge, i.e., to induction,
or analysis. Physics does not include the total range of man's
knowledge, not even his knowledge regarding nature. As we have
seen, physics is a specified and especially accessible zone of
knowledge exclusive of causes. Nevertheless, beyond the realm
of physics these causes remain in all their problematic nature,
inciting us to find ways to understand them. In Newton's words:

185

Whereas the main Business of natural Philosophy is to
argue without feigning Hypotheses, and to deduce Causes
from Effects, till we come to the very first Cause,
which certainly is not mechanical; and not only to
unfold the Mechanism of the World, but chiefly to resolve these and such like Questions. What is there
in places almost empty of Matter, and whence is it
that the Sun and Planets gravitate towards one another,
without dense Matter between them? Whence is it that
Nature doth nothing in vain; and whence arises all
that Order and Beauty which we see in the World? . . .
And these things being rightly dispatch'd, does it
not appear from Phaenomena that there is a Being
incorporeal, living, intelligent, omnipresent, who
in infinite Space, as it were in his Sensory, sees
the things themselves intimately, and thoroughly
perceives them, and comprehends them wholly by their
immediate presence to himself. . . . And though every
true Step made in this Philosophy brings us not immediately to the Knowledge of the first Cause, yet it
brings us nearer to it, and on that account is to be
highly valued."

Now we see that Newton considers the most important questions
in the knowledge of nature to be not only the principles--the
Regulae philosophandi discussed above--that serve as the basis of
his physics, but also the cause of gravitation, which he had
chosen to ignore in his Principia. And this cognitive process,
the general method of which is analysis or induction, has as its
ultimate aim none other than a knowledge of the first cause,
which is to say, God.

My interest has been to show the implications of physics,
mathematics, philosophy, and even natural theology in Newtonian
thought. Of course this leads to hundreds of questions that
ought to be clarified. But this would be possible only through
a careful and detailed study of several of Newton's works, and
for our present purposes it would not be possible to undertake
such an examination. We shall restrict ourselves, therefore, to
pointing out the primary significance and scope of the infinitesimal analysis and a system of concepts that sustained European
natural science for more than two hundred years.[1]

CHAPTER IX
The Two Cartesianisms

1. 1650-1950

Descartes is three hundred years away from us. This rather considerable temporal distance makes him seem somewhat alien to our
time, yet there are certain subtle connections that bring him
essentially close to us. It is quite probable that Descartes is
the most important figure of the Modern Age. But today he does
not interest us simply because of his "greatness," or even because of that quality usually referred to ambiguously by the term
"genius," which, despite its ambiguity, we are hard pressed to
replace. At best such qualities would arouse an academic and
purely formal interest, really a pseudo-interest having little
to do with our precise circumstances. The question arises whether
Descartes stirs another kind of interest on our part, and whether
our own present reality and life may be tied to that interest.
In other words, we may ask whether Descartes has any real historical meaning.
     The fact is that there are no Cartesians in the world today.
Strictly speaking, there have been none since the seventeenth
century. And though it may seem paradoxical to say so, this
same fact must be emphasized to the honor of Descartes. How can
this be? Does it not indicate the sterility of his philosophy?
Not at all. On the contrary, it points to his profound authenticity, which has prevented the adaptation of his philosophy to
situations different from that in which and for which it was
ideated. Like a precision instrument, the philosophy of Descartes
brought about an essential transformation of thought, and it
reflects with maximum purity the still unknown depths of the
European soul in the middle of the seventeenth century. His
perfect and precise adjustment to that strict mission has made
it difficult to extend his thought readily to other situations,
just as it has meant that his thought could hardly be professed
as a doctrine beyond the concrete historical circumstances of its
origin. The question is, what was the nature of that circumstance?

A Biography of Philosophy

2. Twenty Generations

Descartes was born in 1596 and died in an icy Swedish winter in
1650. The three hundred years separating him from us amount to,
according to a more ₓvital and accurate system of reckoning, some
twenty generations. The inevitable magic of the "round number"
marking our commemoration based on astronomical time also appears
in the vital chronology of history. Descartes belonged to the
generation of Louis XIII, whose Catholic religion, the same as
his nursemaid's, the friend of Christine of Sweden never thought
of abandoning. To that generation belonged also Mazarin, the
tragic Charles I of England, Calderón de la Barca, Baltazar Gracián,
and s series of painters: Claude Lorrain, Philippe de Champaigne
(who portrayed the Jansenists so well), Anthony Van Dyck, and
the Spaniards Francisco Zurbarán and Velazquez. It was a generation lacking in great philosophers. The generations immediately
preceding Descartes' had produced the illustrious men who originated
modern science: Francis Bacon, Galileo Galilei, Johannes Kepler,
Herbert de Cherbury, Huig de Groot, and Thomas Hobbes. The generations following Descartes would produce the great names that
to a large degree he made possible: Antoine Arnauld, Blaise Pascal,
Pierre Nicole, Arnold Geulinex, Robert Boyle, Jacques Bénigne Bossuet,
Christian Huyghens, Samuel von Pufendorf, Baruch Spinoza, John Locke
(the last three born in the same year, 1632), Nicolas Malebranche,
Isaac Newton, Gottfried Wilhelm Leibniz. And when the world represented by these men commenced to crumble and the confidence of
triumphant rationalism gradually became tarnished with "historical
Pyrrhonism," Pierre Bayle emerged on the scene to herald a new era.

In the history of philosophy, it seems, Descartes stands alone
in his generation. Such was his destiny: <u>solus recedo</u> (alone I
withdraw), he put it. Not only was his philosophy conceived in
solitude, in his winter quarters in Germany where he was spending
November, 1619 (". . . enfermé seul dans un poêle") thinking to
himself; it is also a philosophy formed of solitude. Alone with
himself, Descartes suspended all previous knowledge, eliminated
and renounced all dependence on tradition, and set out, like another
Adam, to discover the world. We shall see how far this Adamic
attitude took him.

Just what did Descartes propose to do? In simple terms, he
sought to know the world through mathematical physics and to dominate it intellectually by means of the technique inferred from
physics. He persisted in this approach even when the condemnation
of Galileo's physics by the Holy See in 1633 dissuaded him from
publishing his own. Moreover, he still felt obligated to make
known his methodological principles because of the benefits they
offered and because he did not believe he had a right to withhold
them from others. To this end he offered samples--<u>specimina</u>, according to the Latin edition--of his mode of thinking on matters relating
to physics. These works include <u>La Dioptrique</u> (Optics), <u>Les Météores</u>
(Meteorology), and finally as the justification of his entire work,

Discours de la méthode (Discourse On Method), no doubt his most celebrated writing.

Much more than Bacon, Descartes was a man of method, and in this regard, he was very much under the sign of his time. With Renaissance petulance, Bacon had announced: viam aut in veniam aut faciam (Either I shall find the road or I shall make one). Descartes, in doubt-filled solitude, created his way on the basis of that extreme situation itself, by transforming solitary doubt or doubtful solitude into a philosophical method.

In the final analysis, the Cartesian method begins with the elimination of error. Caution, under whose sign Europe has thought for three centuries, is his starting point. Born into the world as children, we begin by learning from our elders. But their beliefs are often erroneous, and in any case they have not been verified by us and thus offer us no personal guarantee. So it is that it becomes necessary, at least once in life, to cast everything into doubt, even those things we do not doubt, provided that we could doubt them. To withdraw from presumed error, the origin of which is social, to solitude, is the equivalent of going from inherited to evident ideas. And this attitude led Descartes, and with him all European philosophy, to fall into two errors: rationalism and idealism. But if these are errors—and they are—they are necessary ones, errors that the European mind had to experience. Furthermore, they are less serious than other errors from which the European mind was emerging, and it was precisely through the new errors that the old ones were overcome.

3. "Functional Cartesianism"

Our own situation is at once essentially different and yet similar. We are rapidly leaving the modern world that Descartes fully inaugurated. Having lived through rationalism, we have taken stock of its limitations and shortcomings. Likewise, we have surpassed idealism in the only effective way: not by falling anew into realism but by taking both it and idealism into account, by acknowledging the partial error and partial truth of each, and thus rising above both of them. Today our problem is precisely the solution advanced by Descartes. Until now we have seen only the differences, even the opposition, between our time and his. Yet from another vantage point our situation is similar to that of Descartes. For we are also at a turning point in the history of thought; we stand at the beginning of a new phase of philosophy. We are homologous to Descartes, and in this sense—but only in this sense—we must also be Cartesians.

It has been twenty years since Edmund Husserl, in his Cartesian Meditations (1931), invoked Cartesianism and spoke of a "Cartesianism of the twentieth century" in the form of phenomenology. But this appeal contained a serious mistake, for phenomenology, in one of its essential dimensions, is one of the most polished and refined

forms of the idealistic error. Phenomenology, precisely because
it is still too close to Descartes, cannot be the Cartesianism
of our century.

Today our problem is much more radical. We cannot be content
with proceeding from inherited to evident ideas, to the "clear
and distinct" ideas claimed by Descartes. That would mean remaining within ideas, and we need to transcend ideas and attain reality.
We must make our way from all ideas and all interpretations to the
underlying reality that makes them possible and necessary. The
vehicle or instrument by which we make this radical regression
is history. Just as physics was a necessity and a method to the
Cartesians of the seventeenth century, so history must serve us
today, albeit in another sense. Yet as an actual form of knowledge,
history is still little more than an inchoate and poorly understood
discipline that must be structured in view of its triple function.
For history, which is first of all the arena wherein things appear
endued with historicity, also functions as a form of knowledge;
it is what permits us to appeal from each interpretation to the
actual origin of interpretations; and in so doing, it frees us
from interpretations altogether and prevents us from mistaking
them for reality itself. But it does not stop here. One after
another, accumulated interpretations are eliminated, like leaves
from an artichoke, until nothing remains. Then it becomes apparent that if it is true that no interpretation in itself is reality,
it is no less true that all interpretations are indeed interpretations of reality. Reality appears in them in an eminent and manifest way, just as it stands out in the system of their actual
succession, which we call history.

Therefore, instead of eliminating social and traditional
interpretations in order to retain only evident ideas, we must
uncover the underlying reality of those interpretations; and this
means beginning with nothing less than their historical reality.
In this sense we could speak of a "functional Cartesianism" in
our time. Of course, its first task would be to avoid Cartesianism,
i.e., the doctrine of Descartes, which we cannot share today, and
instead accept his attitude of reviving and transforming philosophy.

4. Two Cartesianisms

There are really, then, two very different kinds of Cartesianism:
his and ours, and this is precisely what makes it impossible merely
to repeat, petrify, or trivialize his thought. The first Cartesianism, that of Descartes himself, suffered from a bad press, and a
network of well-wrought intrigues prevented it from achieving
sufficient prominence and from reaching whole areas where its
influence would have been far-reaching. Of course, it reached
mathematicians and physicists and, with certain fundamental restrictions, philosophical circles too. It had but the briefest contact
with theology. Among the works of a whole group of theologians,

whose most famous members were Bossuet and Fénelon, Descartes
remains as "evidence"--in the sense that geologists use the term--
of a theology that could have been, had it incorporated the Cartesian point of view into the age-old tradition of the Church
Fathers and medieval Schoolmen. Save for the closest friends
and disciples of Descartes, Cartesianism flourished only in the
hands of original philosophers somewhat removed from him in time:
Malebranche, Spinoza, Leibniz. In other words, it throve in minds
that differed with Descartes, and instead of merely repeating or
prolonging and developing Cartesianism within the same setting,
they were moved and inspired by it to elaborate their own thought.
Later, in the eighteenth century, when "Cartesianism" had assumed
official status, it consisted largely of the more superficial and
antiquated elements of his thought: his physics, the theory of
"tourbillons" (whirlwinds) or of "animal spirits." Philosophy
during that period was dominated by Locke and Francesco Algarotti.
The latter, a Prussian count by the grace of Frederick the Great
and a friend of Voltaire, wrote Newtonisme pour dames (Newtonism
for Ladies). One of the most far-reaching and visible consequences
of the social fate of Cartesianism has been the history of Spanish
philosophy during the past three hundred years.

Descartes has continued to play a silent and covert role in
history--larvatus prodeo, as he stated. He has never removed his
mask. It may be that we are just now beginning to understand the
deepest stratum of his thought, including his idea of reason, the
real sources of his philosophy, and the authentic meaning of the
literary genres of his work. Descartes decided only rather late
to write something resembling a treatise--Principia philosophiae.
Earlier, the most he had written was Meditationes de prima philosophia, in which metaphysics is expressed in a form approaching
that of a book of devotion. This peculiarity is more noticeable
in Discours de la méthode, which is not a book at all but the
confidential revelations of an honnête homme (respectable gentleman).
Furthermore, outside of a good many essential remarks made some fifteen years ago by Ortega at the University of Madrid, almost nothing
has been written on the significance of genre in Descartes.

Today we are beginning to understand more about Descartes,
including his errors. Many of the latter were the price he had
to pay for the privilege of discovering important truths. We
see how the antihistorical attitude of Cartesianism toward the
past, which Descartes ignores and which for that same reason
contradicts him surreptitiously, causes him to accept without
criticism from tradition nothing less than the idea of being and
substance! The ultimate result of this attitude is that Descartes
cannot create a metaphysics. His "Adamism," which ignores the
past, leads him to the paradoxical situation in which the past
wreaks vengeance by overpowering him and making Descartes himself
a part of the past. And this means in an absolute sense that his
Cartesianism cannot be ours, for we must begin by posing in the
most fundamental way possible a problem that indeed did not even

exist in a problematic way for Descartes. The problem may be stated as a question: what is reality?

5. The Idea of Substance

By means of a single but decisive example, let us consider briefly the consequences of this Cartesian "Adamism." In Part IV of the Discours de la méthode (Discourse on Method), after establishing the indubitable truth of the Cogito--Je pense, donc je suis (in Latin, Ego cogito, ergo sum, sive existo [I think, therefore I am, or I exist])--Descartes sets about to examine carefully "ce que j'étais" (what I was), and he concludes after his inquiry: "I knew then that I was a substance whose entire essence or nature consists of thinking."[2] The question is, what is substance?

Descartes makes a rather specific and informative response to this question on several occasions. In his Responses to the Second Objection he writes:

> V. Everything in which there resides immediately, as in a subject, or by means of which there exists anything that we perceive, i.e., any property, quality, or attribute, of which we have a real idea, is called a Substance; neither do we have any other idea of substance itself precisely taken, than that it is a thing in which this something that we perceive or which is present objectively in some of our ideas, exists formally or eminently. For by means of our natural light we know that a real attribute cannot be an attribute of nothing.

> VI. That substance in which thought immediately resides, I call Mind. I use the term "mind" here rather than "spirit," as "spirit" is equivocal and is frequently applied to what is corporeal.

> VII. That substance, which is the immediate subject of extension in space and of the accidents that presuppose extension, e.g. figure, situation, movement in space etc., is called Body. But we must postpone till later on the inquiry as to whether it is one and the same substance or whether there are two diverse substances to which the names Mind and Body apply.

> VIII. That substance which we understand to be supremely perfect and in which we conceive absolutely nothing involving defect or limitation of its perfection, is called God.[3]

In other words, substance is defined exclusively by immanent qualities, properties, or attributes that we perceive, and without

them we have no idea of substance other than that of a subject
in which they formally or eminently exist. And in accord with
this concept, mind, body, and God are defined by the attributes
"thought," "extension," and "perfection." I am a res cogitans
(thinking thing), the world is res extensa (extended thing), and
God, the res perfecta (perfect thing) or infinite substance.
Yet it is clear that the only qualities revealed to me about
these three substances arise, respectively, from their nature as
thinking, extensive, or perfect things; whereas their common
attribute of being a thing, a substance or res, is hidden from
me. In Principia philosophia Descartes takes up the problem
again in greater detail:

Principle LI

By substance, we can understand nothing else than
a thing which so exists that it needs no other thing
in order to exist. And in fact only one single substance can be understood which clearly needs nothing
else, namely, God. We perceive that all other things
can exist only by the help or the concourse of God.
That is why the word substance does not pertain univoce
to God and to other things, as they say in the Schools,
that is, no common signification for this appellation
which will apply equally to God and to them can be
distinctly understood.

Principle LII

Created substances, however, whether corporeal or
thinking, may be conceived under this common concept;
for they are things which need only the concurrence
of God in order to exist. But yet substance cannot be
first discovered merely from the fact that it is a
thing that exists, for that fact alone is not observed
by us. We may, however, easily discover it by means
of any one of its attributes because it is a common
notion that nothing is possessed of no attributes,
properties, or qualities. For this reason, when we
perceive any attribute, we therefore conclude that some
existing thing or substance to which it may be attributed, is necessarily present.[4]

Shortly thereafter he adds: "It is moreover more easy to
know a substance that thinks, or an extended substance, than substance alone, without regarding whether it thinks or is extended.
For we experience some difficulty in abstracting the notions that
we have of substance from those of thought or extension. . . ."[5]
From this new point of view, Descartes defines substance in
terms of autonomy, independence, or sufficiency; substance is

that which needs nothing else in order to exist. Of course, this means that God is the only substance, and such was the conclusion that Spinoza hastened to draw. But Descartes adds an essential restriction: in order for substance to be, it is sufficient that it need nothing other than God. In this way he avoids pantheism, but he does so naturally at the price of the univocality of the concept of substance: no other clear notion common to God and created things can be understood. The reason for this is that the mere existence of things, apart from their attributes or properties, does not affect us. We know of properties and attributes, and through them we infer (or "conclude," according to Descartes) the existence of a substance, in view of the principle that there must needs be a substance to which such properties belong. Thus, admits Descartes, there is a certain difficulty in abstracting the notion of substance from the notions of thought or extension. And with this difficulty in mind, he sets out to study the actual consistency of the latter notions, leaving unclarified the problematical nature of substantia (substance) or res (thing), which has merely been inferred or conjectured on the basis of directly accessible properties. Therefore, inasmuch as Cartesian philosophy is directed to the study of attributes, there is some doubt as to whether the Meditationes really are, as the title indicates, de prima philosophia.

6. The Problem of Analogy

But is it possible to do what Descartes does? Can one restrict oneself to the knowledge of attributes, leaving aside the reality of substance, which serves as their foundation? Let us consider the consequences of this attitude.

As we have seen, Descartes recognizes that the concept of substance is not univocal but instead may be considered analogous. God is not substance in the same sense as created things. However, this presents no serious problem as yet. According to Aristotle (Metaphysics, IV, 2), an analogy exists inasmuch as the various meanings of being, which are expressed in many ways (πολλακῆ), nevertheless exist "always in view of one such meaning and in view of a certain single nature" (πρὸς μὲν καὶ μιαν τινα φυσιν). In other words, the several meanings of being require a foundation in order for analogy to exist, and it must be a single, univocal foundation that permits the different dimensions of that analogy to be predicted analogously. But does this happen in the case of Cartesian substance?

The feature that defines substance is independence or sufficiency: rem quae ita existit, ut nulla alia re indigeat ad existendum (a thing that needs no other thing in order to exist as it is). But independence, which ought to be the foundation of analogy, and hence rigorously univocal, is not; for it is complete only in the case of God, whereas thinking and extensive substance are endowed with only a relative independence. This means that in order to exist, they need no other created thing, nothing that is not the divinity. To put it another way, independence is only analogous, and this fact colors the dimensions of the analogy in question, casting it over with a tenuous and problematic hue that borders on fallacy.

At this point the inadequate presentation of the problem in Cartesianism is evident. Descartes was, above all, interested in the distinction between thinking and extensive substance, and for this reason, he devoted himself to their constituent and differential attributes and ignored the decisive problem concerning the meaning of res itself. The result is that the overly problematic idea of autonomy and sufficiency begins to pose problems when applied to created things, even in the narrow sense given them by Descartes. This explains why today we feel somewhat dissatisfied with the position taken by Descartes. For us, the real question begins where Cartesian metaphysics is assuaged and acquiesces to traditional ideas. Strictly speaking, Descartes turns to traditional ideas at the most important point. Of course, Cartesianism ceases to be Cartesianism at this very point. Husserl asked the positivists to be truly what their name implies; over against the partial positivism of the disciples of Comte, he asked for an authentic and radical positivism that would take things as they were presented. In like manner, we might ask that Descartes remain true to his own method and that above all, within the central problem of metaphysics, he proceed from traditional to evident ideas. Our potential Cartesianism would be much more radical than his, for one of our problems would be to explain the rationale--the historical reason, if you will--of that brilliant interpretation of reality we know under the name of Cartesian philosophy.

CHAPTER X
The Philosophy of Life

1. The Philosophy of the Nineteenth Century

If we consider the chapters devoted to the nineteenth century in
any number of treatises on the history of philosophy, the basic
discrepancies concerning the content of that thought will surprise
us. I am not referring primarily to the divergence of opinion
and interpretation regarding certain thinkers but to something
more fundamental and important: the question of which philosophers
are selected for study. If the books alluded to make any pretense
of being "complete," then the names appearing in their indexes will
all coincide, as one would expect, because all thinkers of any prominence are included. But if, on the other hand, the works are
short and involve a critical selection, the differences are immediately apparent. In any case, the "importance"--the primary historical category--attributed to different thinkers will vary.

It may be that such histories are quite recent, or they may
be otherwise, but in any event a word should be said at this
point about what is understood by a "recent" book. This is important in understanding philosophy and especially so in considering
the history of philosophy. It is not a matter of the publication
date, or that a book "includes" everything down to the present
time, or even that the author supplies up-to-date references and
sources. The important thing is the standpoint from which a book
is written; it is a question of the assumptions and the historical
level on which it rests. This is why we are often misled concerning the "modernity" of certain studies that despite their attempts
to include the "latest"--or perhaps for that very reason--are fundamentally anachronistic and out of date from the beginning. Historical understanding of any sort implies an interpretation, and this
interpretation can be made only from a series of assumptions that
constitute the vantage point of the historian. And the historian,
not the themes of history itself, decides what is modern or otherwise. One may, for instance, study pre-Socratic philosophy from
today's vantage point, and study it with an insight impossible in

196

other times; on the other hand, one can consider living philosophers from the standpoint of outdated intellectual schemes that
cannot afford us an understanding of their thought.

In general, books on nineteenth-century philosophy that were
published some decades ago give an impression of great philosophical richness and abundance. We usually find copious and even
tiresome cataloguing of schools, tendencies, and directions, with
a wealth of representative titles and authors. More recent histories paint a picture of philosophical penury in that century
and carefully present a limited number of thinkers who are given
careful study.

It might be inferred from this that it is simply a matter of
a selection dictated by time and that if now, after many decades,
only the highest values endure, we cannot expect this same discernment from earlier critics. It could perhaps be said that the
nineteenth century is still too close to us and that we lack de-
tachment and the proper historical perspective. Yet if we compare
this view of the past with that of historians of philosophy a
hundred or a hundred and fifty years ago, we see that they apparently had no such problem. Let us consider two examples. The
first, de Gérando's Histoire comparée des systèmes de philosophie
(Comparative History of Philosophical Systems), an erudite and
exhaustive work published in 1804, and the second, Hegel's Vorlesungen über die Geschichte der Philosophie (Lectures on the History
of Philosophy) delivered between 1805 and 1831 and published in
1833. The philosophers of the eighteenth century and even those
of the beginning of the nineteenth studied in these two books--one
French, the other, German--are grosso modo the same ones that any
history of philosophy would consider today. If by chance some
oversight has since been rectified, or if some philosopher therein
discussed has been forgotten, they are but exceptions that make
all the more visible the general agreement concerning the rest.

Furthermore, something very curious and even paradoxical is
apparent about the nineteenth century: whereas the thinkers who
were most influential and renowned in their time have, with few
exceptions, been almost forgotten today, the few thinkers who
seem most important to us are scarcely mentioned in the contemporary histories of philosophy. After the great German Idealists--
who do not belong to the period under discussion--only Comte and
Nietzsche from among the representative philosophers of the nineteenth century seem to have any real importance today. Others
such as Ludwig Feuerbach, Jakob Fries, Friedrich Beneke, Ernst Mach,
Gustav Fechner, Eduard von Hartmann, Wilhelm von Wundt, Ernst Haeckel,
Richard Avenarius, Herbert Spencer, Victor Cousin, Maximilien Littré,
and Alfred Fouillée are men who commanded the greatest attention in
the nineteenth century but whose work today seems to us at best to
be second-rate. In contrast, in those books written in the spirit
of earlier times hardly any attention is given to philosophers such
as Søren Kierkegaard, Bernhard Bolzano, or Auguste Gratry. As a
matter of fact, only lately have they attracted some interest, and

except for Kierkegaard, the interest is still not great. Others
such as Wilhelm Dilthey, Franz Brentano, and even Henri Bergson
and Edmund Husserl have been similarly ignored. Often otherwise
extensive and comprehensive books contain only vague references
that would not arouse even a suspicion of the importance of such
philosophers. What does this anomaly mean? Does it reveal some
oddity in nineteenth-century philosophy?

Another strange fact is that philosophical exposition of the
past century tends to be strongly affected by nationalistic feelings, a rarity in the history of philosophy. Nationalism is
especially predominant in books published in France and Germany,
the countries richest in philosophical tradition. Ortega once
recalled that he could not persuade Hermann Cohen to read Bergson,
despite the fact that both were Jewish and both well-known thinkers.
German books seem to disregard everything foreign, while the French
are largely limited to the thought of their own country with only
marginal allusions to German or English thought. Here one can see
a certain advantage of countries without an old and established
philosophical tradition. Consider, for instance, the case of
Spain. It is quite probable that the studious Spaniard of today
has a somewhat better and more correct idea of the true nature
of philosophy worldwide than the average intellectual of France,
England, or Germany. Since he cannot even pretend to deal exclusively with Spanish thought, the Spanish intellectual from the
outset must keep the rest of the world in mind, and in so doing
he is guided by more independent and less biased criteria.

The fact that I have just alluded to makes it clear that
primarily what has usually been taken for nineteenth-century
philosophy has really been the academic presence of those who
cultivated philosophy, especially those formidable professors of
philosophy in German universities. In certain books--those of
Karl Vorländer and Auguste Messer, to cite the two examples best
known in Spain--the impact of these professors of philosophy, who,
from Göttingen, Marburg, Cologne, and Berlin, wrote and taught
with great authority and prestige, is vividly apparent, and their
influence must be taken into account by historians. No disparage-
ment of this type of thinker--now on the way to extinction--is intended by these statements. They are simply meant to show that
their activities do not necessarily coincide with the real nature
of philosophy.

My interest lies in conveying this impression of strangeness
to the reader, for if one delves into its deepest zones, nineteenth-
century philosophy does indeed turn out to be strange. Dilthey is
an extreme case in point. This brings us to the problematical question
of what caused nineteenth-century philosophy to assume these peculiaritie

Apart from the first thirty years or so, which belong almost
exclusively to German idealism, the whole of the nineteenth century
betrays an essential debt to Hegel. The more one considers the
historical life--and above all the intellectual life--of the past

century, the more one discovers this Hegelian influence. Yet while this is testimony to his greatness, it is no less a serious objection to Hegel himself. For the Hegelian legacy is not always beneficial or fruitful for philosophical thought. In Germany first of all, but also in other countries, philosophy after 1830 consists primarily of taking a stand regarding the towering historical fact of Hegelianism. In general--with the exception of Karl Ludwig Michelet-- this means taking a stand against him, or at least making fundamental alterations in his thought. Kierkegaard and Schopenhauer, both very strongly influenced by idealism, Fries, Beneke, Feuerbach, Marx, Comte, Gratry, and finally, Dilthey and Brentano, all have to contend with Hegelianism and all are conditioned by it either positively or negatively. The same phenomenon occurs in disciplines other than philosophy: theology (at the Tübingen school), history, law, and economics all bear the imprint of Hegel's influence, and their subsequent development is tied either directly to his thought or to an unknowing and confused application of his basic assumptions.

Furthermore, a branch of French thought, traceable to eighteenth-century sources and with only marginal debts to German idealism, also influences nineteenth-century philosophy. As philosophers, the eighteenth-century philosophes offer little by way of originality and depth but their historical influence is unparalleled. The tradition of these modestly endowed intellectuals of the Enlightenment-- Voltaire, Jean Jacques Rousseau, the Marquis de Vauvenargues, Etienne de Condillac, Claude Adrien Helvetius, Baron d'Holbach, Jean d'Alembert, A. R. J. Turgot, the Marquis de Condorcet, as well as A. L. C. Destutt de Tracy and Pierre Laromiguière--continues well into the first third of the nineteenth century. This line of thought, which is free of French sensationalism, combines seventeenth-century rationalism and British empiricism. After the crisis of German idealism, around 1830, French philosophy comes into its own in the form of the positivism of Auguste Comte. Henceforth French thought begins to outstrip and to influence the German, and through Comte it takes its place in post-idealistic European philosophy. Later we shall see that many elements of subsequent European thought may be traced to this source and that in turn the latter, especially with Pierre Paul Royer-Collard and Théodore Jouffroy, incorporates certain features of the Scottish school of "common sense" as developed by Thomas Reid and Dugald Stewart. The direction taken by philosophy during the latter part of the nineteenth century, with repercussions in current thought, reveals the interaction of these two sources, French and German. And although their influence on philosophy is not exerted in equal measures, both are necessary ingredients in its makeup.

The most effectively active Hegelian idea throughout the nineteenth century is that of evolution (Entwicklung). This idea has antecedents in the immediately preceding French tradition--Turgot, Condorcet--in which it appears as the notion of "progress," but with Hegel the concept acquires more philosophical consistency and is presented in different terms and with greater depth than before.

In the first place, Hegel stresses that the arena of evolution is "spirit," not nature. He writes:

> Historical change, seen abstractly, has long been under-
> stood generally as involving a progress to the better,
> the more perfect. Change in nature, no matter how in-
> finitely varied it is, shows only a cycle of constant
> repetition. In nature nothing new happens under the
> sun, and in this respect the multiform play of her pro-
> ducts leads to boredom. One and the same permanent
> character continuously reappears, and all change reverts
> to it. Only the changes in the realm of spirit create
> the novel. This characteristic of spirit suggested to
> man a feature entirely different from that of nature--
> the desire toward <u>perfectibility</u>.[1]

But immediately thereafter Hegel rejects the usual idea of progress because it assumes a quantitative form.[2] He goes on to say:

> If we compare the changes of spirit with those of nature,
> we note that in the latter the individual experiences
> change, but the species continues unchanged. . . . In
> nature, life that is born of death is merely another
> individual life; and if the species itself is considered
> to be the object of that change, then the death of an
> individual does not mean that the species reverts back
> to individuality. The preservation of the species implies
> only the unvarying repetition of the same manner of exist-
> ence. However, the spirit is different, for its changes
> occur not on the surface but in the very concept of itself.
> In nature, the species does not progress, but in the spirit,
> all change is progress. No doubt the series of natural
> forms also constitutes a scale running from light on the
> one hand to man on the other, so that each level represents
> a transformation with regard to the preceding level. Yet
> in nature these different steps exist in mutual separation
> from each other. Furthermore, the transition from one to
> another is apparent only to the thinking spirit that com-
> prehends their connection. Nature has no understanding
> of itself, and thus to it the negative aspect of its trans-
> formation does not exist. On the spiritual level, by way
> of contrast, it is apparent that higher forms have come
> about through elaboration of earlier, lower forms. This
> means that these lower forms have ceased to exist, and
> it means also that if the spiritual changes occur in time,
> it is because each such change is the transfiguration of
> an earlier form. World history is the development of
> Spirit in time, just as nature is the unfolding of Idea
> in space.[3]

The Philosophy of Life

Hegel is more specific in his History of Philosophy. Above all, he interprets evolution as a step between two stages of being which he describes with venerable Aristotelian terms, potentiality and act (δύναμις and ἐνέργεια), which might be described as being-within-self (Ansichsein) and being-for-self (Fürsichsein), respectively. This interpretation influences the Hegelian idea of Entwicklung (evolution) and is especially apparent in three primary aspects of his thought: (1) the priority of act over potentiality which, in keeping with Aristotelian thought, means that the ultimate stages of evolution are already inherent and prefigured in the initial phases; (2) the identification of "reality" in the full meaning of the term with Fürsichsein, or being-for-self, which affects the essential difference between nature and spirit; and (3) the logical conception of evolution as the dialectical unfolding of the completely rational Absolute.

Hegel goes on to compare natural with spiritual evolution and he finds a decisive difference between them. In a plant, for example, the seed evolves through a series of stages until it becomes fruit and thus completes the evolutionary cycle. Yet the fruit, in turn, is also a seed that begins the cycle anew. The same process occurs in the animal world: parents and offspring may be different individuals but in the end all repeat the same natural pattern. It is different with the spirit. Spirit is consciousness; it is free, because within it are contained both the beginning and the end. In nature the fruit does not exist so far as the seed is concerned (only we see that relationship); in the spirit the two antipodes of evolution exist for each other. Thus, spiritual being is being-for-self (Fürsichsein). As Hegel puts it: "Spiritual evolution is an unfolding, whereby self is abandoned so that it may be more truly found."[4] All spiritual evolution is directed toward "knowledge," which is the appearance and presence of the Absolute to itself. For this reason, if spirit alienates itself from self, it is with the ultimate aim of a higher self-realization. "Everything that happens--eternally--on earth and in Heaven, the very life of God and every temporal occurrence, happens so that the spirit may come to know itself, so that it may be the object of its own concern, so that it may find itself, come to be itself, and be reunited with itself. This is duplication and self-estrangement, but it must needs be in order that the spirit may come to find and to know itself more fully."[5]

This is a most revealing passage. It describes happenings as "eternal" and includes therein such disparate realities as the divinity and mere temporal occurrences. Such a notion contains as many pitfalls regarding the idea of God as it does in connection with historical evolution itself. If it leads on the one hand to the concept of a self-evolving God (Gott im Werden) and thus inevitably to pantheism, on the other it "eternalizes" in logical dialectic the true and temporal movement of history. For under these conditions history is reduced to a mere unfolding or explication of what was known from the beginning. We recall that

Hegel begins with the Aristotelian concepts of dýnamis and enérgeia in order to explain the peculiar stresses of the evolutionary process. And while this notion lends vitality to the Hegelian idea of evolution, at the same time it precludes the essential peculiarity of history. The mere realization or unfolding of preexisting realities ignores the radical mutability of being betrayed by human life and history. The naturalistic encumbrances of the Greek notions of potentiality and act render them inadequate to capture the immediate living reality of history as it occurs. Hence, while any interpretation of history must necessarily begin with Hegel, his doctrine is far from an understanding of the intimate reality of history itself.

In 1830, shortly before Hegel's death, Auguste Comte published the first volumes of his Cours de philosophie positive (Course of Positive Philosophy). The philosophy of history contained in the work--and especially the law of three stages--reveals the imprint of Hegel's concept of evolution. However, Comte modifies the logical extremes to which Hegel goes and adopts instead a methodic naturalism. By way of the latter Comte establishes the method used by natural sciences as the only possible means of acquiring knowledge. The pursuit of this notion leads Comte to an idea of "social physics" that prevents him from apprehending history in its true and immediate stage. It should be pointed out, however, that Comtian thought often surpasses its own methodological limitations. In fact, the tension arising between its assumptions, on the one hand, and its results, on the other, leads to a disagreement among the closest disciples of the positivistic school. A case in point is Maximilien Littré's criticism, in his Traité de politique positive (Treatise on Positivistic Politics), of Comte's mature work.[6]

Some thirty years later, in 1859-1860, Charles Darwin's On the Origin of Species by Means of Natural Selection is published.[7] This profoundly influential work, the principal ideas of which date from 1837 following his famous voyage aboard the Beagle, again brings attention to the theme of evolution, but this time in the realm of biology. This idea of biological evolution influences all areas of the intellectual life of the time and has an especial impact on the concept of history.[8] Thus Karl Marx and Friedrich Engels, who otherwise display their well-known adherence to Hegelian concepts, are also obliged to consider Darwinian doctrines in formulating their thought. Moreover, as Rádl correctly notes, although the Marxists believe the Darwinian idea of natural selection to be overly aristocratic in nature, they nonetheless accept the general tenets of evolution. The dialectical concept of history advocated by Hegel underlies, in an altered form, all materialistic interpretations of history. Marx holds dialectical progression to be the "last word in philosophy," though he adds that it must be shorn of its mystical fluff. A dialectic of economics must replace that of idea.[9] At the same time, notwithstanding his objections to the coarseness of English

202

thought, Marx considers the Darwinian theory to be the "foundation of natural science" as he understands it.[10]

Finally, in the famous book of Rudolf Stammler, Wirtschaft und Recht nach der materialistischen Geschichtsauffassung (Economics and Law According to the Materialistic Concept of History), the struggle for existence is expressly considered to be the basis of human society.[11] This work is a synthesis of the two conceptions of history, dialectical and biological evolution.

Evolution is also the central philosophical idea of the English philosopher Herbert Spencer (1820-1903), who began his work before Darwin and whose influence was greatest in the latter part of the nineteenth century. In a sixteen-thesis résumé of his system, which reduces his basic principles to three pages, Spencer states: "(1) In the Universe generally and specifically there is endlessly renewed distribution of matter and motion. (2) This redistribution constitutes evolution whenever the integration of matter and the dissipation of movement predominate. . . . "[12] This alteration, together with the transformation of the uniform into the diverse, occurs throughout the universe and its dominions, from the nebulae to spiritual and social life. The principal cause of evolution is the instability of the homogeneous, and the quantitatively invariable substratum of all evolutionary processes is a limitless potentiality that Spencer prefers to call the "unknowable." It should not be overlooked that in its time this doctrine was the most profound and penetrating, the most flexible and encompassing as far as reality itself was concerned, yet advanced. Bergson himself is quite explicit in admitting that Spencer's thought was an exception and that his youthful philosophical aim was "to complete and consolidate it." It was due to this influence that Bergson came to discover temporal reality as "duration" and to make it the focal point of his philosophy.[13]

Such were the most important philosophical attitudes of the nineteenth century. All were dominated, in one way or another, by the idea of evolution and by the need to arrive at a satisfactory interpretation of the course of history as well as of those varied phenomena referred to somewhat equivocally as "life." We have observed the persistent, albeit inadequate, treatment of the theme of evolution throughout the century. Yet the question arises whether these activities constituted the whole of nineteenth-century philosophy. Not at all. Indeed, obscured by prevailing trends, or perhaps misinterpreted, two branches of thought were laying the groundwork for a new philosophical climate. The first of these, which begins with Bernhard Bolzano and culminates in Franz Brentano, renews a concern for metaphysics and offers a new philosophical method; the second, with initial indications during the early years of the century and its highest expression in Dilthey, is nourished by the discovery and exploration of a hitherto ignored reality: human life.[14] A cursory history of that discovery is in order at this point.

2. Steps in the Discovery of Life

Were we to trace the idea of life--in its proper meaning of <u>human</u>
life--to its earliest beginnings, we should have to go back at
least to the middle of the eighteenth century, to Turgot (1727-
1771) and d'Alembert (1717-1783). But the work of these men was
soon eclipsed by the complete triumph of sensationalism with such
men as Abbé Condillac--who belonged to the same generation as
d'Alembert--and his followers, the "ideologues": Destutt de Tracy,
Pierre Cabanis, and others. For our present purposes we need only
consider trends in the nineteenth century, beginning with Laromiguière
(1756-1847), who initiates the first reaction against sensationalism
and yet must still be classified with the sensationalists. His
thought bears the decisive imprint of Condillac, whom he acknowledges.[1]
Yet traditional sensationalism seems insufficient to him. He cannot
accept "passivity" as the fundamental condition of the soul. The
mere reception of certain sensations and the subsequent formation
of ideas from them seems inadequate to him. Laromiguière emphasizes
two aspects of sensation: the reception of a sensation in which
the soul is passive and a reaction in which the soul is active.
Seeing is not the same as looking, nor hearing the same as listen-
ing. To the mere passivity with which I receive external impressions that arouse sensations and "feelings" within me must be added
the active reality of "attention," which originates in me and encompasses external objects.[16] The "I" is therefore active, but
its activity is by no means creative. Behind the entire process
lie the sensory impressions, and this means that human activity
is not creative but reactive. I react to things by attention--in
the form of understanding--and by desire--in the form of will.

Laromiguière offers the first indications of a movement to
surpass both sensationalism and idealism. Yet he accepts the conventional belief concerning the existence of things and is unable
to make any decisive progress because of his assumption that sensation is the primary consideration. He fails to see that it is
merely an abstract element of perception and thus secondary to it.
Nor does he understand that feeling is the motive force of reaction.
These limitations are the tribute Laromiguière pays to his era.

In 1804--the year Kant died--Joseph Marie de Gérando published
the three huge volumes of his <u>Histoire comparée des systèmes de
philosophie, relativement aux principes des connaissances humaines</u>
(Comparative History of Philosophical Systems Regarding the Principles of Human Knowledge). At the very beginning of the century,
four years earlier, he had published his four-volume work <u>Théorie
des signes et de l'art de penser considérés dans leurs rapports
mutuels</u> (Theory of the Signs and Art of Thinking Considered in
Their Mutual Relationships). Baron de Gérando (1772-1842), or
Degérando, was of the same generation as Laromiguière but was
more deeply committed to the Sensationalist school. His favorite
authors were Bacon, Locke, and Condillac. Yet he was also mindful
of German idealism, which troubled him and made his intellectual

stance more difficult. Sensationalist thought was still predominant at the time, but it was already entering into a period of
crisis. Beginning with it, de Gérando sought to postulate a new
kind of philosophy, which he would call "philosophy of experience."

"My point of departure is the principle, recognized today
by all philosophers, that the source of all our knowledge lies in
our sensations, and I so begin by an analysis of sensation."[17]
Beginning with this assumption, de Gérando goes on to derive all
mental activities from sensation. He also alludes to the function
of attention. More importantly, however, in the course of his
analysis perception by the "I" becomes problematic and its derivation from mere sensation becomes more difficult. At this point,
de Gérando is forced to appeal to a "feeling of resistance," experienced whenever "I" touch an object (for example, a ball). Thus
to begin with, de Gérando is obliged to posit the notion of clear
"perception"; yet immediately thereafter he declares "resistance"
to be more important, inasmuch as it permits the revelation of a
reality other than myself through which "I" come to discover myself in an appositional relationship. "The feeling of resistance
is composed of two others: the sensation of something different
from oneself and the impression of something that is oneself.
There are, then, two perceptions: one of objects and another of
self. And one understands that the two are different from each
other, that one is outside the other, and through their apposition
one learns to distinguish between them."[18]

But this poses the problem of an irreducible duality. Over
against the vague notion of a so-called "modification of the 'I'
by sensations"--later strongly rejected by Maine de Biran--stands
the necessity of two opposing, external, and different elements.
But we should not attribute more to de Gérando than he deserves.
His purpose is simply to discover the "I," to become aware of it,
and the presence of something other than the "I" is necessary in
order to do this. Yet the "other" is relatively secondary in the
hierarchy of sensations, and the "I" was certainly active and
functional before this discovery. Therefore, it is incorrect to
conceive of the "I" existing only as a consequence of resistance
encountered. This assertion would come later with Maine de Biran,
but it is totally absent in de Gérando. The clearest statement of
de Gérando's views appears in Volume III of his Comparative History
of Systems, in which he juxtaposes two categories of objects that
impress themselves on the mind: on the one hand, the "I" with
its existence and subsequent modifications; and on the other,
the existence of things that are both contiguous to and different
from the "I." The fundamental properties found in the "I" are
permanence, identity, and unity.[19]

Toward the end of his Comparative History of Systems, after
reviewing all the philosophical positions of the past, de Gérando
postulates--but does no more than postulate--a unifying philosophy
based on "experience" that transcends prior antinomies. This
experience is by no means mere sensory impressions. Furthermore,

de Gérando makes a distinction between internal and external
experience, just as he does between a simple experience (mere
contact with things), complex experience (a series of simple experiences), and a reasoned experience (consisting of meditation
on the content of experience). He goes on to say: "The germ of
human science is completely contained within the phenomenon of
conscience, and philosophy has no other function than to study
and develop this phenomenon."[20]

De Gérando's aim is to unite rationalism and empiricism and
to preserve the worthwhile elements of both methods. Likewise,
he proposes to reestablish in its entirety the phenomenon of conscience, which idealism and materialism had weakened by focusing
attention only on certain of its aspects to the exclusion of others.
The philosophy of experience finds in conscience ". . . a state of
dependence and source of strength, action and reaction. It redis-
covers along parallel lines and at an equally fundamental level,
self-knowledge and knowledge of something beyond self that sheds
light on each other through both their simultaneous occurrence
and their contrast."[21]

What in Laromiguière was hardly more than a hint within the
context of his sensationalist thought becomes in de Gérando the
ultimate aim and summary of philosophic intentions. But de Gérando
also betrays a tendency toward eclecticism that culminates in the
work of Victor Cousin and precludes a direct treatment of problems.
Only with Maine de Biran does this groping suspicion about the
strange reality of our own life achieve a certain coherence.

Elsewhere I have studied at length this new step forward in
philosophy, and I refer the interested reader to that work.[22] In
the present writing I shall restrict myself to those points wherein
Maine de Biran surpasses the philosophy of his time and enters unfamiliar regions.

To begin with, Maine de Biran seeks a "primary fact" on which
the science of principles must needs rest. But this approach,
which is clearly sensationalist in origin, leads from the outset
to a solution that for fundamental reasons differs from that proposed by Condillac. "Sensation" as such cannot be a primary fact
since it is not a "fact" at all. This discovery then motivates
Maine de Biran to consider the problem at a prior and more profound
level. In order for a fact to be at all, it must be known, that
is, it must be for someone. This means, then, that the sensory
impressions must coincide with the "I."[23] But such a coincidence
presupposes a prior context or arena wherein it occurs, a setting
where I come into contact with knowledge. Knowledge always implies
a duality, for to know is to acquaint myself with an object. Any
fact, therefore, presupposes a double set of terms that cannot
be conceived singularly and separately.[24] With this decisive
insight Maine de Biran surpasses the inchoate tendencies of earlier
French philosophy. What had been antipodal extremes are now revealed
as functions of each other. The "I" is an active force that exists
only insofar as it acts on the inertia, or "resistance." Their

relationship is one of reciprocal action by a single force--the
"I"--and a single opposing point--"that which is resistant." In
other words, Maine de Biran converts "objective" concepts into
"functional" terms: force and resistance. The coexistence of
these functions implies a dynamic reality manifested as action
and effort. And it is this dynamic relationship, with its action
and effort, that lends meaning and reality to the ingredients that
go into its formation.

The long and difficult intellectual journey through what
Maine de Biran calls "a deserted and uncultivated land that few
visitors have any curiosity to see" leads to a most important
consequence: I am not a thing.[25] Man stands as the antithesis
of the entire universe. Not only is the primary reality behind
the active force or effort not a mere thing; the same is true of
both elements that derive their reality by constituting the dynamic interaction. Strictly speaking, Maine de Biran interprets
the being of man from the standpoint of human life, which is
understood as an active tension between the "I" and the world
whose reality is revealed as aspects or ingredients in the primary reality of "effort." The "I" fashions its being within the
stress created between effort and resistance, and it cannot be
regarded as a thing complete and independent. For this reason,
man, who may initiate a series of free acts--which are unlike
simple animal reactions--enjoys a personal life that is, strictly
speaking, human life in the biographical sense. In the work
of Maine de Biran there appears dimly, and yet with depth and
insight, the strange reality of "human life" that was alien to
the prevailing intellectual habits of the time.

Nominally, the influence of Maine de Biran was quite extensive and important in France. "We all regarded him as our teacher,"
recalled Royer-Collard on the occasion of Maine de Biran's death.
Cousin paid him similar tribute and always acknowledged a debt
to him. Yet in reality Maine de Biran's influence was superficial
in the spiritualist and eclectic school that dominated French
philosophy around the middle of the century. For this reason,
it is not always easy to discover notable repercussions of his
nebulous concept of human life, a concept that his contemporaries
and successors almost invariably misunderstood. Only in the work
of Father Gratry (1805-1872) was there any fruitful treatment of
Maine de Biran's intuitions. Following a different course,
Father Gratry came to a similar point of view, which he later
enriched with Maine de Biran's ideas.[27] To Gratry man is "a
word of God," as indeed are all things. But man differs from
other things in that he is a "growing" word, an utterance never
completely finished (a faciamus and not a simple fiat). As Gratry
states: "My life is composed of waves that come pressing in suc-
cessively on one another. . . . Each and everyone of us is created
with a consecutive nature like a discourse or a song. . . . I am
not yet complete, nor shall I ever be so. . . . I shall never
see the day when I am finished. Light from the beginning has

been what it is today and what it shall be tomorrow. But tomorrow
I shall be as I have not yet been. Yet even then I shall have
limitless hopes of what I may become. It is an endless process. . . .
Continuous growth is the only conceivable image of the infinite."
And he adds: "Searching and unrest, desire and hope, these make
up the very basis of our life here below. . . . Desire is the
root of the soul, its source and primary strength."[28]

Gratry strongly insists on the dynamic, unfinished, ever-open
and growing nature of man. It is true that not all these intuitions are correlated into a formal metaphysics in his thought,
yet one cannot overlook the importance of intuiting a new kind
of reality that is irreducible to the being of things. Indeed,
human life stands in formal opposition to the world of things.
Doubtless, Gratry was guided in his meditation by an overall aim
of interpreting conceptually and rationally the being of man
within a Christian context.

The preceding are the principal stages in the discovery of
"human life" as a distinct reality through which nineteenth-century
French philosophy passed. After Gratry and in contention with
positivism, an indirect influence of Maine de Biran can be traced
to Bergson. As for Auguste Comte, his work contains hints of a
profound though undeveloped understanding of the being of man,
but his discoveries deal more with the problem of history and
social reality than with the theme of life in the individual sense.
Of course, the positivists who dominated European thought in the
second half of the nineteenth century were blind to the most
meaningful areas of these discoveries and to the insights of the
man they regarded as their teacher.

I have insisted, albeit briefly, on the French precursors
of the philosophy of life because, though they are relatively
ignored, the first mature treatment of the theme by Wilhelm Dilthey
and its higher development in recent years cannot be fully understood without them. French thought on the topic merges with better
known and studied German contributions. The latter begin with
Maine de Biran's contemporary, J. G. Fichte,[29] appear also in
the work of the Dane Søren Kierkegaard--who was influenced somewhat
polemically by German idealism--and reappear in quite altered form
in Friedrich Nietzsche and Dilthey.

The thematic opposition of the "I" and the "non-I" in Fichte
is well known, and so is his concept of the dynamic interdependence
of both. Fichte, to be sure, interprets this interdependence according to idealistic criteria: he maintains that the relationship
depends primarily on the "I" and that it is posited prior to the
"non-I." Likewise, much attention has been given the Fichtean
interpretation of reality as Tathandlung (activity or "deed").
Together with the "Historicist School," this German idealistic
philosophy--Fichte, Friedrich Schelling, Friedrich Schleiermacher,
Hegel, and, finally, Friedrich Jacobi--forms the intellectual
foundation on which Dilthey structures his philosophy.

The Philosophy of Life

Søren Kierkegaard (1813-1855), whose thought bears the imprint of both the prevailing German philosophy—especially Hegelianism—and Protestant theology, rejects "abstract thought" and the attempt to consider reality sub specie aeterni, from the eternal point of view. He bases his rejection on the fact that abstract thought excludes "existence," i.e., man's very mode of being (and incidentally, that of the abstract thinker himself). Kierkegaard observes:

> Since abstract thought is categorized sub specie aeterni, it makes mere abstractions of things concrete and temporal, of the unfolding of existence, and of the anguish of man, whose life is the meeting ground for the temporal and the eternal. . . . To conceive of existence abstractly and sub specie aeterni is to negate it essentially. . . . Existence cannot be thought of without movement, and movement cannot be apprehended sub specie aeterni. . . . What is true of movement is true of existence. By thinking them, I abolish them and then it becomes impossible to think them. Thus one could say that existence is something that cannot be thought. But the fact remains that since whoever thinks, exists, existence must be postulated simultaneously with thought.[30]

Kierkegaard stresses the temporal, concrete, and mobile nature of human existence, and he criticizes Hegelian thought for its tendency—discussed earlier in this work—to "eternalize" history and evolution. There are well-known repercussions of the Danish thinker's early-day "existentialism" in the twentieth century. One thinks immediately of Miguel de Unamuno and, in a rather different situation, of Martin Heidegger. Though scarcely noticed for many years, the view of life represented by Kierkegaard would one day take its place in philosophy.

Finally, two philosophers, chronologically later than Dilthey, either begin or deepen their work during the last decades of the nineteenth century. With these two, Bergson and Nietzsche, the problem of human life reverts to an earlier and less developed state, despite the chronology of their birth. This is especially true if one compares their thought to the later writings of Dilthey, in which he achieves a certain intellectual consistency of expression and a real, though still deficient, grasp of his own discoveries. Nietzsche was born in 1844 and his lucid thought ended in 1889. Under the influence of Goethe and Arthur Schopenhauer,[31] he discovered the value of life as such, as well as the possibility of levels and hence of "reality" within life. Henri Bergson begins with a concept of life as biological reality but he immediately encounters the problems of time in the vital sense, which he refers to as durée réelle (real duration). In this way he discovers the

aspect of "quasi-creation" revealed by life and the enlightenment
it offers of new possibilities. No adequate and exhaustive effort
has been made to show the contributions made by Nietzsche and
Bergson to the matters under consideration. Nor is this the opportune time to do so. My only purpose for the moment is to point
out cursorily the various stages necessary in order to situate
Diltheyan philosophy historically and to shed light on its concepts.
Thus the problem of life as a philosophical concept in the full
sense has yet to be broached.

If at this point we pause to review the salient stages of
the thought examined so far, albeit somewhat hastily, we perceive
that the discovery of human life as a philosophical reality--until
now vague and insufficiently understood--has been made from several
points of view. Furthermore, each view captures a certain dimension
of that reality, and as they accumulate, a more complete and systematic picture begins to emerge. French philosophy of the first half
of the nineteenth century approaches the question of vital reality
from the standpoint of the psyche and the problem of knowledge.
This viewpoint induces French thought to acknowledge duality as
a primary fact of human life. However, attempts to describe the
substance of that duality reveal that it is not a matter of the
simple coexistence of dissimilar elements but rather of a dynamic
tension between them, such that their very being is fashioned by
an active and mutual dependence. From a similar position, Father
Gratry veers away somewhat from the notion of duality and stresses
instead the "successive" and unperfected nature of human life, with
its life-long but never completed task of self-creation. As for
Fichte, he begins from a different set of assumptions--the primacy
of practical reason and the notion of pure ego--but reaches similar
conclusions in the end.
Proceeding along other lines, Kierkegaard emphasized the
finite, concrete, and temporal nature of existence. The religious
concepts underpinning his thought cause Kierkegaard to dwell on
the rigorous individuality and strictly personal destiny of man.
To Kierkegaard existence is always individual existence, that experienced by each and every person in specific and unique self-
hood. At the same time, a noticeable opposition develops between
his view of being and the abstract, universal, and atemporal concepts of conventional philosophy of that time. A vague irrationalism appears that is both promising and perilous--promising in
that it contains the germ of a higher form of reason than the
narrowly abstract, perilous insofar as it fosters the merely
irrational and fails to inculcate a higher and more advanced
idea of reason.
In Nietzsche we find an awareness and an appreciation of
the value of life itself. Indeed, his view stems from a deeper
and more interesting idea that life is invested with an essential,
intrinsic meaning of its own. At the same time he emphasizes the
importance of the individual in his views on society and history.

In Bergson, finally, together with an understanding of time itself, in its own peculiar and mobile being, as "duration"--not merely as finitude and limitation in comparison with eternity-- we find life interpreted from the standpoint of biology and in relation to universal vitality. Notwithstanding the interest his interpretation holds, it is made perhaps at the cost of partially overlooking life's most authentic meaning found in its personal and biographical aspects.

With this we come to Dilthey. His insights are broader, deeper, and subtler than those of all the philosophers mentioned. Yet, as Ortega has shown, Dilthey's approach to this newly dis- covered reality is halting and his conceptualization and expres- sion of it are especially inadequate. On the one hand, the general philosophical assumptions of the time and Dilthey's own historical situation, and, on the other hand, the radical nature of his thought, caused his philosophy to remain rather more in- sinuated than expressed. Let us attempt to outline some essential points of his approach so as to make possible an understanding of his thought.

3. The Idea of Life in Dilthey

Wilhelm Dilthey (1833-1911) belonged to the same generation as Franz Brentano, Friedrich Nietzsche, and William James. Born in 1798, Auguste Comte was three generations earlier. This means that Dilthey experienced not the influence but rather the intellectual prestige associated with Comte. This is important in Dilthey's case. He belonged to the positivist group that had come to feel a dissatisfaction already beginning to be apparent in the previous generations. For the most part, they were content to overcome the limitations of their movement in rather oblique ways. Indeed, this was true of Dilthey himself: though dissatisfied with posi- tivism, he was unable to escape its influence. This dependence and his struggle to free himself of it left a mark on all his work. (The same thing happened in the case of the neo-Kantians.)

Dilthey had a long and rich tradition behind him. He had read very extensively and deeply in history and literature, and his knowledge ranged over every area having a bearing on his con- ception of cultural history. In one way or another, any modern philosopher is influenced by the whole history of philosophy, but in Dilthey's case the philosopher's thought is extraordinarily rich in modern influences: the Renaissance humanists, the Reforma- tion, Leibniz, German idealists, the entire Romantic movement: Goethe, Hölderlin, Novalis, and especially Schleiermacher; the entire Historical School; Maine de Biran, Comte, and of course his contemporaries.

In Dilthey's work, metaphysics, psychology, and history are interwoven in a peculiar way. Indeed, so artfully and covertly does he unite them that for a long time the first passed unnoticed

and his principal contribution was considered to be his treatment
of the latter two.[32] Yet in the strictest sense, Dilthey formulates neither a theory of life nor a historical doctrine, nor
even a system. What he does is at once more and less: he makes
contact with the reality of life and he does so in a more unusual
and complete way than anyone had done before him. As Ortega puts
it, Dilthey ". . . discovers the Idea of life."

But to moder man this metaphor of "discovery," together with
its immediate meaning of "uncovering" or "unveiling," conjures
up visions of ocean voyages. It would appear that it is a matter
of seeing a new reality--like a new continent--from afar and of
finding a road or means of reaching it. But in reality the discovery of life and history is more like finding the sea over which
we are already sailing. All men live within history, willy-nilly,
yet many are unaware of this truth. Other men know that one day
their time will become a part of history, but they do not presently
live historically. Dilthey gave us "historicism," and this is of
course a doctrine; but in a deeper ser.se, it is a way of being.
It implies historical consciousness in a basic sense, which is to
say, without mere intellectual or doctrinal coloration. Today
we live so fully immersed in historicism that we find it hard to
realize how novel this discovery once was. We are aware that we
live in a certain time and that this time will pass and be replaced
by another, just as all past times have come and gone. We are able
to transport ourselves, in a certain sense, to other ages. We
live in a world that derives its structure directly from temporality. In order to understand anything at all, we must have the
date of its emergence and inclusion in history; unless we have
such knowledge we cannot understand it. Everything that is revealed to us is revealed within a historical setting. As we look
out over a city, for example, we see not only its visible structures
but also a historical accumulation of various chronological periods:
the city appears to us as the end result of a historical process
in which the past survives and the future is implied.

Dilthey sees a close relationship between this historical
process and the scepticism that arises from clashing ideas and
systems. Our attitude today precludes all definitive statements.
We do not believe that any question can be answered once and for
all. We can answer it only according to the views of our age,
and we are fully aware that our answer is destined to be superseded
or amended in times to come. Dilthey views history as "an immense
field of ruins." But history has not always been interpreted so.
Whole eras have believed that many things withstand and transcend
the ravages of time: all classical ages imply as much. But even
in less serene and self-assured ages, and especially in those
which have broken with the past, the present is proclaimed to be
the new and absolutely valid order of things. Over against the
view of history as a repertory of errors, the present is regarded
as a period of rectification and elimination of previous mistakes.
Today we keenly sense that all history is antiquated, yet we are

212

aware also that our time must needs be included also in that
history. To understand any man we must know the two dates of
birth and death, which define the setting of his life. Even
those of us still living anticipate with a great question mark
that second, as yet uncertain date. Never before has man, each
man, lived his life with such an awareness that "his days are
numbered." This, in short, is history.

A similar attitude toward the past marks all periods in
their final phases--at least on the surface. For this is the way
man reacts whenever he has a long and more or less well-known
past behind him. But in our own time this is true to an unprec-
edented degree, for two main reasons. First, the tremendous
development of history as a discipline since the end of the
eighteenth century and the expansion of man's vital horizons
have given contemporary man evidence that he possesses a past of
great magnitude. He is aware, furthermore, that the past weighs
on him as such, and not as "tradition," and that precisely because
the past has a certain magnitude, it ceases to be merely "immemorial." Because it is symptomatic of how modern men regard the
past, let us recall the opening lines of Cardinal Newman's famous
treatise on Development of Dogma: "Christianity has existed in
this world long enough for us to speak of it as a fact of history."
The second, and more important reason is that our age has discovered
that it is man himself who changes. Man not only dwells in history,
and not only does he "have" a history: he is history. Man's historicity affects his very being.[33]

Now, historical man has what Dilthey calls a Weltanschauung,
i.e., an idea or conception of the world that is not primarily a
mental construction. Philosophy, religion, art, science, and
political, juridical, or social beliefs are elements, ingredients,
or manifestations of this broader idea of the world. Yet the idea
of the world itself is previous to all such ingredients and rests
on a fundamental assumption of the reality of human life. The
ultimate root of any Weltanschauung is, according to Dilthey, life
itself. And this life can be understood only from within itself;
knowledge cannot begin from a point prior to life. This means
that Dilthey's method must be descriptive and comprehensive instead of explicative and casual. More specifically, it must be
a form of interpretation, or hermeneutics; and indeed some of
Dilthey's most significant thought is associated with this method.
Thus Dilthey alters the meaning of contemporary psychology as well
as that of historiography.

Dilthey seeks to apprehend life in its historical dimensions.
The other points of view discussed earlier, all rooted in an older
tradition, are apparent in his work, but their influence is secondary. As Dilthey sees it, the very substance of life is history.[34]
He usually speaks of life as a totality rather than as individual
life. Life is dispersed throughout the world in many currents,[35]
like a river containing a multitude of forms. Individual life
belongs to life in general.[36] But it is precisely at this point

213

that the problem of life for Dilthey arises as he begins to delve deeper into its structure.

Vital reality does not reveal itself to us as a "world" of things and people, but as an interdependent complex, or network (Zusammenhang), of vital relationships. Singularly, things are properly only an ingredient or element of our life; and as they condition life, they also acquire their meaning within it as a function of the totality. The world is but a correlative of that complexity of relationships, but at the same time the complexity itself can never exist without that "other" which we call the "world."[37]

Life reveals itself to man as an enigma that demands understanding. In the face of the maximum enigma, death, man attempts to fashion images of the reality of death in order to render it understandable. From this strange attitude and the reaction to it, there arises a certain tenor of life that influences man's conception of the world. Optimism and pessimism regarding life are the two extreme expressions of this life feeling. Dilthey is obliged to formulate a topology of world conceptions as a possible intellectual means of apprehending the reality of life. But there are still other assumptions supporting his view.

Dilthey comes under the influence of the positivist heritage. Two of his most important ideas stem from Comte. The first is that all previous philosophy has been partial and incomplete and that this was in fact the source of its error, its declining to accept universal reality as it is. The second is that metaphysics is impossible and that only the positive sciences are valid. But Dilthey adds his own genius to these inherited ideas and even makes essential modifications in their meaning. Nevertheless, he is handicapped by his erroneous notion of the second idea.

Dilthey states that the fundamental idea of his philosophy is that until now philosophy has never been founded on full, total, and unmutilated experience, which is to say that it has never been rooted in total and complete reality. In assuming that it accepted reality in its entirety, positivism was guilty of excessive abstraction, for it arbitrarily reduced the real to mere empirical data. In short, positivism was not "positive." Dilthey, on the other hand, claims to be positive, but he is aware from the outset that intelligence is not an isolated and "absolute" faculty but is rather a process in the evolution of mankind. In the light of this notion, Dilthey reasons, philosophy so understood is the science of the real. Knowledge alone cannot encompass universal reality. In everything known there remains an inscrutable and ineffable kernel of the unknown. The mind stops short of absolute and exhaustive penetration into reality; it is only capable of "comprehending" things, and this does not exclude a degree of impenetrability. This idea of the limitation of knowledge is reinforced by Diltheyan historicism. For he holds that all views verified by history are true (or at least may be true), but that no single view is the whole truth because all are

214

partial. No one vantage point in history can encompass all reality, and error arises when a single view is mistaken for the whole and men believe it to be the only one. Dilthey shuns all intellectual absolutes and finds in history the means of obviating the scepticism that history itself has aroused. Claims of absolute validity are the very reasons why the history of various systems is a "field of ruins," as Dilthey remarked. Once such claims are surrendered, a partial and historically conditioned truth remains.

Yet true to his positivist heritage, Dilthey identifies metaphysics with the search for absolute and universally valid knowledge. This explains why he declares metaphysics to be impossible. His only purpose in inquiring into the types of world ideas is to find a means of reaching the reality of life. Instead of following the positivist tendency of consolidating all scientific method by reducing it to natural science, Dilthey stresses the irreducible peculiarity of cultural and psychological sciences and postulates a "critique of historical reason." The Diltheyan dialectic begins with self-knowledge or autognosis, proceeds to a hermeneutics of the life of others, and culminates in the knowledge of nature. Thus he goes from the thing closest to us--we ourselves--to the remotest--nature. Dilthey's postulate of "historical reason" and the hermeneutic method are his greatest contributions to thought.[38] Nevertheless, they involve an error that should be noted.

Whenever Spaniards hear the expression "historical reason" they tend to give it an Ortegan meaning that has become fairly familiar to us in late years but is not what Dilthey meant by it. However, the meaning Ortega gave the term allows us to understand more fully what Dilthey was <u>trying</u> to say, provided of course that we do not confuse the two.

The usual nineteenth-century reaction to the discovery that life is a radically temporal reality consisting of constant movement and differing from things was irrationalism of some sort. Dilthey was an exception. Noticing the shortcomings of pure reason as applied to life and history, he postulates a new form of reason that is broad enough to include history. In other words, he would apply reason to history while disclaiming, of course, any absoluteness. Dilthey's genius lies in his view of historical reason, yet he ends up by considering basic conceptions of the world to be beyond the scope of history. And since history cannot touch these world views, neither can Dilthey account for them.[39]

By "historical reason" Ortega means something much more profound and radical. He does not merely <u>apply</u> reason to historical themes, as has been the case hitherto. Nor is it enough to say that reason arises as a function of life. Rather, history itself is reason--"reason," naturally, in a new meaning of the term. "Vital reason" is not simply reason more or less accurately modified but reason extracted from life itself. Stated in another way, reason is life in its function of causing us to apprehend reality intellectually. The misunderstanding of the term is due to a failure not only to consider rigorously and seriously the terms used but also to clarify the meaning of the expressions "historical reason" and "vital reason" in the light of a third term, "living reason" (razón viviente), also used by Ortega. The latter expression implies that life, far from being something secondary and derived, informs and constitutes reason in a rigorous and formal sense.

Let us recall some of Ortega's statements, in one of his most important works: "To me, reason, in the true and rigorous sense, is every such act of the intellect as brings us into contact with reality, every act by means of which we come upon the transcendent." And he adds:

> Until now history has been the contrary of reason. In Greece the two terms "reason" and "history" were opposites. And in fact, scarcely anyone till now has taken it upon himself to examine history for its rational substance. At most, attempts have been made to impose on it a reason not its own, as when Hegel infused the formalism of his logic into history, or [Henry Thomas] Buckle his physiological and physical reason. My purpose is the very contrary: to discover within history itself its original, autochthonous reason. Hence the expression "historical reason" must be understood in all the rigor of the term: not an extrahistorical reason which appears to be fulfilled in history, but, literally, a sub-stantive reason constituted by what has happened to man, the revelation of a reality that transcends theories about man, and, indeed, which is man himself underneath his theories. [. . .] Until now, what reason offered was not historical, and what was historical was not rational. Historical reason is, then, ratio, logos, a rigorous concept. . . . Historical reason accepts nothing as mere fact, but makes every fact fluid in the fieri whence it comes and sees how every fact takes place.[40]

It is evident that great strides have been made since Dilthey and that the concept of historical reason has assumed proportions it neither had nor could have had in Dilthey. But here we must stop. For the final steps in this mode of thought are being taken before our very eyes and are far from being complete. They must be accomplished before they can be told, for only the inner and as yet unfinished movement of this philosophy holds the secret to its ultimate form.

Notes

Notes to Chapter I

1. Cf. José Ortega y Gasset, "Prólogo a la Historia de la Filosofía, de Bréhier," Obras completas, Vol. VI.
2. Cf. my Introducción a la Filosofía, Obras, Vol. II; see especially Chapters V and X.
3. Metaphysics, I, 3, 983b, 2-3.
4. Ibid., I, 3, 983b, 27 ff.
5. Introducción a la Filosofía, Section 63, pp. 264 ff.
6. Cf. Metaphysics, I, 7, 988a, 20; II, I, 993a, 30; b, 17, 20.
7. Ibid., I, 2, 982b, 18-19.
8. Ὁ φιλόμυθος φιλόσοφός πώς ἐστιν ὁ γὰρ μῦθος σύγκειται ἐκ θαυμασίων (Metaphysics, I, 2, 982b, 18-19).
9. Ὅσω μονώτης εἰμί, φιλομυθυτερος γέγονα (Fr. 668).
10. Heraclitus, fr. 92 Diels.
11. Introducción, Chapter VIII; see especially Section 62.
12. Herodotus, I, 91.
13. In my Introducción a la Filosofía, Section 58, I have gone into greater detail concerning the derivation of the idea of nature.
14. Cf. Introducción, Section 57.
15. Introducción, Section 56.
16. See Introducción, Section 57.
17. Herodotus, I, 46-49.
18. See I, 2, 982b, 17-22.
19. See V, I.
20. Ibid., I, 5, 985b, 23ff.
21. Ibid., I, 6, 987b, 11-12.
22. Ibid., I, 3.
23. Ibid., I, 6, 897b, 28.
24. Cf. Introducción, Section 38.
25. For the logical function of the epithet and its relationships to predication and consistency, see my Introducción, Section 64.

26. One might expect the traditional counterpoising of essence and existence; but each involves excessive implications, which make them ambiguous terms so long as we have no other details beyond those offered by the present context. Regarding existence especially, with the accumulations left heaped on it by scholasticism and existentialism, one would have to say with Don Luis Mejía of Doña Ana de Pantoja:

> . . . con lo que habéis osado,
> imposible la hais dejado
> para vos y para mí.
> (. . . with what you have dared,
> You have left her impossible
> For you and for me.)

27. Herodotus, VI, 106.
28. Metaphysics, I, 2, 982a, 17-19.
29. Note the difficulties Ross encounters in commenting on this passage. He concludes by stating: "It should be remembered that the present passage is a statement of ἔνδοξα, so that some looseness in the thought may be expected" (Aristotle's Metaphysics, I, 121-122).
30. Thucydides, II, 60.
31. Διαλέγεται μὲν γὰρ ὑπὲρ ὧν οἱ φιλοσοφοῦντες. Philostratus, Vit. Sophist. Prooem. (Ritter-Preller), p. 224.
32. Φαινομένη σοφία οὖσα δ' οὔ. Aristotle, Soph. elench., I, 165a, 21.
33. In addition to Prothagoras, see Theaetetus, 152 ff.
34. Metaphysics, 1053a, 35-b, 3.
35. Theaetetus, 152b.
36. Adversus Mathematicos, VII, 60.
37. Introducción a las ciencias del espíritu (translated into Spanish by J. Marías), pp. 188-189: "Este relativismo suyo afirmaba ciertamente de las cualidades de las cosas que no existían más que en esa relación, pero no de la objetividad misma. Lo dulce, si se suprime el sujeto que gusta el dulzor, ya no es nada; sólo existe en relación con la sensación. Pero su teoría de la percepción muestra luego que no ha desaparecido para él con esa sensación de dulce el objeto mismo. Si un objeto afecta al órgano sensorial y se comportan así aquél de un modo activo, éste de un modo pasivo, por una parte se origina en ese órgano sensorial la visión, la audición, la impresión sensible correspondiente, y por otra aparece ahora el objeto como coloreado, sonoro; en una palabra: con diversas cualidades sensibles. Solo esta explicación del proceso hizo posible para el relativismo de Protágoras una teoría de la percepción, y se ve bien que no podía suprimir la realidad del movimiento exterior al sujeto, que originaba en él la percepción, porque ponía a su vez al mismo tiempo en cuestión toda objetividad. Explicó los diversos estados del sujeto sensible y mostró así que las cualidades de los objetos que se manifiestan

están condicionadas por esos estados. Así resultó de su teoría
de la percepción la paradoja de que las percepciones están en
contradicción entre sí y, sin embargo, son todas igualmente verda-
deras." (Translation into English by translator from the Spanish
version by Marías [translator's note]).

38. Sextus Empiricus, Adversus Mathematicos, VII, 65 ff; cf.
the pseudo-Aristotelian De Melisso, Xenophane, Gorgia, 5 and 6.

39. "Sócrates, en efecto no hablaba, como la mayoría de los
otros, acerca de la Naturaleza entera, de cómo está dispuesto eso
que los sabios llamen Cosmos y de las necesidades en virtud de
los cuales acontece cada uno de los sucesos del cielo, sino que,
por el contrario, hacía ver que los que se rompían la cabeza con
estas cuestiones eran unos locos.

Porque examinaba, ante todo, si es que se preocupaban de
estas elucubraciones porque creían conocer ya suficientemente
las cosas tocantes al hombre, o si porque creían cumplir con su
deber dejando de lado estas cosas humanas y ocupándose con las
divinas. Y, en primer lugar, se asombraba de que no viesen con
claridad meridiana que el hombre no es capaz de averiguar seme-
jantes cosas, porque ni las mejores cabezas estaban de acuerdo
entre sí al hablar de estos problemas, sino que se arremetían
mutuamente como locos furiosos. Los locos, en efecto, unos no
temen ni lo temible, mientras otros se asustan hasta de lo más
inofensivo; unos creen que no hacen nada malo diciendo y hablando
lo que se les ocurre ante una muchedumbre, mientras que otros no
se atreven ni a que les vea la gente; unos no respetan ni los
santuarios, ni los altares, ni nada sagrado, mientras que otros
adoran cualquier pedazo de madera o de piedra y hasta los animales.
Pues bien: los que se cuidan de la Naturaleza entera, unos creen
que 'lo que es' es una cosa única; otros, que es una multitud infinita; a unos les parece que todo se mueve; a otros, que ni tan
siquiera hay nada que pueda ser movido; a unos, que todo nace y
perece; a otros, que nada ha nacido ni perecido.

Esto era lo que decía de los que se ocupaban de estas cosas.
Por su parte, él no discurría sino de asuntos humanos, estudiando
qué es lo piadoso, qué lo sacrílego; qué es lo honesto, qué es lo
vergonzoso; qué es lo justo, qué lo injusto; qué es sensatez, qué
insensatez; qué la valentía, qué la cobardía; qué es el Estado,
qué el gobernante; qué mandar y quién el que manda; y, en general,
acerca de todo aquello cuyo conocimiento estaba convencido de que
hacía a los hombres perfectos, cuya ignorancia, en cambio, los
degrada, con razón, haciéndolos esclavos" (I use the translation
by Zubiri in his magnificent study, "Sócrates y la sabiduría
griega," which I recommend to the reader; see Xavier Zubiri,
Naturaleza, Historia, Dios, pp. 244-46). (Translation into
English by translator from Zubiri's Spanish version [translator's
note]).

40. 96a-99d.

41. See the richly suggestive book by Antonio Tovar: Vida
de Sócrates (Revista de Occidente: Madrid, 1947), Chapter IV.

42. Cf. Zubiri, "¿Qué es saber?," Naturaleza, Historia, Dios, pp. 51 ff.

43. Cf. Ortega, Del Imperio romano (Obras completas, VI, pp. 71 ff.).

44. Politics, I, 2, 1253a, 29.

45. Epistle VII, 326a-b; cf. Republic, V, 473b.

46. Epistle VII, 341c-e, 344b-d.

47. See "Scholasticism in its Own World and in Ours" (Chapter VI of the present work).

48. Summa Theologica, II-IIae, q. 51, art. 2.

49. Sophist, 263e.

50. Topics, Book I, Chapter I.

51. Introducción a la Filosofía, Section 61.

52. To cite a single example, note what Gredt says: "Essentia metaphysica est id quo primo constituitur res seu id quo primo distinguitur ab omnibus aliis et quod est radix ceterorum, quae de re concipiuntur. Essentia metaphysica definitione metaphysica exhibitur" (Elementa Philosophiae Aristotelico-Thomisticae, II, p. 200). (Metaphysical essence is that which is first constituted as a thing, or that which is first distinguished from all other things and is the origin of the rest, which are perceived through that thing. Metaphysical essence is revealed in metaphysical definition.) (English translation by translator [translator's note]).

53. Concerning the reasons for this, see "El problema de la lógica," Introducción a la Filosofía, Chapter VII, Section 61.

54. Cf. Ortega, "Apuntes sobre el pensamiento: su teurgia y su demiurgia," Obras completas, V.

55. Phaedrus, 237b-d.

56. Ibid., 245c-e.

57. Ibid., 246a.

58. Laws, X, 895d.

Notes to Chapter II

1. History, I, 1.

2. Ibid., I, 22.

* A Spanish noblewoman; widowed with two children, she was hanged in 1831 at the age of twenty-seven for political activities [translator's note].

3. History, IV, pp. 168-97.

4. "And now, even as I speak,
My silent strength
Enters your eyes and youthful hues,
And despoils and ruins them . . .
I flee, I run, I fly;
Nor will you see (oh blind ones!)
The fleeing, the race, the flight" (English version by translator [translator's note]).

Notes

Notes to Chapter III

* Chapter I of the present work [translator's note].
1. Fritz Taeger, Das Altertum (1939), I, p. 326.
2. Cf. supra, I, p. 7.
3. Taeger, Das Altertum, I, p. 327.
4. Epistle VII, 325e.
5. Cf. M. Rostovtzeff, The Social and Economic History of the Hellenistic World (Oxford, 1941), I, p. 100.
6. Rostovtzeff, op. cit., p. 93. Cf. III, p. 1329.
7. ". . . the general uncertainty, which may have prevented Greek citizens from indulging in the luxury of large families. There developed at the same time a growing individualism and selfishness, a strong tendency to concentrate effort on securing the largest possible prosperity for oneself and one's limited family" (Rostovtzeff, op. cit., I, p. 96).
8. Ibid., I, pp. 96 ff.
9. "En el siglo iv hacía mucho que esta vida (la vieja y auténtica vida griega) había quedado quebrantada por la preponderancia de las fuerzas e intereses comerciales en el estado y en los partidos políticos, y por el individualismo intelectual que se había hecho general durante el período. Probablemente veía con claridad toda persona inteligente que el estado no tenía salvación a menos que se superase tal individualismo, o siquiera la forma más cruda de él, desenfrenado egoísmo de cada persona; pero era difícil desembarazarse de él cuando hasta el estado estaba inspirado por el mismo espíritu--había hecho realmente de él el principio de sus actos--. La política predatoria de finales del siglo v había empujado gradualmente a los ciudadanos a rodar por estos nuevos caminos del pensamiento, y ahora el estado sucumbía víctima de la idea egoísta, tan impresionantemente descrita por Tucídides, que él mismo había convertido en principio. El viejo estado con sus leyes había representado para sus ciudadanos la totalidad de las normas 'consuetudinarias'. Vivir de acuerdo con las leyes era la más alta ley no escrita en la antigua Grecia, como Platón lo recuerda tristemente por última vez en su Critón. Este diálogo presenta el trágico conflicto del siglo iv agudizado hasta el absurdo consciente; el estado es ahora tal, que de acuerdo con sus leyes tiene que beber la cicuta el hombre más justo y más puro de la nación griega. La muerte de Sócrates es una reductio ad absurdum del estado entero, no simplemente de los dignatarios contemporáneos" (Werner Jaeger, Aristóteles. Translated by José Gaos [Mexico, 1946], pp. 453-54).
* The Basic Works of Aristotle. Edited by Richard McKeon (Random House: New York, 1941), 1260b, 28-36, p. 1146. Unless otherwise indicated, all subsequent English translations of Aristotle's work are from this book [translator's note].
10. Cf. W. L. Newman, The Politics of Aristotle (4 vols.) (Oxford, 1887-1902), vol. I, pp. 374-75.
* The Basic Works of Aristotle, p. 1161 [translator's note].

11. <u>Politics</u>, VIII, 6, 1341a, 28-32 (McKeon, <u>The Basic Works</u>, p. 1314).
12. <u>Ibid</u>., II, 8, 1268a, 9-10; 1268b, 23-24 (McKeon, <u>The Basic Works</u>, pp. 1162-63).
13. Cf. K. Freeman, <u>The Pre-Socratic Philosophers</u> (Oxford, 1946), pp. 74 ff.
14. <u>Republic</u>, V, 473d; Epistle VII, 326a-b.
15. See Chapter I, 37-42 of the present work.
16. <u>Memorabilia</u>, I, 1, pp. 11-17; cf. "Greek Philosophy from Its Origin to Plato" (Chapter I of the present work), pp. 37-50.
17. <u>Republic</u>, 358e ff.
18. See my <u>Historia de la Filosofía</u> (Obras, I), pp. 61 ff.
19. Cf. my <u>Introducción a la Filosofía</u> (Obras, II), Section 67; also, <u>Idea de la metafísica</u> (Obras, II), Chapter VI.
20. Ἡμῖν δ'ὑποκείσθω τὰ φύσει ἢ πάντα ἢ ἔντα κινούμενα εἶναι δῆλον δ'ἐκ τῆς ἐπαγωγῆς.
21. Cf. <u>supra</u>, I.
22. <u>Physics</u>, II, 1, 192b, 8-23 (McKeon, <u>The Basic Works</u>, p. 236).
23. <u>Ibid</u>., II, 1, 193a, 9-17 (McKeon, <u>The Basic Works</u>, p. 237).
24. <u>Metaphysics</u>, VII, 2, 1028b, 8-13 (McKeon, <u>The Basic Works</u>, p. 784).
25. <u>Metaphysics</u>, VII, 3, 1029a, 3-5.
26. <u>Ibid</u>., I, 6, 988a, 4.
27. <u>Physics</u>, III, 1, 201a, 10-11 (ἡ τοῦ δυνάμει ὄντος ἐντελέκελα ἢ τοιούτου, κίνησις ἐντιν).
28. <u>Metaphysics</u>, IX, 5, 1047b, 31; and 1048a, 11.
29. <u>Ibid</u>., IX, 6, 1048b, 18-36. This passage, omitted in some manuscripts but certainly authentic, does not appear in the translation by William Moerbeke, and is thus not found in the commentary of Saint Thomas. Neither does Bessarion translate it.
30. <u>On the Soul</u>, II, 5.
31. "A 'Historia de la Filosofía' de Emile Bréhier," <u>Obras completas</u>, VI, pp. 377-418 (see especially pp. 410-17).
32. "El cambio de ser algo blanco a ser negro empieza en la cosa blanca y <u>termina</u> cuando se ha vuelto negra. Todo cambio, al ser paso y <u>tránsito</u>, tiene un término del que viene y otro término al que va. El vocablo 'término'--πέρας--dice muy bien que cuando a él se llega, el cambio ha acabado. Ahora bien, en el ejemplo anterior el término es 'ser negro' y ser negro es realidad distinta del ennegrecerse. Entre el cambio mismo y su término hay, pues, radical diferencia, o, lo que es igual, el término está fuera, es distinto del cambio mismo. Los otros ejemplos que trae Aristóteles son del mismo tipo: no es lo mismo adelgazar que haber adelgazado (=estar ya delgado), aprender y haber aprendido, sanar y haber sanado.
Pero he aquí otra realidad: el hombre pensando, 'teorizando', meditando. Pensar es un cambio en el hombre. De ser el que no piensa en A pasa a ser el que piensa en A. Ese pensar es, precisamente, pensar. <u>Pasar</u> a pensar A es <u>estar</u> ya pensando A y seguir

222

pensando la misma A mientras dure ese pensar. De otro lado, por
'no pensar en A' el hombre, ha de entenderse 'no pensar actual-
mente A', pero estar siempre en potencia de ello. Como todo
movimiento, pensar es liberación de la potencia en cuanto tal.
Pero aquí el cambio no es distinto de su término, como lo es
ennegrecerse de ser negro. En el cambio que es pensar, el término
es inmanente al cambio o, dicho en otra forma, el cambio no se
produce en beneficio de un ser otro que él, sino del propio cambio.
Intentemos expresarlo en otra forma: todo movimiento es un hacer
o hacerse algo; a saber: su término. En el construir se construye
la obra. Construir es el hacer, obra es lo hecho, y cuando aquél
llega a la obra, concluye, quedando ésta. Pero imagínese que la
obra a que aspiramos consiste precisamente en un hacer, como
cuando lo que nos proponemos no es ir a un sitio, sino pasear.
En el pensar hay, como en todo cambio, tránsito y paso, pero en
éste se da la condición paradójica de que el pensar no es pasar
a otra cosa, sino que, al contrario, es un incremento, marcha,
avance o 'progreso hacia sí mismo' εἰς αὐτὸ γὰρ ἡ ἐπίδοσις.
    . . . Todo el párrafo del <u>Tratado del Alma</u>, a que la cita
comentada pertenece, tiembla de indecisión. 'No es acertado
llamar cambio--alteración--a la meditación o habría tal vez que
distinguir dos géneros de cambio'. . .
    Si hubiera Aristóteles insistido más en la cuestión que
descubre y le azora, se le habría impuesto esta inmediata conse-
cuencia: que el cambiar o moverse <u>tipo</u> 'pensamiento', al ser por
él contrapuesto al 'cambio a lo otro' (alteración, traslación, etc.),
esto es, a lo que él llama <u>sensu stricto</u> movimiento, reclama una
definición también opuesta a la de éste. Y si ha dicho que el
'movimiento' es la potencia en cuanto actualidad, el pensar sería
el acto convirtiéndose en potencia de sí mismo, la actualidad
en cuanto potencia . . . El paso de la potencia inicial al acto
de pensar no implica <u>destrucción de la potencia</u>, sino que es,
<u>más bien, una conservación de lo que es en potencia por lo que
es en perfección (entelequia), de modo que potencia y acto se
asimilan</u>" (Obras completas, VI, pp. 411-14). Ortega's commentary
contains many other things, for it is replete with fertile ideas;
but for now my only concern is to illuminate with his comments
my prior contention that the Aristotelian schemata of matter/form,
potential/act are inadequate <u>from Aristotle's own point of view</u>
to explain substance insofar as it is a question of dealing with
realities that are more truly substantial. Natural things are
less readily explained than the artificial, and living things are
harder still. Finally, after grounding his theory in the idea of
potentiality and action (in the sense of realization or <u>entelékheia)</u>
and <u>kínesis</u>, the human modes of being remain as a marginal "exception" in his outline. And since within the sublunar world man
is ontologically the highest and most substantial being, this
means that Aristotle's profoundest idea of substance does not fit
into his scheme of traditional interpretation. The question becomes even more acute in the case of God.

223

33. εἰς αὐτὸ γὰρ ἡ ἐπίδοσις καὶ εἰς ἐντελέκειαν (On the Soul, II, 5, 417b, 6-7).

34. πολὺ διαφέρουσιν οἱ τῶν ἀνθρώπων βίοι (Eudemian Ethics, I, 4, 1215a, 25).

35. Nicomachean Ethics, I, 2, 1094a, 18-29 (McKeon, The Basic Works, pp. 935-36).

36. Ibid., I, 4, 1095a, 14-21 (McKeon, The Basic Works, p. 937).

37. αὐτὸς δὲ περὶ τῶν ἀνθρωπίνων ἀεὶ διελέγετο (Memorabilia, I, 1, 16).

38. Nicomachean Ethics, X, 9, 1181b, 14-15.

39. Ibid., X, 9, 1180b, 28-1181b, 23 (McKeon, The Basic Works, pp. 1111-12).

40. Politics, II, 6, 1265a, 17-18 (McKeon, The Basic Works, p. 1155).

41. Ibid., II, 1, 1260b, 33-36 (McKeon, The Basic Works, p. 1146).

42. See Dilthey, Introducción a las ciencias del espíritu (trans. by Julián Marías), II, Section II, Chapter VII, pp. 229-47.

43. Politics, I, 2, 1253a, 2-3.

44. Ibid., I, 2, 1252b, 30-34 (McKeon, The Basic Works, p. 1129).

45. Ibid., I, 2, 1253a, 19-20 (McKeon, The Basic Works, p. 1129).

46. Ibid., I, 2, 1253a, 29.

47. Ibid., I, 2, 1253a, 18.

48. Ibid., I, 2, 1253a, 9-10.

49. Cf. Hesiod, Works and Days, V, 275 ff.; Herodotus, History, IV, p. 106; and Plato, Protagoras, 327d-e; Laws, 765e.

50. Politics, I, 2, 1253a, 33-34 (McKeon, The Basic Works, p. 1130).

51. Ibid., I, 2, 1253a, 23.

52. Ibid., III, 6, 1278a, 20-29.

53. Ibid., II, 2, and III, 3.

54. Ibid., III, 9, 1280b, 40-1281a, 1-4 (McKeon, The Basic Works, p. 1189).

55. Ibid., III, 4, 1276b, 26-29 (McKeon, The Basic Works, p. 1180).

56. Ibid., III, 1276b, 1-8 (McKeon, The Basic Works, p. 1179).

57. Ibid., VI (IV), 1, 1289a, 15-17 (McKeon, The Basic Works, p. 1206).

58. Ibid., VI (IV), II, 1295a, 40.

59. Laws, 817b.

60. Politics, II, 8, 1268b, 25-38 (McKeon, The Basic Works, p. 1163).

61. Ibid., II, 8, 1269a, 12-23 (McKeon, The Basic Works, p. 1164).

62. Ibid., III, 16, 1287b, 5-8.

63. See Heinrich Maier, Sokrates, Sein Werk und seine geschichtliche Stellung (1913), pp. 157-63; also Jaeger, "Paideia," op. cit., I

64. Jaeger, Aristóteles, p. 456.

65. Politics, VIII (VI), 5, 1319b, 33-1320a, 4 (McKeon, The Basic Works, pp. 1270-71).

66. Ibid., VI (IV), 13.
67. Ibid., III, 14, 1285a, 25-29 (McKeon, The Basic Works, p. 1198).
68. Ibid., VI (IV), 11, 1296a, 32-36 (McKeon, The Basic Works, p. 1222).
69. Ibid., VI (IV), 11, 1296b, 7-12 (McKeon, The Basic Works, p. 1222).
70. In his course "A New Interpretation of Universal History" in the Instituto de Humanidades (1948-49). Later, in 1949-50, the Instituto de Humanidades studied, with the collaboration of Ortega himself and professors Díez del Corral, Valdecasas, García Pelayo, and Ollero y Ramiro, the general theme of "The Mixed Regime as Idea and Political Form." (Marías and Ortega were co-founders of the Institute of the Humanities [translator's note]).
71. Politics, VI (IV), 11, 1295a, 25-31 (McKeon, The Basic Works, p. 1220).
72. Ibid., VI (IV), 8, 1294a, 3-7.
73. Ibid., VI (IV), 9, 1294b, 34-40 (McKeon, The Basic Works, p. 1219).
74. Ibid., VI (IV), 11, 1296a, 7.

Notes to Chapter IV

1. Diogenes Laertius, Lives and Opinions of the Most Famous Philosophers and a Brief Summary of the Main Doctrines of All Schools, VII, 1, 16, 25.
2. Ibid., VII, 183.
3. The reader is referred to Part VI of the book by Paul Barth, The Stoics (Los estoicos), despite its shortcomings and errors, especially regarding the Stoic influences in Christian texts.
4. "At scire negatis quemquam rem ullam nisi sapientem. Et hoc quidem Zeno gestu conficiebat. Nam cum extensis digitis adversam manum ostenderat, visum, inquiebat, hujus modi est. Dein cum paulum digitos contraxerat, adsensus hujus modi. Tum cum plane compresserat pugnumque fecerat, comprensionem illam esse dicebat; qua ex similitudine etiam nomen et rei, quod ante non fuerat, κατάληψιν imposuit. Cum autem laevam manum admoverat et illum pugnum arte vehementerque compresserat, scientiam talem esse dicebat; cujus compotem nisi sapientem esse neminem" (Cicero, Academicae quaestiones, II, p. 145).
5. Diogenes Laertius, Lives and Opinions, VII, p. 136.
6. Ibid., VII, p. 156.
7. Ibid., VII, pp. 137; 147-48.
8. Ibid., VII, p. 147.
9. According to Zeno (Diogenes Laertius, Lives and Opinions, VII, p. 87), the aim of man is ὁμολογουμένως τῇ φύσει ζῆν. Cicero translates this phrase as convenienter naturae vivere (De finibus, IV, 6, p. 14). Seneca uses the same expression. As Ch. Werner

A Biography of Philosophy

recalls (La Philosophie grecque [Paris, 1938], p. 288), Heraclitus, to whom the Stoics appealed, had said: ποιεῖν κατὰ φύσιν ἐπαιοντας.

10. Marcus Aurelius, Εἰς ἑαυτόν, IV, p. 23.

11. Numerous books may be consulted concerning the Stoic doctrine. Besides the imposing treatises of Zeller, Gomperz, or Uberweg; and, of course, the extant fragments of the ancient Stoa (Arnim, Stoicorum veterum fragmenta, 3 vols. [1903-05]); and the works of the later Stoics, interesting commentaries can be found in Book VII of Diogenes Laertius (Lives and Opinions) and a selection of texts in Ritter and Preller, Historia philosophiae graecae (in their original languages), and in Wilhelm Nestle, Die Nachsokratiker (in German). Important studies on Stoicism include the work by Barth already mentioned; Emile Bréhier, Chrysippe; and Karl Reinhardt, Posidonios. Shorter discussions may be found in chapters devoted to the topic by Léon Robin, La Pensée grecque; Charles Werner, La Philosophie grecque; and W. Windelband, Lehrbuch der Geschichte der Philosophie.

12. See my Historia de la Filosofía (Obras, I).

13. X. Zubiri, "Sócrates y la sabiduría griega," Naturaleza, Historia, Dios, III, p. 194.

14. τὸ γε φιλομαθὲς καὶ φιλόσοφον ταὐτόν (Republic, II, 376b).

15. τοὺς τῆς ἀληθείας φιλοθεάμονας (Ibid., V, 475e).

16. Theaetetus, 155d.

17. τὸ μὲν μανίαν, τὸ δὲ ἀμαθίαν (Timaeus, 86b).

18. φιλοσοφία κτῆσις ἐπιστήμης (Euthydemus, 288d).

19. διὰ τὸ θαυμάζειν (Metaphysics, IV, 2).

20. Ibid.

21. περὶ τοῦ ὄντος ἦ ὄν (Metaphysics, IV, 1).

22. Ibid., I, 2.

23. Nicomachean Ethics, I, 4, 5.

24. τοὺς ἐπακτικοὺς λόγους καὶ τὸ ὁρίζεσθαι καθόλου (Metaphysics, XIII, 4).

25. Memorabilia, I, 1, Para. 16.

26. Adversus Mathematicos, VII, p. 11.

27. Ibid., XI, p. 169.

28. Cf. De rerum natura, especially I, pp. 62-101, wherein human life is presented as being oppressed by the weight of religion, until a Greek (Epicurus) dares to confront and conquer it. And after recalling the sacrifice of Iphigenia, he ends the passage with the famous verse: tantum religio potuit suadere malorum. See also II, pp. 47-61; and V, pp. 1161 ff.

29. Arnim, Stoicorum veterum fragmenta, II, note 35.

30. Plutarch, De Stoicorum repugnantiis, 2, 3, p. 1033d. See also Ritter-Preller, Historia philosophiae graecae, note 481a.

31. Cf. Léon Robin, La Pensée grecque, pp. 413-14.

32. For the historical facts indicated, see R. Cohen, La Grèce et l'hellénisation du monde antique; W. W. Tarn, Hellenistic Civilization; A. Piganiol, Rome; U. Wilcken, Griechische Geschichte; Ortega y Gasset, Del Imperio romano; and F. Taeger, Das Altertum.

33. Cf. my Historia de la Filosofía; "Marco Aurelio o la

exageración," San Anselmo y el insensato (Obras, IV), pp. 101-2; 104-6.

Notes to Chapter V

    1. Introducción a las ciencias del espíritu (trans. by Julián Marías), pp. 272, 274.

    2. "Nihil potui invenire me in ea dixisse, quod non catholicorum patrum et maxime beati Augustini scriptis cohaereat. Quapropter, si cui videbitur, quod in eodem opusculo aliquid protulerim, quod aut nimis novum aut a veritate dissentiat, rogo, ne statim me aut praesumptore novitatum aut falsitatis assertorem exclamet, sed prius libros praefati doctoris Augustini de trinitate diligenter percepiciat, deinde secundum eos opusculum meum dijudicet. . . . Precor autem et obsecro vehementer, si quis hoc opusculum voluerit transcribere, ut hanc praefationem in capite libelli ante ipsa capitula studeat praeponer" (Monologion, Prologue). (I have not been able to find that I have made in it any statement which is inconsistent with the writings of the Catholic Fathers, or especially with those of St. Augustine. Wherefore, if it shall appear to any man that I have offered in this work any thought that is either too novel or discordant with the truth, I ask him not to denounce me at once as one who boldly seizes upon new ideas, or as a maintainer of falsehood; but let him first read diligently Augustine's books on the Trinity, and then judge my treatise in the light of those. . . . But it is my prayer and earnest entreaty, that if any shall wish to copy this work, he shall be careful to place this preface at the beginning of the book, before the body of the meditation itself.) (English translation by Sidney Norton Deane, St. Anselm [The Open Court Publishing Co., 1944], pp. 36-37 [translator's note]).

    3. San Anselmo y el insensato (Obras, IV), Chapter I.

    4. Cf. A. Koyré: "Le monde n'est pour eux qu'un vestige, qu'une image d'une réalité plus haute, d'une réalité suprasensible et divine. Le monde porte à leurs yeux la marque non méconnaissable de son imperfection, de sa dépendance, de son irréalité. . . . Il est ab alio, il est 'créature' dans le double sens de ce mot qui exprime à la fois et sa réalité relative, et son imperfection foncière" (L'Idée de Dieu dans la philosophie de St. Anselme, p. 7). (For them the world is only a vestige, an image of a higher, suprasensible, and divine reality. The world reveals to their eyes the unmistakable mark of its imperfection, its dependence, and its unreality. . . . It is ab alio, or "creature," in the double meaning the word conveys of its relative reality and its fundamental imperfection) (English translation by translator [translator's note]).

    5. "Les dogmes sont des faits, ou plutôt, pour être plus exact, l'énoncé de faits, de matters of fact. Ils sont incompréhensibles, certes, mais la réalité, l'est-elle jamais? . . . Les dogmes sont l'énoncé de réalités, aussi réelles, aussi certaines--

non, plus réelles et plus certaines et, par conséquent, encore plus incompréhensibles et irrationnelles que notre réalité à nous" (A. Koyré, op. cit., p. 32 [note]). (Dogmas are facts, or rather, to be more precise, they are the statement of facts, matters of fact. Of course they are incomprehensible, but is reality itself ever less so? . . . Dogmas are statements of reality, and, consequently, they are as real and certain, indeed, more real and certain, and even more incomprehensible and irrational than our reality) (English translation by translator [translator's note]).

6. "Qui non crediderit, non experietur, et qui expertus non fuerit, non intelliget. Nam quantum rei auditum superat experientia, tantum vincit audientis cognitionem experientis scientia" (Saint Anselm De fide Trinitatis, Chapter 2) (He who does not believe will not experience, and he who is not experienced does not understand. For just as experience surpasses the knowledge of things heard, so experimental knowledge is superior to that based on hearing) (English translation by translator [translator's note]).

7. Monologion, Chapter LXXVIII.

8. "Christianus per fidem debet ad intellectum proficere, non per intellectum ad fidem accedere, aut, si intelligere non valet, a fide recedere. Seb cum ad intellectum valet pertingere, delectatur; cum vero neguit, cum capere non potest, veneratur" (Epistle XLI) (The Christian ought to proceed by faith to understanding, not by understanding to faith, so that he may return to faith should understanding fail. But inasmuch as it is good to obtain understanding, it is to be enjoyed, and if it cannot be reached, it is to be venerated) (English translation by translator [translator's note]).

9. Note the expressions he uses to give thanks to God for his discovery of the ontological argument: "Quod prius credidi te donante, jam sic intelligo te illuminante. . . ." (Prologion, Chapter IV) (That which I first believed by thy gift, I now understand by thy illumination) (English translation by translator [translator's note]).

10. "Audivi, cum fui scholaris de Aristotele, quod posuit mundum aeternum, et cum audivi rationes et argumenta quae fiebant ad hoc, incepit concuti cor meum et incepit cogitare quomodo potest hoc esse? Sed haec modo sunt ita manifesta ut mullus de hoc possit dubitare" (Collationes de decem praeceptis, Coll. II, no 29 [Opera omnia, V, p. 515]. Cited by Father Amorós in Obras (B.A.C.), I, p. 5). (As a student of Aristotle, I heard how the world might be eternal, and as I listened to the reasons and arguments offered in support of this notion, my heart began to pound and I wondered how this could be? But the arguments are so manifest that nothing of what they assert can be doubted) (English translation by translator [translator's note]).

11. "Les formules où s'exprime une pensée sont liées à l'ordre qu'elle suit. Pour exposer Saint Thomas selon l'ordre inverse du sien, il faudrait d'abord disloquer continuellement ses textes, mais il faudrait surtout disloquer sa pensée en l'obligeant à

remonter un courant qu'elle-même affirme avoir descendu. . . .
Assurément, on peut constuire une philosophie faite d'éléments
empruntés au thomisme et qui ne parle pas de Dieu dans tout ce
qu'elle dit: on le peut, pourvu qu'on ait claire conscience de
ce que l'on fait et qu'on en mesure exactement les conséquences"
(Le Thomisme, 4th Edition [1942], p. 26 [note]). Gilson adds in
another work: "C'est un fait, rien de plus, que ses ouvrages
systématiques sont des sommes de théologie et que, par conséquent,
la philosophie qu'elles exposent nous est offerte selon l'ordre
théologique. Les premières choses que nous connaissons ne sont
autres que les choses sensibles, mais la première chose que Dieu
nous révèle, c'est son existence; on commencera donc théologique-
ment par où l'on arriverait philosophiquement après une longue
préparation" (La Philosophie au Moyen Age, 2nd Edition [1944],
p. 529). (The formulae by means of which a thought is expressed
are linked to the order followed by that thought. In order to
explain Saint Thomas in an inverse order from his own, it would first
be necessary to juggle his texts continually. But above all, it
would be necessary to alter his thought, forcing it to retrace its
steps over a pathway that it admits having followed to its present
state. . . . Most assuredly, one may construct a philosophy from
elements borrowed from thomism, one that does not mention God in
everything it states. One may do so, provided one has a clear
awareness of what is being done and provided one takes a careful
account of the consequences.) (It is an undeniable fact that his
philosophical works are theological summae and that, consequently,
the philosophy they present is offered in theological order. The
first things we know are but sensible things, but the first thing
God reveals is his existence. Thus one begins theologically from
a point attainable philosophically only by a long preparation.)
(English translation by translator [translator's note]).

    12. Gilson, Le Thomisme, p. 34.

    13. "Cum enim aliquis ad probandum fidem inducit rationes quae
non sunt cogentes, cedit in irrisionem infidelium. Credunt enim
quod hujusmodi rationibus innitamur, et propter eas credamus.--Ea
igitur quae fidei sunt, non sunt tentanda probare nisi per auctoritates his qui auctoritates suscipiunt; apud alios vero sufficit
defendere non esse impossibile quod praedicat fides" (Summa
theologica, I, q. 32, art. 1 ad. resp.). He also states: "Mundum
incepisse est credibile, non autem demonstrabile, vel scibile.--Et
hoc utile est ut consideretur, ne forte aliquis, quod fidei est
demonstrare praesumens, rationis non necessarias inducat, quae
preaebeant materiam irridenti infidelibus existimantibus nos propter
hujusmodi rationis credere quae fidei sunt" (Summa theologica, I, q. 46,
art. 2 ad. resp.) (For when someone wants to support faith by
unconvincing arguments, he becomes a laughingstock for the unbelievers, who think that we rely on such arguments and believe because of them. Therefore one should try to prove the truths of
faith only by authoritative tests to those who are ready to accept
them. In talking to others it is enough to defend the position

that what faith upholds is not impossible.) (That the world had a beginning, therefore, is credible, but not scientifically demonstrable. And it is well to take warning here, to forestall rash attempts at demonstration by arguments that are not cogent, and so provide unbelievers with the occasion for laughing at us and for thinking that these are our reasons for believing the things of faith.) (English version taken from Summa theologiae, translated by the Dominican Order [London, 1963], Vol. 6, p. 105; and Vol. 8, p. 81 [translator's note]).

14. "Et praeterea adhuc non est demonstratum, quod Deus non possit facere, ut sint infinita actu" (De aeternitate mundi contra murmurantes [end]).

15. "Ich musste also das Wissen aufheben, um zum Glauben Platz zu bekommen" (Kritik der reinen Vernunft. 2nd Edition, p. XXX). (Thus I had to forego knowledge in order to make way for belief) (English translation by translator [translator's note]).

16. Gratry, El conocimiento de Dios (translated by J. Marías), p. 163.

17. "Etiam in speculativis alia rationalis scientia est dialectica, quae ordinatur ad inquisitionem inventivam, et alia scientia demonstrativa, quae est veritatis determinativa" (Summa theologica, II-IIa, q. 51, art. 2). (Regarding speculation, rational science may be said to be dialectical if it deals with original investigation, and demonstrative if its aim is to determine the truth) (English translation by translator [translator's note]).

18. "Le XIIIe siècle a généralement cru possible d'unir en une synthèse solide la théologie naturelle et la théologie révelée. . . . Ses représentants les plus illustrés se sont donc efforcés de déterminer un point de vue d'où toutes les connaissances rationnelles et toutes les données de la foi puissent apparaître comme autant d'éléments d'un unique système intellectuel" (Gilson, La Philosophie au Moyen Age, p. 638). (In general, the thirteenth century thought it was possible to bring natural and revealed theology together in a solid synthesis. . . . Its most illustrious representatives therefore attempted to specify a point of view from which all rational knowledge and all the premises of faith might appear as elements of a single intellectual system) (English translation by translator [translator's note]).

19. "Le caractère propre du XIVe siècle, c'est d'avoir désespéré de l'oeuvre tentée par le XIIIe, ou peut-être plutôt d'avoir usé de la philosophie pour montrer combien avaient vu juste ces théologiens méfiants qui, dès de XIIIe siècle, dénonçaient l'impossibilité d'appuyer le dogme sur la philosophie. Mieux vaut poser la foi comme telle que de la fonder sur de pseudo-justifications" (Gilson, La Philosophie, p. 638). (The distinguishing trait of the fourteenth century is its despair over the work attempted by the thirteenth century. Perhaps one could say that it exhausted philosophy and in so doing showed just how correct had been the view of those distrusting theologians, who, beginning in the thirteenth century, had stated the impossibility of supporting

dogma by philosophy. They held that it was better to offer faith
on its own merits than to base it on pseudo-justification.) (English translation by translator [translator's note]).

20. "Secundum varietatem passionum erit varietas scientiarum.
Unde de homine potest sciri, ex hoc quod est compositum ex contra-
riis, quod est corruptibilis et scientia hujus conclusionis est
physica sive naturalis. De eodem etiam potest sciri quod est
beatificabilis et hec conclusio pertinet ad theologiam. De eodem
iterum potest sciri quod est liberi arbitrii et hujusmodi et hec
pertinet ad moralem.--Secundum hoc ponit quod alterius et alterius
scibilis est alia scientia. . . ." (Tractatus de principiis theologiae, Ed. Baudry, pp. 68-69); cf. also p. 72). (There will be as
many varieties of knowledge as there are varieties of feelings.
Whatever may be known of man reveals that he is composed of con-
traries and is corruptible, and this conclusion is based on physical or natural knowledge. It may also be ascertained from such
contrary qualities that he may attain to blessedness, and this
conclusion belongs to the realm of theology. Likewise, one may
know the nature of free will, and such speculation pertains to
morality. . . . We find this or that branch of knowledge depending
on how what is known is presented) (English version by translator
[translator's note]).

21. "Non potest probari per aliquam rationem. Potest tamen
evidenter cognosci per experientiam, per hoc, quod homo experitur,
quod, quantumcumque ratio dictet aliquid, potest tamen voluntas
hoc velle vel nolle" (Quodlibeta septem, I, q. 16). (It cannot
be proved by any other kind of reason. However, it can be known
evidently by means of experience, so that whatever man experiences,
regardless of whether reason holds otherwise, the will can nevertheless accept or reject it) (English translation by translator
[translator's note])

22. "Fieri nequit, ut quis Theologus perfectus evadat, nisi
firma prius Metaphysicae jecerit fundamenta intellexi semper"
(Disputationes metaphysicae ["Ratio et discursus totius operis"]
[Cologne, 1608]). (I was ever aware that it was impossible to
become a complete theologian without first having laid down a
firm foundation of metaphysics) (English translation by translator
[translator's note]).

23. "Indies tamen luce clarius intuebar, quam illa divina ac
supernaturalis Theologia, hanc humanam et naturalem desideraret
ac requiret: adeo ut non dubitaverim illud inchoatum opus paulisper
intermittere, quo huic doctrinae Metaphysicae suum quasi locum,
ac sedem darem, vel potius restituerem" (Disputationes ["Ratio"]).
(Daily I saw clearer than light itself how divine and supernatural
theology desires and requires human and natural metaphysics. Hence
I did not hesitate to interrupt this work that had hardly been
begun in order to bring or, better, to restore metaphysics to its
rightful place) (English translation by translator [translator's
note]).

24. "Ita vero hoc opere Philosophum ago, ut semper tamen prae

oculis habeam nostram Philosophiam debere Christianam esse, ac
divinae Theologiae ministram. . . . Eamque ob causam philosophico
cursu nonnunquam intermisso ad quaedam Theologica diverto, non
tam ut in illis examinandis, aut accurate explicandis, immorer
(quod esset abs re, de qua nunc ago) quam ut veluti digito indicem
lectori, quanam ratione principia Metaphysicae sint ad Theologicas
veritates confirmandas referenda, et accommodanda" (Disputationes
["Ratio"]). (So I proceed as a philosopher, but I never lose sight
of the fact that our philosophy ought to be Christian and the minion
of theology. . . . For this reason, the course of philosophy is
sometimes interrupted in order to turn to matters of theology,
not for the purpose of examining or accurately explaining them
at length (for my present task this would be beside the point),
but rather to point out to the reader as though with my finger
how the principles of metaphysics are to be directed and adapted
to the confirmation of theological truths) (English translation
by translator [translator's note]).

25. "Haec scientia accipere potest aliquid a philosophicis
disciplinis, non quod ex necessitate eis indigeat, sed ad majorem
manifestationem eorum quae in hac scientia traduntur. Non enim
accipit sua principia ab aliis scientiis, sed immediate a Deo
per revelationem. Et ideo non accipit ab aliis tanquam a superiori-
bus, sed utitur eis tanquam inferioribus et ancillis" (Summa
theologica, I, q. 1, art. 5 ad 2 n.). (This science can receive
elements from the philosophical disciplines, not that it does so
out of necessity, but rather so that their content may be made
more manifest in this science. However, it does not receive its
principles from other sciences but rather owes them immediately
to the revelation of God. Furthermore, it does not accept things
from other sciences as though they were superior to it, but
rather makes use of them as inferior and subsidiary sciences)
(English translation by translator [translator's note]).

26. "[Prima Philosophia] naturalis principia explicat atque
confirmat, quae res universas comprehendunt, omnemque doctrinam
quodammodo fulciunt atque sustentant" (Disputationes ["Proemium"])
(First philosophy explains and confirms the natural principles
that comprehend all things and support and sustain all doctrine)
(English translation by translator [translator's note]).

27. "Factum est, ut Theologi scholastici disputantes de Deo
utramque Theologiam promiscue tradiderint" (Tractatus de divina
substantia ["Proemium"] [Maguncia, 1607], p. 1). (It is a fact that
in discussing God the scholastic theologians have indiscriminately
dealt with both theologies) (English translation by translator
[translator's note]).

28. "In opere, in quo Metaphysicam sapientiam tradidimus,
necessarium nobis ad illius doctrinae complementum naturalem Theologiam distincte, ac separatim pro viribus elaborare" (Tractatus
de divina substantia ["Proemium"], p. 1). (In this work in which
we dealt with metaphysical knowledge, it was necessary for us to
elaborate separately and distinctly the natural theology that

complements that doctrine) (English translation by translator [translator's note]).

    * Marías believes that a generation comprises approximately fifteen years and he has fashioned an interesting historiographical method on this concept. See El método histórico de las generaciones (Obras, VI); in English: Generations: A Historical Method (The University of Alabama Press, 1970) (translator's note).

    29. "En matière de théologie on doit aimer l'antiquité, parce qu'on doit aimer la vérité, et que la vérité se trouve dans l'antiquité. Il faut que toute curiosité cesse, lorsqu'on tient une fois la vérité. Mais en matière de philosophie on doit au contraire aimer la nouveauté, par la même raison qu'il faut toujours aimer la vérité, qu'il faut rechercher, et qu'il faut avoir sans cesse de la curiosité pour elle" (Malebranche, Recherche de la vérité, Book II, 2nd Part, Chapter V). (In matters of theology one ought to love antiquity; for one ought to love the truth, and truth is found in antiquity. Once one has the truth all curiosity must cease. But in matters of philosophy one ought on the contrary to love the new for the same reason that one must always love the truth; one must always seek it and at all times be curious about it) (English translation by translator [translator's note]).

    30. Ed. Gerhardt, III, p. 514.

    31. Discours de la Métaphysique, Note 11.

    32. See the texts mentioned in my notes on Discours de la Métaphysique (Chapter VII, pp. 172-74 of the present work).

    33. Cf. Hegel, Vorlesungen über die Geschichte der Philosophie (Jubiläumsausgabe, III, pp. 99-212).

    34. See the First Part of El conocimiento de Dios and the final chapter of Logique. Cf. also my book, La filosofía del Padre Gratry, especially Chapters I-II (Obras, IV).

    35. For example, see his posthumous book Vom Dasein Gottes (1929).

    36. Book II, Section III.

    37. For the meaning of historical reason in Dilthey, cf. the final chapter of the present work and, especially, my Introducción a la Filosofía, Section 46.

    38. El conocimiento de Dios, p. 188.

    39. Metaphysics, II, 1, 933b, 20.

    40. Cf. supra, 1.

    41. "Echte Wissenschaft kennt, soweit ihre wirkliche Lehre reicht, keinen Tiefsinn . . . Tiefsinn in Sache der Weisheit, begriffliche Deutlichkeit und Klarheit Sache der strengen Theorie" (Husserl, "Philosophie als strenge Wissenschaft," Logos, Band I, Heft 3 [1911], p. 339). (True science knows no depth so far as its theory is concerned . . . depth in the manner of wisdom, conceptual distinctness and clarity in the manner of rigorous theory) (English translation by translator [translator's note]).

    42. El tema del hombre (1943), pp. 125-26. (The present work develops many themes outlined in El tema [translator's note]).

    43. Cf. my Historia de la Filosofía (Obras, I), p. 103.

44. Interesting and pertinent discussions on the problem and
notion of Christian philosophy are found in Gilson, L'Esprit de
la philosophie médiévale, Vol. I, pp. 1-44; in addition to an ample
bibliography on the topic in the same work, Vol. I, pp. 297-324,
and Vol. II, pp. 279-90. However, given the meticulousness of
Gilson, it is surprising to find a total absence of any allusions
to Gratry and his concepts of "separate philosophy" and "grafted
philosophy" (philosophie greffée). Concerning Gratry, see my
La filosofía del Padre Gratry (Obras, IV).

Notes to Chapter VI

    * In the French of Montaigne: ". . . je suis moy-mesmes
la matiere de mon livre." "Certes, c'est un subject merveilleuse-
ment vain, divers et ondoyant, que l'homme" (Essais, Livre I,
pp. 1 and 5, respectively [translator's note]).
    * "Ésta es la filosofía que abre los sentidos, contesta el
espíritu, magnifica el entendimiento y reduce al hombre a la
verdadera beatitud que puede tener como hombre" (translated by
translator from the Spanish version cited by Marías [translator's
note]).
    * "Enseñábanse en aquellos tiempos algunas opiniones, cuya
falsedad estaba entonces tanto más oculta cuanto había sido menos
examinada. Establecíanse como inconcusos y firmes algunos prin-
cipios venerados por una ciega fe como máximas de la filosofía
y como ciertas deidades de la razón a quienes sólo el disputarle
la verdad parecía un linaje de irreverencia" (English version by translator from the Spanish version cited by Marías [translator's
note]).
    1. See the excellent book by Enrique Gómez Arboleya, Francisco
Suárez, S. I. (Granada, 1949), pp. 64-91.
    2. Disputationes metaphysicae ("Ratio et discursus totius
operis") (Cologne, 1608).
    3. Disputationes ("Proemium").
    4. Disputationes, I, Section I, XXIV.
    5. Disputationes, I, Section I, XVII.
    6. De Deo uno et trino (Tractatus de divina substantia
["Proemium"] [Maguncia, 1607]).
    7. Disputationes, I, Section I, XIX-XXXIII.
    8. Disputationes, I, Section V, XVII-XXI.
    9. Disputationes, I, Section V, XXVIII-XXX.
    10. Disputationes, XXXI, Section I, III.
    11. It is evident that now and then Suárez points out the
necessity of that historical consideration, at times with great
insight. As a single example, recall his study of the notions
of hypostasis and person in Disputationes metaphysicae, XXXIV,
Section I, XIV. For the relationship of philosophy to its history,
see my Introducción a la Filosofía (Obras, II), Chapter XII
(especially Section 91).

12. Enrique Gómez Arboleya, <u>Francisco Suárez</u>, p. 64.

Notes to Chapter VII

1. "Les modernes, pas plus que les anciens, n'ont philosophé
dès l'instant qu'ils ont essayé de le faire; il leur a même fallu
un temps quatre fois aussi long. <u>Les tentatives des uns durèrent</u>
<u>deux siècles, depuis Thalès jusqu'à Socrate; celles des autres en</u>
<u>ont duré huit, depuis Alcuin jusqu'à Descartes; sept, il est vrai,</u>
sont absorbés par la scolastique, et à peine en reste-t-il un
pour les spéculations de Telesio, Bruno, Campanella, Ramus, Bacon,
qui cherchent à innover. Or, <u>la scolastique loin d'ouvrir la voie</u>
<u>à la philosophie, n'est propre qu'à lui fermer,</u> puisqu'elle jette
la pensée hors de soi, et l'enchaîne dans les mots, tandis que
l'objet de la philosophie est de la rappeler à elle-même. <u>C'est</u>
<u>malgré la scolastique</u> que saint Thomas, saint Bonaventure,
<u>saint Anselme, Henri de Gand, Albert le Grand,</u> ont compris quel-
que chose, et surtout que Roger Bacon donne le signal de la réforme,
deux siècles avant Telesio. <u>Ils étaient secrètement excités par</u>
le christianisme, dont l'esprit les vivifiait, quoique la théocratie,
qu'il avait alors revêtue, tendît, avec la scolastique, à les
étouffer." "Sans doute elle est une tentative de philosopher,
mais <u>une tentative à rebours,</u> qui tourne le dos à la raison et à
la vérité. Aussi plus elle avance, plus elle s'enfonce dans les
ténèbres, et tombe enfin, avec Scot, dans l'abîme des subtilités.
Cependant, l'esprit humain, <u>qu'a raminé le christianisme,</u> acquiert
le sentiment de sa force, et <u>attaque la scolastique</u> comme la féo-
dalité." (Marías' italics).
2. "Et maintenant, quelle peut être l'attitude de la pensée
thomiste à l'égard de la pensée dite moderne? Il faudrait distinguer, pour répondre à cette question, la <u>science moderne</u> et
la <u>philosophie</u> spécifiquement moderne, et, <u>dans cette dernière,</u>
<u>l'esprit qui l'anime en propre et les matériaux de vérité</u> qu'elle
<u>contient en puissance."</u> "<u>Nous rejetons l'esprit de la philosophie</u>
<u>moderne, ses principes</u> spécifiques, son <u>orientation</u> d'ensemble,
<u>le terme</u> final auquel elle tend. De tout cela <u>il n'y a rien à</u>
<u>garder,</u> que d'utiles leçons." "<u>Saint Thomas seul</u> apparaît aujourd'hui
comme le représentant par excellence de la philosophie chrétienne
et parce que seul il en contient dans ses principes toute l'univer-
salité, et, toute la largeur, la hauteur et la profondeur, seul il
peut la défendre efficacement contre des erreurs auxquelles nul
palliatif ne saurait plus remédier. <u>La scolastique moderne ne</u>
<u>peut mettre sa fierté qu'à l'imiter humblement, et non pas à</u>
repenser sa doctrine à la mode de notre temps, mais à repenser,
selon le mode de sa doctrine, tous les problèmes de notre temps."
"La philosophie moderne après cela est très utile à la pensée <u>par</u>
<u>ses erreurs mêmes,</u> dont la <u>réfutation</u> force sans cesse à approfondir
la vérité, à préciser les principes, à mettre en lumière des aspects
nouveaux." "Il convient à la philosophie scolastique de tout

assimiler, de tout rectifier, de tout équilibrer, et de transporter
dans la vraie lumière ces intentions intellectuelles que la philosophie moderne viciait. C'est là la seule manière acceptable
de sympathiser avec les philosophes modernes." (Marías' italics).
    3. ". . . pour la logique, ses syllogismes et la plupart de
ses autres instructions servent plutôt à expliquer à autrui les
choses qu'on sait, ou même, comme l'art de Lulle, à parler sans
jugement de celles qu'on ignore, qu'à les apprendre."
    4. "Per intuitum intelligo mentis purae et attentae tam
facilem distinctumque conceptum ut de eo, quod intelligimus,
nulla prorsus dubitatio relinquatur; seu, quod idem est, mentis
purae et attentae non dubium conceptum, qui a sola rationis luce
nascitur, et ipsamet deductione certior est, quia simplicior. . . .
Ita unusquisque animo potest intueri, se existere, se cogitare,
triangulum terminari tribus lineis tantum, globum unica superficie,
et similia . . ." (Regula III) (English version by Elizabeth S. Haldane
and G. R. T. Ross, The Philosophical Works of Descartes [2 Vols.]
[Cambridge, 1931], Vol. I, p. 7).
    5. "Dicimus tertio, naturas illas simplices esse omnes per
se notas, et nunquam ullam falsitatem continere. Quod facile
ostendetur, si distinguamus illam facultatem intellectus, per
quam res intuetur et cognoscit, ab ea quas judicat affirmando
vel negando" (Regula XII) (English version by Haldane and Ross,
op. cit., p. 42).
    6. "Solus intellectus equidem percipiendae veritatis capax
est" (Regula XII) (English version by Haldane and Ross, op. cit,
p. 43).
    7. "Comme les idées des choses qui sont en Dieu renferment
toutes leurs propriétés, qui en voit les idées en peut voir
successivement toutes les propriétés; car lorsqu'on voit les choses
comme elles sont en Dieu, on les voit toujours d'une manière
très parfaite, si l'esprit qui les y voit était infini. Ce qui
manque à la connaissance que nous avons de l'étendue, des figures
et des mouvements, n'est point un défaut de l'idée qui la représente, mais de notre esprit qui la considère" (Malebranche,
Recherche de la vérité, Book III, 2nd Part, Chapter VII).
    8. "La différence essentielle de l'homme consiste dans l'union
nécessaire qu'il a avec la raison universelle" (Ibid.).
    9. "Mais s'il est vrai que la raison à laquelle tous les
hommes participent est universelle, s'il est vrai qu'elle est in-
finie, s'il est vrai qu'elle est immuable et nécessaire, il est
certain qu'elle n'est point différente de celle de Dieu même. . . ."
(Ibid., Clarification X).
    10. "Il y a donc nécessairement quelque chose qui est avant
tous les temps, et de toute éternité; et c'est dans cet éternel
que ces vérités éternelles subsistent. C'est là aussi que je les
vois . . . Ainsi nous les voyons dans une lumière supérieure à
nous-mêmes . . . Ces vérités éternelles, que tout entendement
aperçoit toujours les mêmes, par lesquelles tout entendement est
réglé, sont quelque chose de Dieu, ou plutôt sont Dieu même"

(Bossuet, De La Connaissance de Dieu et de soi-même, Chapter IV).

11. "Ordo et connexio idearum idem est ac ordo et connexio rerum" (Spinoza, Ethices, pars II, prop. VII).

12. "Omnes ideae, quatenus ad Deum referuntur, verae sunt.-- Nihil in ideis positivum est, propter quod falsae dicuntur.-- Omnis idea quae nobis est absoluta, sive adaequata et perfecta, vera est" (Ethices, propositions XXXII-XXXIV).

13. "Je connus . . . que j'étois une substance dont toute l'essence ou la nature n'est que de penser et que, pour être, n'a besoin d'aucun lieu ni ne dépend d'aucune chose matérielle."

14. "Haec ipsa est notio substantiae, quod per se, hoc est absque ope ullius alterius substantiae, possit existere."

15. "Omnis res cui inest immediate, ut in subjecto, sive per quam existit aliquid quod percipimus, hoc est, aliqua proprietas, sive attributum, cujus realis idea in nobis est, vocatur substantia" (Meditationes de prima philosophia. Responsio ad Secundas Objectiones [Definition V]). (English version by Haldane and Ross, The Philosophical Works, II, p. 53 [translator's note]).

16. "Substantia, cui inest immediate cogitatio, vocatur mens." "Substantia, quae est subjectum immediatum extensionis localis, et accidentium quae extensionem praesupponunt, ut figurae, situs, motus localis, etc., vocatur corpus" (Meditationes. Responsio [Definitiones VI, VII]).

17. "Per Substantiam intelligimus id, quod ad existendum solo Dei concursu indiget."

18. "Per substantiam intelligo id, quod in se est, et per se concipitur; hoc est id, cujus conceptus non indiget conceptu alterius rei, a quo formari debeat."

19. "Dicimus igitur, creationem esse operationem, in qua nullae causae praeter efficientem concurrunt, sive res creata est illa, quae ad existendum nihil praeter Deum praesupponit."

20. "Ex hac difinitione satis sequi, accidentium et modorum nullam dari creationem: praesupponunt enim praeter Deum substantiam creatam" (Cogitata metaphysica, Part II, Chapter X).

21. Aristotle understands by entelechy a being that is real by virtue of having reached its end (telos), i.e., not only real, but realized; therefore, it possesses entire reality through the unfolding of its internal possibilities.

22. "Notionem virium seu virtutis (quam Germani vocant Kraft, Galli la force) . . . plurimum lucis afferre ad veram notionem substantiae intelligendam. Differt enim vis activa a potentia nuda vulgo scholis cognita, quod potentia activa Scholasticorum, seu facultas, nihil aliud est quam propinqua agendi possibilitas, quae tamen aliena excitatione, et velut stimulo indiget,ut in actum transferatur. Sed vis activa actum quemdam sive ἐντελέκειαν continet, atque inter facultatem agendi actionemque ipsam media est, et conatum involvit; atque ita per se ipsam in operationem fertur; nec auxiliis indiget, sed sola sublatione impedimenti. Quod exemplis gravis suspensi funem sustinentem intendentis, aut arcus tensi, illustrari potest." "Et hanc agendi virtutem omni

substantiae inesse ajo, semperque aliquam ex ea actionem nasci."

23. "Pour trouver ces unités réelles je fus contraint de recourir à un atome formel. . . . Il fallut donc rappeler et comme réhabiliter les formes substantielles, si décriées aujourd'hui. . . . Je trouvai donc que leur nature consiste dans la force, et que de cela s'ensuit quelque chose d'analogique au sentiment et à l'appétit; et qu'ainsi il fallait les concevoir à l'imitation de la notion que nous avons des âmes. . . . Aristote les appelle entéléchies premières. Je les appelle, peut-être plus intelligiblement, forces primitives qui ne contiennent pas seulement l'acte ou le complément de la possibilité, mais encore une activité originale.

24. "Les changements naturels des monades viennent d'un principe interne, puisqu'une cause externe ne saurait influer dans son intérieur." "On pourrait donner le nom d'Entéléchies à toutes les substances simples ou monades créées, car elles ont en elles une certaine perfection (ἔχουσι τὸ ἐντελές), il y a une suffisance (αὐτάκεια) qui les rend sources de leurs actions internes et pour ainsi dire Automates incorporales" (Thesis 18).

25. Julián Marías, La filosofía del Padre Gratry. La restauración de la metafísica en el problema de Dios y de la persona (Obras, IV

26. "Je révérois notre théologie et prétendois autant qu'aucun autre à gagner le ciel; mais ayant appris, comme chose très assurée, que le chemin n'en est pas moins ouvert aux plus ignorants qu'aux plus doctes, et que les vérités révelées qui y conduisent sont au-dessus de notre intelligence, je n'eusse osé les soumettre à la foiblesse de mes raisonnements, et je pensois que pour entreprendre de les examiner et y réussir il étoit besoin d'avoir quelque extraordinaire assistance du ciel et d'être plus qu'homme."

27. "Cette idée [de Dieu] est née et produite avec moi dès lors que j'ai été créé, ainsi que l'est l'idée de moi-même. Et de vrai on ne doit pas trouver étrange que Dieu, en me créant, ait mis en moi cette idée pour être comme la marque de l'ouvrier empreinte sur son ouvrage; et il n'est pas aussi nécessaire que cette marque soit quelque chose de différent de cet ouvrage même; mais de cela seul que Dieu m'a créé, il est fort croyable qu'il m'a, en quelque façon, produit à son image et semblance, et que je conçois cette ressemblance, dans laquelle l'idée de Dieu se trouve contenue, par la même faculté par laquelle je me conçois moi-même; c'est-à-dire que, lorsque je fais réflexion sur moi, non seulement je connois que je suis une chose imparfaite, incomplète et dépendante d'autrui, qui tend et qui aspire sans cesse à quelque chose de meilleur et de plus grand que je ne suis, mais je connois aussi en même temps que celui duquel je dépends possède en soi toutes ces grandes chose auxquelles j'aspire, et dont je trouve en moi les idées, non pas indéfiniment, et seulement en puissance, mais qu'il en jouit en effet, actuellement et infiniment, et ainsi qu'il est Dieu. Et toute la force de l'argument dont j'ai ici usé pour prouver l'existence de Dieu consiste en ce que je reconnois qu'il ne seroit pas possible que ma nature fût telle qu'elle est, c'est-à-dire que j'eusse en moi l'idée d'un Dieu, si Dieu n'existoit véritablement." (Marías' italics [translator's note]).

28. "Dieu est très étroitement uni à nos âmes par sa présence, de sorte qu'on peut dire qu'il est le lieu des esprits, de même que les espaces sont en un sens le lieu des corps. Ces deux choses étant supposées, il est certain que l'esprit peut voir ce qu'il y a dans Dieu qui représente les êtres créés, puisque cela est très spirituel, très intelligible et très présent à l'esprit." "Si nous ne voyions Dieu en quelque manière, nous ne verrions aucune chose" (Recherche de la vérité, Book III, 2nd Part, Chapter VI).

Notes to Chapter VIII

* English translation from Newton's Principia. Translated by Motte; revised by Florian Cajori (University of California Press, 1947), p. xvii (translator's note).
* Opticks. Reprinted from the 4th Edition (London, 1730) (London, 1931), pp. 404-5 (translator's note).
* Ibid., p. 404 (translator's note).
* Newton's Principia, pp. 398, 400 (translator's note).
* Opticks, p. 402 (translator's note)
* Newton's Principia, pp. 546-47 (translator's note).
* Opticks, pp. 369-70 (translator's note).
1. I have used the following editions of Newton's writings: Philosophiae naturalis principia mathematica. 3 vols. (Cologne, 1760); Optique (French translation) (Paris, 1787).

Notes to Chapter IX

* Marías is applying his generation method to historiography to this period. See translator's note in Chapter VI (translator's note).
1. See my Introducción a la Filosofía (Obras, II), Chapter IV.
2. Discours de la méthode. Edited by Gilson. Part IV, p. 33.
3. "Omnis res cui inest immediate, ut in subjecto, sive per quam existit aliquid quod percipimus, hoc est, aliqua proprietas, sive qualitas, sive attributum cujus realis idea in nobis est, vocatur Substantia. Neque enim ipsius substantiae praecise sumptae aliam habemus ideam quam quod sit res, in qua formaliter, vel eminenter existit illud aliquid quod percipimus, sive quod est objective in aliqua ex nostris ideis; quia naturali lumine notum est nullum esse posse nihili reale attributum.

"Substantia, cui inest immediate cogitatio, vocatur Mens: loquor autem hic de mente potius quam de anima, quoniam animae nomen est aequivocum, et saepe pro re corporea usurpatur.

"Substantia, quae est subjectum immediatum extensionis localis, et accidentium, quae extensionem praesupponunt, ut figurae, situs, motus localis, etc. vocatur Corpus. An vero una et eadem substantia sit quae vocatur Mens, et Corpus, an duae diversae, postea erit inquirendum.

"Substantia, quam summe perfectam esse intelligimus, et in qua nihil plane concipimus quod aliquem defectum sive perfectionis limitationem involvat, Deus vocatur" (Meditationes de prima philosophia. Responsio ad Secundas Objectiones. Definitiones V-VIII). (English translation by Haldane and Ross, The Philosophical Works of Descartes, II, p. 53 [translator's note]).

4. "Per substantiam nihil aliud intelligere possumus, quam rem quae ita existit, ut nulla alia re indigeat ad existendum. Et quidem substantia quae nulla plane re indigeat, unica tantum potest intelligi, nempe Deus. Alias vero omnes, non nisi ope concursus Dei existere posse percipimus. Atque ideo nomen substantiae non convenit Deo et illis univoce, ut dici solet in Scholis, hoc est, nulla ejus nominis significatio, potest distincte intelligi, quae Deo et creaturis sit communis.

"Possunt autem substantia corporea, et mens, sive substantia cogitans, creata, sub hoc communi conceptu intellegi: quod sint res, quae solo Dei concursu egent ad existendum. Verumtamen non potest substantia primum animadverti ex hoc solo, quod sit res existens; quia hoc solum per se nos non afficit: sed facile ipsam agnoscimus ex quolibet ejus attributo, per communem illam notionem, quod nihili nulla sint attributa, nullaeve proprietates, vel qualites. Ex hoc enim, quod aliquod attributum adesse percipiamus, concludimus aliquam rem existentem, sive substantiam cui illud tribui possit, necessario etiam adesse" (Principia philosophiae, I, pp. 51-52). (English translation by Haldane and Ross, The Philosophical Works of Descartes, I, pp. 239-40 [translator's note]).

5. "Facilius intelligimus substantiam extensam, vel substantiam cognitantem, quam substantiam solam, omisso eo quod cogitet vel sit extensa. Nonnulla enim est difficultas in abstrahenda notione substantiae, a notionibus cogitationis vel extensionis" (Principia philosophiae, I, p. 63). (English translation by Haldane and Ross, The Philosophical Works of Descartes, I, p. 246 [translator's note]).

Notes to Chapter X

1. Lecciones sobre la filosofía de la historia universal (translated into Spanish by José Gaos) (Madrid: Revista de Occidente, 1928), I, p. 118. (English translation by Carl J. Friedrich, The Philosophy of Hegel. Edited by Carl J. Friedrich. [New York: The Modern Library, 1953], p. 15 [translator's note]).

2. Lecciones, p. 119.

3. Lecciones, pp. 121-22. (Portions of the English version of this passage were taken from The Philosophy of Hegel, pp. 35, 41. Those not appearing in the work mentioned are by the translator [translator's note]).

4. "Die Entwicklung des Geistes ist Herausgehen, Sichaussein-anderlegen, und zugleich Zusichkommen" (Vorlesungen über die Geschichte der Philosophie [Jubiläumsausgabe], I, p. 51).

5. "Alles was im Himmel und auf Erden geschieht--ewig geschieht--, das Leben Gottes und alles was zeitlich gethan wird, strebt nur darnach, hin, dass der Geist sich erkenne, sich sich selbst gegen-ständlich mache, sich finde, für sich selber werde, sich mit sich zusammenschliesse. Er ist Verdoppeling, Entfremdung, aber um sich selbst finden zu können, um zu sich selbst kommen zu können" (Ibid., I, p. 52).

6. See Littré, Auguste Comte et la philosophie positive, pp. 527-37.

7. The complete--and expressive--title of the work is: On the Origin of Species by Means of Natural Selection, or the Preserva-tion of Favoured Races in the Struggle for Life.

8. See Rádl, Historia de las teorías biológicas (Revista de Occidente), II, pp. 108-87.

9. "So sehr diese Dialektik unbedingt das letze Wort aller Philosophie ist, so sehr es andererseits nötig, sie von dem mystichen Schein, den sie bei Hegel hat, zu befreien" (Letter from Marx, May 31, 1858, quoted by Vorländer, Marx, Engels und Lassale als Philosophen, p. 52). (It is so true that this Dialektik is the last word of all philosophy that it must be freed from the mystical air it assumed under Hegel) (English translation by trans-lator [translator's note]).

10. "Obgleich grob englisch entwickelt, ist dies das Buch, das die naturwissenschaftliche Grundlage für unsere Ansicht enthält" (Letter of December 19, 1869, ibid., p. 52). (Despite its coarse English development, this is the book that contains the foundation of natural science from our point of view) (English translation by translator [translator's note]).

11. Rudolf Stammler, Wirtschaft und Recht nach der material-istischen Geschichtsauffassung (2nd Edition), p. 23 ff.

12. F. Howard Collins, Résumé de la philosophie synthétique de Herbert Spencer (French translation). Preface by Spencer, pp. viii-xi.

13. Bergson, La Pensée et le mouvant, p. 8.

14. An exposition of these two philosophical currents can be found in my Historia de la Filosofía (Obras, I).

15. P. Laromiguière, Leçons de Philosophie (2nd Edition [Paris, 1820], I, p. 20.

16. Ibid., pp. 100-06.

17. "Je pars ici du principe reconnu aujourd'hui par tous les philosophes que l'origine de toutes nos connaissances est dans nos sensations, et c'est par l'analyse de la sensation que je commence" (Des Signes, I, p. 6).

18. "Le sentiment de la résistance se compose de deux autres; le sentiment de quelque chose d'étranger à lui, et le sentiment de quelque chose qui est lui. Il aura deux perceptions, celle d'un corps, celle de son moi, il comprendra que l'un n'est pas

l'autre, que l'un est hors de l'autre, et c'est par l'opposition qui règne entr'eux qu'il apprendra à les distinguer" (Ibid., pp. 13-14).

19. Histoire comparée des systèmes, III, pp. 415-17.

20. "Le germe de la science de l'homme est renfermé tout entier dans le phénomène de la conscience, et la philosophie n'a d'autre fonction que d'étudier et de développer le phénomène de la conscience" (Ibid., III, pp. 551-53).

21. ". . . un état de dépendance et une source de puissance, une action et une réaction; elle retrouve sur une ligne parallèle, dans un ordre également primitif de connaissances, la connaissance du moi, celle de quelque chose hors du moi, qui s'éclairent l'une l'autre par leur simultanéité même et leur contraste" (Ibid., III, p. 568).

22. Julián Marías, "El hombre y Dios en la filosofía de Maine de Biran," San Anselmo y el insensato (Madrid: Revista de Occidente, 1944) (Obras, IV), pp. 120-46.

23. Maine de Biran, Essai sur les fondements de la psychologie et sur ses rapports avec l'étude de la nature (Oeuvres, VIII), p. 18.

24. Ibid., VIII, pp. 19-20.

25. Ibid., p. 127 (note).

26. Ibid., p. 114.

27. Concerning this topic, see my book, La filosofía del Padre Gratry (Obras, IV), especially Chapter IV.

28. "Ma vie se compose de flots qui se succèdent et qui se pressent. . . . Vous nous faites successifs, tous et chacun, comme un discours ou comme un chant." "Je ne suis pas encore achevé! et je ne le serai jamais. . . . Jamais un temps n'arrivera où je serai fini. La lumière fut, dès l'origine, ce qu'elle est aujourd'hui, ce qu'elle sera. Mais je serai ce que je ne suis pas encore, et alors même j'aurai encore un abîme d'espérances, et cela sans fin. . . . La croissance continue est la seule image concevable de l'infini." "La recherche, le désir, l'inquiétude, l'espérance sont ici-bas, le fond de notre vie. . . . Le désir est la racine de l'âme, sa source, sa première force" (La Connaissance de l'âme, Book I, Chapter I, note 11) (Marías' italics).

29. See especially Die Anweisung zum seligen Leben.

30. Post-scriptum no científico a las Migajas filosóficas, Part II, Section II, Chapter III, Para. 1. (English title of this work: Concluding Unscientific Postscript to the "Philosophical Fragments"). The English translation herein given is based on the Spanish version offered by Marías: "Porque el pensamiento abstracto es sub specie aeterni, se hace en él abstracción de lo concreto, temporal, del devenir de la existencia, de la angustia del hombre, situado en la existencia por un cruce de lo temporal y lo eterno." "Pensar abstractamente la existencia y sub specie aeterni significa suprimirla esencialmente . . . la existencia no puede ser pensada sin movimiento, y el movimiento no puede ser pensado sub specie aeterni . . . Pasa con la existencia como con

el movimiento. Si los pienso los he abolido, y ya no los pienso.
Así pudiera parecer correcto decir que hay una cosa que no se
deja pensar: la existencia. Pero entonces subsiste la dificultad
de que por el hecho de que quien piensa existe, la existencia se
encuentra puesta al mismo tiempo que el pensamiento" (translator's
note).

31. Notwithstanding the fact that the conclusions of Schopenhauer
regarding the value of life are, in a certain way, contrary to those
of Nietzsche, this does not alter the fact that both move in the
same arena of problems and that Nietzsche grasped the nature of the
problem from Schopenhauer. Any serious study of this theme would
have to take into account the work of Guyau (1854-1888) and Simmel
(1858-1918).

32. See Ortega y Gasset, Guillermo Dilthey y la idea de la
vida (Obras completas, VI, pp. 165-96).

33. "Gerade so wie Natur bin ich Geschichte" (Breifwechsel,
71); "--Der Mensch ist ein Geschichtliches" (G. S., VII, p. 291).
(Just as nature [is historical], I am also history . . . Man is
a historical being) (English translation by translator [translator's
note]).

34. "Leben . . . ist seinem Stoffe nach eins mit der Geschichte . . .
Geschichte ist nur das Leben, aufgefasst unter dem Gesichtspunkt
des Ganzen der Menschheit, das einen Zusammenhang bildet" (G. S.,
VII, p. 256). (Life is fashioned out of the same stuff as history . . .
History is but life itself apprehended from the viewpoint of all
mankind) (English translation by translator [translator's note]).

35. Cf. the observations of Bollnow, Dilthey, p. 31 ff.

36. Dilthey, op. cit., VII, p. 359.

37. Ibid., VIII, pp. 17-18.

38. Once again I refer to the essay by Ortega (cited in note
32 above), which is still the most helpful work to date in understanding Dilthey. See also the work by Pedro Laín Entralgo,
Dilthey y el método de la historia.

39. For a view of the scope of historical reason in Dilthey,
see the chapter "Leben und Vernunft" in the book by Bollnow
(cited in note 35 above).

40. "Para mí es razón, en el verdadero y rigoroso sentido,
toda acción intelectual que nos pone en contacto con la realidad,
por medio de la cual topamos con lo trascendente." "Hasta ahora,
la historia era lo contrario de la razón. En Grecia, los términos
razón e historia eran contrapuestos. Y es que hasta ahora, en
efecto, apenas se ha ocupado nadie de buscar en la historia su
sustancia racional. El que más, ha querido llevar a ella una
razón forastera, como Hegel, que inyecta en la historia el forma-
lismo de su lógica, o Buckle, la razón fisiológica y física. Mi
propósito es estrictamente inverso. Se trata de encontrar en la
historia misma su original y autóctona razón. Por eso ha de entenderse en todo su vigor la expresión 'razón histórica'. No
una razón extrahistórica que parece cumplirse en la historia,
sino literalmente, lo que al hombre le ha pasado, constituyendo

la sustantiva razón, la revelación de una realidad trascendente a las teorías del hombre y que es él mismo por debajo de sus teorías." "Hasta ahora, lo que había de razón no era racional. La razón histórica es, pues, ratio, logos, rigoroso concepto." "La razón histórica . . . no acepta nada como mero hecho, sino que fluidifica todo hecho en el fieri de que proviene: ve cómo se hace el hecho" (Historia como sistema [Obras completas, VI], Chapter IX; printed for the first time in Spanish in 1935; in English, in 1941).

Index

245

Index